WITHDRAWN
UTSA LIBRARIES

RENEWALS 458-4574

Dependent Self-Employment

Dependent Self-Employment

Workers on the Border Between Employment and Self-Employment

Ulrike Muehlberger
Vienna University of Economics and Business Administration

© Ulrike Muehlberger 2007

All rights reserved. No reproduction, copy or transmission of this publication may be made without written permission.

No paragraph of this publication may be reproduced, copied or transmitted save with written permission or in accordance with the provisions of the Copyright, Designs and Patents Act 1988, or under the terms of any licence permitting limited copying issued by the Copyright Licensing Agency, 90 Tottenham Court Road, London W1T 4LP.

Any person who does any unauthorized act in relation to this publication may be liable to criminal prosecution and civil claims for damages.

The author has asserted her right to be identified as the author of this work in accordance with the Copyright, Designs and Patents Act 1988.

First published 2007 by
PALGRAVE MACMILLAN
Houndmills, Basingstoke, Hampshire RG21 6XS and
175 Fifth Avenue, New York, N.Y. 10010
Companies and representatives throughout the world

PALGRAVE MACMILLAN is the global academic imprint of the Palgrave Macmillan division of St. Martin's Press, LLC and of Palgrave Macmillan Ltd. Macmillan® is a registered trademark in the United States, United Kingdom and other countries. Palgrave is a registered trademark in the European Union and other countries.

ISBN-13: 978–0–230–51549–9 hardback
ISBN-10: 0–230–51549–5 hardback

This book is printed on paper suitable for recycling and made from fully managed and sustained forest sources. Logging, pulping and manufacturing processes are expected to conform to the environmental regulations of the country of origin.

A catalogue record for this book is available from the British Library.

A catalog record for this book is available from the Library of Congress.

10 9 8 7 6 5 4 3 2 1
16 15 14 13 12 11 10 09 08 07

Printed and bound in Great Britain by
Antony Rowe Ltd, Chippenham and Eastbourne

Library
University of Texas
at San Antonio

Contents

List of Tables and Figure   ix

Acknowledgements   xi

1 The Blurring Boundaries Between Employment and Self-Employment   **1**
  1.1 Introduction and motivation   1
  1.2 What is dependent self-employment?   4
  1.3 The theoretical and methodological approach   8
   1.3.1 Research design and methods   8
   1.3.2 The countries: varieties of capitalism?   9
   1.3.3 The industries   12
  1.4 Overview of the book   14

2 Work on the Border Between Employment and Self-Employment   **18**
  2.1 Recent trends of self-employment   18
  2.2 Dependent forms of outsourcing and the development of self-employment   20
  2.3 The special case of franchising   22
  2.4 Evidence of independent contractors in the US   23
  2.5 Evidence of dependent self-employment and dependent forms of outsourcing   26
  2.6 Conclusions   32

3 The Institutional Factor: Labour Law and Regulations Across Europe   **34**
  3.1 The legal uncertainty of dependent self-employment   34
  3.2 The scope of labour law in comparative perspective   37
  3.3 Conclusions   44

4 The Supply Side: Identifying Workers on the Border Between Employment and Self-Employment   **46**
  4.1 The determinants of self-employment   46
  4.2 The motives to supply-dependent self-employed work: qualitative findings   50

4.3	Dependent self-employment in Austria	54
4.4	Dependent self-employment in the UK	58
4.5	Dependent self-employment in Italy	66
4.6	Conclusions	77

5 The Organisational Governance of Dependent Forms of Self-Employment — 80

- 5.1 The importance of informal structures — 80
- 5.2 Markets, hierarchies and relational contracts — 81
  - 5.2.1 The market-versus-hierarchy approach — 81
  - 5.2.2 Relational contracts, repeated games and reciprocity — 86
- 5.3 Governing dependent forms of outsourcing — 91
  - 5.3.1 Relational contracts and dependent forms of outsourcing — 91
  - 5.3.2 The key features of dependent business relationships — 94
  - 5.3.3 Explaining dependent outsourcing from an organisational sociology perspective — 97
- 5.4 Conclusions — 105

6 The Creation of Dependent Self-Employment in Comparative Perspective — 107

- 6.1 The research design — 107
- 6.2 Dependent self-employment in the British and Austrian insurance industry — 110
  - 6.2.1 Employment in the British and Austrian insurance industry — 110
  - 6.2.2 The creation of dependent self-employment in the insurance industry — 115
  - 6.2.3 The organisational logic of tied agency — 132
    - 6.2.3.1 The effects of labour law and the cost structure — 132
    - 6.2.3.2 Managerial control, risk exposure and industrial regulation — 134
    - 6.2.3.3 The effect of company culture — 139
    - 6.2.3.4 Motivation and productivity — 140
- 6.3 Dependent self-employment in the Austrian service sector — 142
  - 6.3.1 Employment trends in the Austrian service sector — 142
  - 6.3.2 The dependent self-employed workers in the Austrian service industry — 145

		6.3.3	Effects and consequences of dependent self-employment	151

Contents

6.4	Dependent self-employment in the Austrian freight industry			155
	6.4.1	Recent developments in the Austrian freight industry || 155
	6.4.2	The contractual organisation of dependent self-employment in the Austrian freight industry || 157
	6.4.3	Motives for outsourcing the fleet of trucks || 158
	6.4.4	Effects, risks and consequences of outsourcing || 161
6.5	The creation of dependency			165
	6.5.1	Dependency as a result of support || 165
	6.5.2	Dependency as a result of managerial control || 167
	6.5.3	Relational risk and mutual dependency || 169
6.6	Dependency, relational contracts and the creation of hybrid forms of organisational governance			170
6.7	Power and trust in dependent business relations			173
6.8	Conclusions			176

7 Conclusions — 178

7.1	Explaining dependent self-employment: an evaluation of the research questions			178
	7.1.1	The key features of dependent business relationships		178
		7.1.1.1	The normative basis of dependent self-employment	178
		7.1.1.2	The control mechanism	179
		7.1.1.3	Methods of conflict resolution	181
		7.1.1.4	Tone or climate	182
		7.1.1.5	Commitment	182
		7.1.1.6	Degree of flexibility	183
	7.1.2	The factors determining the creation of dependent business relationships		183
		7.1.2.1	Managing resource dependency	183
		7.1.2.2	The influence of environmental changes	184
		7.1.2.3	The influence of institutional changes	184
		7.1.2.4	The role of imitative behaviour	185
		7.1.2.5	The role of organisational routines and norms	186
		7.1.2.6	The influence of the state	186

7.2 The borders of dependent self-employment and legal regulation 187
7.3 Within-system diversity and mixed governance structures 191

Notes 195

References 202

Index 213

List of Tables and Figure

Tables

2.1	Annual average growth rates of self-employment and total civilian employment	19
2.2	Self-employment in some EU countries, 1995–2005	20
4.1	Dependent self-employment in Austria (2001)	55
4.2	Further characteristics of dependent self-employed workers in Austria (2001)	58
4.3	Summary statistics by employment status (British Labour Force Survey)	59
4.4	Employment status, $t-1$ and t (row percentages)	62
4.5	Estimated risk of self-employment and dependent self-employment (multinomial logit)	63
4.6	Descriptive statistics of the sample (Italian Labour Force Survey)	68
4.7	Estimated risk of being self-employed or being an employee in comparison to being a collaborator	71
4.8	Estimated risk of being employed or self-employed in comparison to being a collaborator	72
4.9	Transitions between three different labour market statuses	75
4.10	Probit estimation of the likelihood to work at time t (work = 1, unemployed = 0)	76
4.11	Estimated risk of being self-employed or being an employee in comparison to being a collaborator	77
5.1	Efficient governance of transactions	84
5.2	Combinations of ownership and governance regimes that define four organisational forms	90
5.3	Key features of various governance structures	95
6.1	Number of employees in the Austrian insurance sector	111
6.2	Number of employees in the UK insurance sector (Two digit SIC 1992: 66)	114
6.3	Number of employees in the UK insurance sector (Microcensus, two digit SIC 1992: 66)	114
6.4	Sources of new regular premiums in the British long-term insurance business (total individual regular premiums)	126

6.5 Sources of new premiums in the Austrian insurance
business 127
6.6 Multi-channel distribution of the insurance companies
included in the case study (Status: June 2001) 131
6.7 Overview on the personal characteristics and findings of
the interviews conducted 153

Figure

6.1 Multi-channel distribution 116

Acknowledgements

This book was written while working and studying at the European University Institute in Florence, the London School of Economics, Harvard University, the International Center of Economic Research (ICER) in Turin and the Vienna University of Economics & B.A. The academic environments of these institutions were highly stimulating for writing this book.

I am grateful to Colin Crouch (Warwick Business School), who was my PhD supervisor at the European University Institute, for the many discussions, helpful guidelines and advise throughout the years. Thanks to Jackie O'Reilly (University of Sussex), Silvana Sciarra (University of Florence), Franz Traxler (University of Vienna) and Herbert Walther, the head of my academic unit and supervisor of my PhD thesis at the Vienna University of Economics & B.A., for helpfully commenting on various parts of this book. Stimulating joint research with René Böheim (University of Linz), Silvia Pasqua and Sonia Bertolini (University of Turin) is reflected and cited in this book. I am, moreover, thankful to all my interview partners who offered their time and gave me a deep insight into their working environment.

I am indebted to the Austrian Central Bank (OeNB) for financing a related research project (Jubiläumsfonds Project No. 11090) and a post-doc fellowship (Dr Maria Schaumayer Post-doc Fellowship) as well as the ICER in Turin for a fellowship to work with Italian data.

I am very grateful for the support of my family and my friends. Looking back over the last years I realise their immense importance as they have always been the light house and the save haven in my life. You make my life so wonderful.

I thank my father who saw the beginning of this research project, but not the end. His natural belief in me and his fatherly pride was always a source of stamina although I hardly realised it. This book is dedicated to him in loving memory.

1
The Blurring Boundaries Between Employment and Self-Employment

1.1 Introduction and motivation

The focus of this book is work relationships where the worker is formally self-employed but the conditions of work are similar to those of employees. Although they work exclusively (or mainly) for a specific firm (i.e. the outsourcing firm), workers are neither clearly separated from the firm they contract with nor clearly integrated. These work relationships are not based on employment contracts, but on private contracts between a self-employed worker and the outsourcing firm.

This study analyses the externalisation of labour and, thus, the transformation of employment relationships into business relationships. Business organisations increasingly source out parts of their workforce and establish business relationships that are based on both relational contracts and hierarchical structures, creating *dependent* forms of self-employment. This development has two major effects. Firstly, the boundary between employment and self-employment becomes blurred, resulting in a need to rethink the restrictions of labour and social security law. Secondly, the boundaries of firms become fuzzy. This study will demonstrate that dependent self-employed workers are neither clearly separated from the firm they contract with nor clearly integrated. However, the sharp delineation of markets and hierarchies used in conventional theories of the firm does not permit to explain the increasingly blurred boundaries of the firm. Thus, social scientists have to develop new models of the firm with respect to issues such as firm behaviour, work relationships, corporate control and ownership, incentive structures, hold-up problems or trust.

The motivation to write this book lies in the observation that although dependent forms of self-employment and outsourcing are widely discussed in national [e.g. Burchell et al. (1999) and Collins (1990) for the UK; Dietrich (1996) for Germany; Lyon-Caen (1990) for France; Fink et al. (2001) for Austria], international (ILO 2003; OECD 2000) and in European political and legal forums (Supiot 2001; Eiro 2002; Perulli 2003; Sciarra 2004), there is a surprising lack of both sociological and economic research to understand the emergence and the consequences of this development.

The macroeconomic and societal background of the expansion of dependent forms of outsourcing lies in both recent economic developments and labour market changes. European business organisations are facing severe challenges. The enlargement of markets through increasing integration, the accession of Central and East European countries to the European Union (EU) and WTO agreements are some recent developments that strongly affect both public policy and the behaviour of business organisations. Of course, these two spheres are closely related and interdependent.

These recent economic developments and supply-side public policy measures are significantly changing the governing modes of economic exchange. On the one hand, we observe a rise in mergers and acquisitions, which substitutes markets for hierarchies, leading to further economic concentration. On the other hand, we see an increase in outsourcing and subcontracting activities, which appear to be replacing hierarchy by market forms of governance. However, there is empirical evidence that an increasing share of outsourcing activities is based on dependent business relationships (Semlinger 1993; Dietrich 1996; Burchell et al. 1999; OECD 2000; Chapters 2 and 5 of this book). This study aims at developing a systematic understanding of dependent forms of outsourcing and the creation of dependent self-employment.

In addition to changes in the economic environment, European labour markets are confronted with new, challenging developments. Firstly, workers' lifestyles are increasingly heterogeneous and flexible due to various facts. For example, the increasing share of highly qualified women in the workforce has lead to more demand for flexible work forms (O'Reilly and Fagan 1998; O'Reilly et al. 2000). As a consequence, women's growth rates in self-employment have been above that of men. Secondly, the 'Fordist' model, which is based on large industrial businesses engaging in mass production with a narrow definition of job competencies and a hierarchical structure of labour management, no longer reflects the governance of European labour markets. The trend towards a heterogeneous production process is accompanied by an increasing heterogeneity amongst workers, describing the flexible post-industrial society. New contractual arrangements are a major consequence of these new developments on both sides of the production process (Crouch 1999; DiMaggio 2001; Supiot 2001). Thirdly, sectoral change towards the service sector has increased the opportunities for becoming self-employed since starting a business is usually connected with lower costs compared to the capital-intensive industrial sector (Zagler 2003; Arum and Müller 2004: 10).

Externalising business activities, or outsourcing, opens new ways for business organisations to profit from the division of labour. A firm can either acquire some intermediate input by taking on an employee who works under the employer's auspices, using the employer's tools, and usually being paid a fixed salary, or instead by hiring an agent who works with her own tools and methods, being paid proportionally to the quantity supplied. The motives for externalising parts of the production process are manifold. The most important rationales are to (partly) transfer entrepreneurial risk, to transform fixed costs into variable ones and thus gaining financial flexibility, to circumvent labour and social security laws, to weaken the bargaining power of internal labour, to circumvent institutionalised hierarchical structures or to increase incentive pay structures. In sum, firms attempt to increase their organisational flexibility through such tactics (see Chapter 6). Grimshaw and Rubery (2005) argue that the externalisation of labour is more common if introduced by key competitors, if new sources of cheap labour supply are emerging (unemployment, immigrants, women) and if employment regulations allow for an easy transfer from internal to external labour.

Using dependent forms of outsourcing increases the firm's flexibility for various reasons. Since these business relationships are based on commercial contracts rather than employment contracts, there are fewer regulations restricting the contractual arrangement, allowing contracts customised to the special needs of the firm. However, this also means, that the dependent self-employed worker is usually not covered by labour protection measures. Additionally, these contractual arrangements are used to allow quick adaptation when new contingencies arise, sourcing out (part of the) entrepreneurial risk. Finally, using dependent self-employed workers strongly decreases the bargaining power of employed labour.

Another rationale behind dependent forms of outsourcing is to extend the control function of management across organisational boundaries. By mixing governance structures, firms are able to benefit from the advantages of outsourcing without losing control over labour. Grimshaw and Rubery (2005) suggest that this strategy demonstrates a compromise between the control and cooperation dilemmas. Although numerous empirical studies of hybrid forms of organisations provide useful material for understanding the interactions between blurred organisational boundaries and the structural change of employment relations, much less work has been aimed to theoretically explain these empirical observations. Traditional theories of the firm and employment relations have substantial problems in explaining new forms of work or organisational changes such as dependent forms of outsourcing. Labour-related issues such as workers' control, coordination of labour and production or even the issue of labour segmentation are traditionally focused on single organisations with strictly defined borders. Analyses of inter-organisational coordination, on the other hand, have mainly been carried out on the industrial (e.g. networks) or regional level (e.g. industrial districts). However, recent empirical research on the changing nature of work has shown that theoretical research has to go beyond organisational boundaries in order to explain work relationships on a micro-level (Rubery et al. 2002; Marchington et al. 2004). The contribution of this book is to focus on one specific development in labour markets and organisations – i.e. dependent forms of outsourcing and self-employment – and to demonstrate on both the theoretical and the empirical level the interaction between hazy organisational boundaries and the changing nature of work relations, combining organisational and labour market research.

1.2 What is dependent self-employment?

Self-employed persons usually work for a large number of customers without placing themselves in hierarchical subordination to them. They bear the entrepreneurial risk but also gain the entrepreneurial possibilities implied by self-employment. However, if the self-employed person works mainly for one customer in hierarchical subordination we observe dependent forms of outsourcing or subcontracting and, consequently, dependent self-employment.[1]

Thus, dependent outsourcing or subcontracting refers to business relationships where the subcontractors (i.e. agents)[2] are formally self-employed (or declare themselves as self-employed)[3] but their conditions of work are similar to those of employees. They are economically – and in extreme cases also personally – dependent on the firm they are contracted to (i.e. principal). Dependent self-employed persons assume entrepreneurial risk without gaining the entrepreneurial possibilities of independent self-employed persons, because contracting only to one firm they do not appear on the external market. Consequently, they are labelled 'dependent self-employed workers'. In this context, dependency refers not only to economic and personal dependence in a legal sense but also to the fact that these subcontractors are restricted in their presence on the external market and are, thus, restricted in their alternatives.

Dependent self-employment refers to a type of contract that falls between independent self-employment and dependent employment, thus displaying the characteristics of both. Although these workers are formally self-employed, they face elements of authority which determine their work. Dependent self-employed workers do not have a contract of employment, but still supply labour – in the form of a personal service or a produced good – to their principal. They work on the basis of a private contract according to private law.

The best approach to the concept of dependent self-employed workers is probably to define other employment statuses relevant for this study.[4] An *employee*, to begin with, is an individual who is employed by a firm with an explicit or implicit contract of employment. Basic remuneration is normally not directly dependent upon the revenue of the firm for which she or he works. An employee uses the assets owned by others and is supervised by others. An *independent self-employed person*, at the opposite end of the continuum, is an individual who provides labour or goods to various firms and/or customers, normally under a contract for services or a contract of purchase, and who is in business on his or her own account. Remuneration is directly dependent upon the profits derived from the goods and services produced and purchased. A *worker* is an individual who is deployed by a firm either as an employee or as an independent contractor (but not on his or her own account) and who is economically dependent on the business of the other (Deakin and Morris 1998). The notion *dependent self-employed worker* expresses contractual situations where an individual is self-employed in legal terms (or, at least maintains that this is so), but who is economically, and sometimes also personally, dependent on his or her principal. An important point here is that the dependent self-employed worker does not appear on the external market since he or she has only one firm they are contracted to.

What does it mean to be economically dependent on a principal? Economic dependence basically means that the dependent self-employed worker takes the entrepreneurial risk. Since such workers have only one (main) principal they generate their whole (or a substantial part of their) income from this business relationship.[5] This implies that the dependent self-employed person is dependent on the orders of the principal. If we assume that the two parties do not usually agree on a constant quantity of orders but quite the contrary, namely that the quantity of business deals depends on the economic situation of the principal, then the dependent self-employed worker obviously takes the entrepreneurial risk.

Another form of dependence is personal dependence (or subordination). This refers to dependence in terms of time, place and content of work. In the case of personal dependence it is the principal who decides when and where the work must be performed. Moreover, the principal determines what work must be carried out and how. A dependent self-employed worker is by definition economically dependent but is not necessarily personally dependent on his or her principal. This problematic area is precisely the grey zone which these workers inhabit. Those who are both economically and personally dependent border on the employee status, while those who are economically dependent to a lesser degree are closer to the borderline of independent self-employment. Thus, although we are referring to all the workers in the grey zone between an employee status and independent self-employment as dependent self-employed workers, we are nevertheless addressing manifold forms of work.[6]

The following outlines two common examples in order to further clarify the concept of dependent self-employment. A classic case of dependent self-employment is the private transport sector. Many of the big carriers pursue a dual organisational strategy to ensure a certain amount of flexibility. On the one hand they deploy employees who use the employer's vehicles and on the other they deploy dependent self-employed workers who use their own trucks. However, the two perform exactly the same role, namely that of delivering freight to customers. The important difference between these two types of workers is that the employees do not bear the entrepreneurial risk. The dependent self-employed workers do, in contrast, bear the entrepreneurial risk. First, they often do not have a contractually fixed quantity of deliveries. Second, they have to ensure that their assets (i.e. the trucks) are ready for service when needed. Third, they face economic risk when they are prevented from carrying out work due to technical problems with the trucks or when they get ill or take holidays. In other words, they do not get any money when they are prevented from carrying out their work.[7]

Another example is the multi-channel distribution strategy in the life and pension insurance industry. Most insurance companies organise their distribution using different channels such as direct sales agents, tied agents and independent agents. Again, these different workers and/or subcontractors perform exactly the same kind of work, namely selling insurance contracts to clients. In contrast to tied and independent agents, direct sales agents are employees of the insurance companies. Both tied and independent agents are self-employed but have different contracts with insurance companies. Whilst a tied agent is only allowed to represent one particular insurance company, an independent agent is able to sell insurance contracts from different companies. These three distribution channels, namely the direct sales force, the tied agents and the independent agents, are exemplary of three forms of work: the employee status, dependent self-employment and independent self-employment, respectively. Again, while the direct sales force (i.e. the employees) of an insurance company do not bear the entrepreneurial risk, the tied agents (i.e. the dependent self-employed workers) do for various reasons. First, whilst the direct sales force earns a (small) basic salary plus commission for every insurance policy they sell, the tied agent receives only commission. Second, in contrast to the direct sales force, tied agents must finance their own assets (i.e. office, car, IT). Third, tied agents, such as freight subcontractors, face economic risk when they are prevented from carrying out their work (e.g. illness, holidays).[8] Fourth, they invest in specific human capital since they sell insurance products from only one firm. For this and for other reasons, switching contract partner would create switching costs.[9]

Both examples show that most disadvantages for the dependent self-employed workers are, in turn, advantages for the principals. Although the principals have control over the asset, they do not have to maintain it. Moreover, they do not have to pay social security benefits or any other benefits and do not bear the financial risk when the worker gets ill. Another advantage for the principals, which may be even more important, is that they face less legal constraints of employment protection in terms of working time or security. Furthermore, dependent self-employment workers are usually beyond the scope of collective bargaining and trade union representation. In sum, most employment protection laws are not applicable in such business relationships. Thus, dependent self-employment undercuts laws that are designed to protect workers.

The division between employment and self-employment in a legal system indirectly involves the assessment of how certain social and economic risk are to be shared between employers, workers and the state. While employees have access to specific social security benefits and a certain protection of income and employment, self-employed persons have only restricted or no access to these social benefits. Employees, on the other hand, do not have the same opportunities as the self-employed to set off their work-related expenditures against income tax (Burchell et al. 1999).[10] Other motives for the worker to contract exclusively with one company on a tied basis are, on the one hand, the absence of opportunities for employment following redundancies and strategic moves towards outsourcing and, on the other hand, the fact that hierarchical forms of self-employment are associated with lower start-up costs and a simpler work process (in terms of coordination). In comparison to employment, these workers face similar, yet less control, more flexibility and often a reduced legal liability (Burchell et al. 1999; see also Chapter 6 of this book).

However, as Sciarra (2004: 22) points out: 'What is most difficult to assess is under which circumstances (be they social or caused by deep changes in the enterprise organisation) a grey area emerges, in which criteria of subordination are not immediately visible and yet dependence is an indisputable feature.' Chapter 6 of this book presents case study research in three different industries (i.e. insurance, freight and business services) in the UK, Italy and Austria, demonstrating how dependency is created by both formal and informal means to bring some light into this grey area of labour markets.

1.3 The theoretical and methodological approach

1.3.1 Research design and methods

The basic idea of the research design of this book is, on the one hand, to combine sociological and economic research and, on the other, to use both quantitative and qualitative empirical research techniques to explore the reasons and organisational consequences of dependent forms of outsourcing.

Chapter 4 presents quantitative research on the characteristics of dependent self-employed workers in the British (Spring 2002) and the Italian (Fourth quarter of 2004) Labour Force Surveys, using cross-section logistic regression. Unfortunately, quantitative investigation of micro-data was unfeasible for Austria due to a severe problem with the quality of the Austrian micro-data. For this reason, only aggregate data are presented in the Austrian case.

The individual data of the British and Italian Labour Force Surveys allows us to gain information on both personal characteristics (e.g. age, education) and the work environment (e.g. sector) of dependent self-employed workers. However, it hardly provides any information on the firm to which the dependent self-employed worker is contracted. Thus, in order to fully understand the logic of dependent outsourcing, it was necessary to carry out qualitative case study research in various industries based on in-depth, semi-structured interviews, business material and social science literature. Only this firm-centred approach enables us to illuminate the mechanisms of organisational governance that lead to dependent forms of outsourcing.

Qualitative research can provide exceptional insights which are not achievable through quantitative methods. Neither official or business statistics nor the analysis of written contracts would provide the necessary information. Hence, in order to study business behaviour or, more concretely, to analyse the principles of dependent outsourcing, the only solution is to interview people in business. In addition, the phenomenon of dependent outsourcing has to be studied in its real-life context since the boundaries between the phenomenon of dependent outsourcing and the context (i.e. firm-internal governance) are not clearly evident. For this reason, the interviews conducted did not focus exclusively on outsourcing activities, but on the whole firm-internal labour market organisation. The research design of the case studies is described in more detail in Chapter 6.

1.3.2 The countries: varieties of capitalism?

This study compares the logic of the creation of dependent self-employment in three different countries, the United Kingdom, Italy and Austria. These countries represent different forms of macroeconomic governance, especially in terms of production regimes, industrial relations and the welfare state systems. Whilst the UK can be seen as a prime example of an uncoordinated, deregulated economy, Austria (stronger) and Italy (weaker) are characterised as coordinated, institutionalised economies (e.g. Crouch and Streeck 1997; Soskice 1999; Hall and Soskice 2001).

According to the 'varieties of capitalism' literature, the production system in the UK is based on low-skilled mass production and the application of numeric flexibility. Italy's and Austria's production systems, on the other hand, are identified as high-skilled production organised around a flexible specialisation system (e.g. Soskice 1999; Ebbinghaus and Manow 2001). Collective bargaining arrangements are strongly decentralised in the UK (mostly at the firm-level), while they on a sectoral level in Italy and in Austria (with a stronger coordination between the sectors in Austria). The organisation of the welfare state strongly differs in the three countries. The UK is associated with a free-market or liberal capitalism approach with a strictly reduced welfare state regime. Austria is a typical example of the conservative 'continental European' model with a strong role of the state in shaping the organisation and inter-linkages between families and work (Esping-Andersen 1990). The same is true for Italy, but with a more important role of kinship and family networks and other informal institutions (Ferrera 1997; Naldini 2003).

The 'varieties of capitalism' literature argues that different national economic institutions shape the opportunities for firms to organise production, leading to specific economic outcomes (e.g. Kitschelt et al. 1999; Hall and Soskice 2001). It sees firms as the central actors in an economy, determining national economic performance. Firms have to interact with each other in different spheres of the economy: on financial markets, in the industrial relations system, in the education and training system, via inter-firm relations, on product markets and in the area of firm–employee relations. Thus, coordination in these different spheres of the economy is seen as the major determining factor of national economic outcomes. Hall and Soskice (2001) identify two different groups of countries that differ in their institutional setting and, hence, in their economic opportunities and comparative economic advantage: 'coordinated market economies'[11] (such as Germany, Sweden, Italy and Austria) on the one hand and 'liberal market economies'[12] (such as the USA and the UK) on the other. While the former group is associated with a dense institutional environment and a high level of coordination among actors ('strategic interaction'), the latter refers to countries with a sparse institutional environment where coordination mainly takes place through competitive markets. The 'varieties of capitalism' literature perceives institutional combinations as consistently stable over time and rule out, firstly, the possibility of mixing institutional spheres from different types of economic governance and, secondly, the possibility of change within one sphere without affecting the others. Thus, change occurs only if the entire economic system shifts simultaneously from one to another system (Hall and Soskice 2001; Hall and Gingerich 2004).

The 'varieties of capitalism' approach has recently been strongly criticised (e.g. Amable 2003; Crouch 2003, 2005; Allen 2004). Allen (2004), for instance, criticises that the 'varieties of capitalism' literature assumes that national institutions are uniformly present across sectors, inducing homogeneity. In contrast, he argues that institutions are spread unevenly within nations, allowing heterogeneity of organisational outcomes. Crouch (2003) points out that the classification of different types of capitalist economies and the allocation of national economies to these different types runs the risk of becoming 'functionalist, deterministic and stereotypical' and may lead to 'an over-simple relationship between types and cases', disregarding within-system diversities (see also Crouch 2005: Chapter 2). Amable (2003) criticises the deterministic approach of Hall and Soskice (2001) and departs from a vast empirical assessment of the main domains in an economy (i.e. product and labour market, financial system, social protection and education) and finds five different groups in organising these institutions: market-based (Anglo-Saxon countries), social democratic (Nordic), Asian, Mediterranean and continental European (although he stresses the diversity within this latter group).

In accordance with this critique of the 'varieties of capitalism' literature, this study clearly reveals within-system diversity, which results in surprising outcomes that would not be explainable within the dualistic approach of economic systems. Instead, we found no single model in the British, Italian and Austrian economies but several within them. Still, this study uncovers some clear national patterns as a result of specific constellations of within-system diversity. For instance, we find that tighter employment regulation (e.g. working time regulation, collective agreements and codetermination) in Italy and Austria as compared to the UK leads to innovative ways of avoiding costly labour protection measures such as dependent forms of outsourcing. An interesting point here is that both the Italian and Austrian public policies support this development, actively contributing to an insider–outsider labour market. On the other hand, we found, for instance, that the insurance industry – and especially the selling process – is highly regulated in the UK than in Italy and Austria. This leads to the result that insurance companies in the UK are more eager to have direct control over their sales agents in order to comply with regulations. Thus, they either employ their agents on the basis of an employment contract (to have direct control) or they source out not only labour but also legal liability by working with independent agents. Furthermore, the high degree of competition in the British insurance industries fortifies the necessity to have stronger control over their agents. Consequently, there are very different institutions at work that produce this particular national patterns, namely a higher rate of dependent self-employment in Italy and Austria than in the UK.

This study demonstrates how types of economic governance are mixed by introducing hierarchical elements to market relationships, thus opposing typological approaches such as the 'varieties of capitalism', which exclude hybrids of this kind. It is shown that the 'varieties of capitalism' literature is too rigid in this argument.

1.3.3 The industries

Chapter 2 demonstrates that dependent forms of outsourcing are prevalent in many industries. The most common examples are the trucking industry (Fernández et al. 2000; Baker and Hubbard 2003, 2004; Chapter 6 in this book), the media industry (Dex et al. 2000; Baumann 2002) and the construction industry (Eccles 1981; Nisbet 1997; Bosch and Philips 2003). The case studies in this book address the insurance (UK, Italy and Austria), business service (Italy and Austria) and transport industry (Austria). As already discussed above, most insurance companies in the UK and in Austria organise their distribution using three main channels. Firstly, direct sales agents are employed by the insurance company and sell only their employer's insurance product. Secondly, tied agents are self-employed but have a tied business relationship with the insurance company they contract with. They are only allowed to sell insurance product from this same company. Thirdly, independent agents who are self-employed but sell insurance products from different insurance companies. Obviously, these three distribution channels represent three forms of work: the employee status, dependent self-employment and independent self-employment. Thus, the organisational governance of the insurance industry demonstrates that firms do not face the classical make-or-buy decision, but rather simultaneously make, buy and cooperate. Consequently, case study research in the insurance industry enables us to investigate the rationales and consequences for internalising or externalising specific transactions.

In contrast to the UK and Austria, tied agents ('produttori liberi') have already had a long tradition in Italy. Virtually all sales agents of an insurance company are tied agents, representing only one particular insurance company and accessing the market under the logo and name of the insurance company they contract with. As in the other two countries, they are only paid on the basis of the products they sell. However, in contrast, these tied agents are not directly controlled by managers of the insurance company but by other dependent self-employed ('titolari di settori'), who are responsible for the coordination of tied agents of a specific region. Those, in turn, are managed by company managers ('agenti generali'). Thus, although the managerial structure differs in the three countries, we find that in all countries the insurance industry represents an example where companies use legally self-employed workers who work exclusively for them in managerial subordination.

The unit of analysis in this case study of the insurance industry is the organisation of distribution of insurance products. This means – in more technical terms – that the dependent variable is whether an insurance company uses tied agency or not. Although the determination of the unit of analysis helps us to limit the boundaries of this case study research, we are nevertheless interested in the broader system of business organisation, determining the embeddedness of firms' internal social relations. Transactions are not only embedded in a social context but also in the context of other transactions. Hence, transactions controlled by one mechanism have an effect on transactions controlled by another mechanism. For instance, firms can use the information the in-house distribution channel (i.e. the direct sales force) generates for negotiating contract terms with tied agents. Likewise, using different distribution channels simultaneously increases competition between governance structures and creates pressures on bargaining power. Consequently, we have to study not only the tied agent channel but also the other distribution channels in order to fully understand the logic of dependent outsourcing in the insurance industry.

The business relationships between the insurance companies and their tied agents are long-term and continuous, based on relational contracts, and not short-term, project-based relationships. As we will see in Chapter 6, the long-term nature of these business relationships is pivotal for the creation of dependency and trust. Another reason for choosing the insurance industry for a case study is that tied agents are among those that are legally more or less clearly defined as being self-employed. Nevertheless, Chapter 6 will demonstrate that tied agents are both economically and personally dependent on the insurance company they are tied to. Thus, this study will clearly show that some workers are *dependent* self-employed despite the fact that they are legally independent self-employed. In sum, the insurance industry represents an excellent case to study dependent forms of outsourcing and self-employment.

While the insurance industry works in all three countries with legally self-employed workers, the business service industries in Italy and Austria mainly deploys them on the basis of hybrid legal forms (see Chapter 3 for legal details). This research set-up allows us to investigate whether the legal form of the dependent self-employed workers has an effect on the organisational governance of these forms of work.

In both countries, firms in the business service industry are mainly small and medium-sized companies that massively deploy staff with short-term employment contracts or on the basis of hybrid legal forms. This refers particularly to the executive staff involved in particular projects (e.g. field experts, tutors, teaching staff), while management and administrative personnel are mostly hired with standard employment contracts.

Industrial restructuring in Italy and Austria have led to a trend of sourcing out both core and non-core activities, leading to a fundamental change in the demand for input factors. The intermediary (business to business) demand for business services has been rising steadily due to increasing demand spurred by technological innovation, market changes and increased complexity of labour processes.

Since the business service industry subsumes many different jobs in both countries, the organisation of dependent self-employment is, of course, not uniform. The common criteria are that dependent self-employed workers only work for one company in (more or less) hierarchical subordination. Some of our interviewees stated that they work from the premises of the company they contract with, others from their own. Although the business service sector uses extensively the legal hybrid forms in both countries, we nevertheless find also legally self-employed that work only for one company in subordination.

The final case is the transport industry in Austria where dependent self-employment is a massively increasing phenomenon. Also here we find a dichotomic organisation. Both employees and dependent self-employed workers deliver goods to customers, but while employees use the carriers' trucks, the dependent self-employed workers drive their own (although often with the carrier's logo on it). Deregulation of road transport has resulted in increasing competition because a great number of foreign forwarders entered the Austrian market. Reacting to the harsher competition, Austrian forwarders pursue the following strategies: cost-cutting, mergers and acquisitions and concentration on core business. A company-owned truck pool constitutes significant fixed costs. Thus, sourcing out physical transport reduces these fixed costs substantially. Furthermore, for many forwarders physical transport is not part of their core business and, thus, source out (part of) their truck pool for strategic reasons. Overall, we observe a strong tendency to reduce the number of company-owned vehicles. Like in the insurance industry, we mainly observe legally self-employed individuals being dependent self-employed.

1.4 Overview of the book

The rest of the book is organised as follows. Chapter 2 presents a literature overview, analysing work on the border between employment and self-employment across Europe and the US and embedding this research into a broader analysis of recent labour market developments. It discusses research on self-employment, franchising and gives international evidence of outcontracting. So far, dependent forms of self-employment have been mainly analysed in the trucking, construction and media industries. This chapter brings together literature from Europe and the US, highlighting the role of both microeconomic factors and political institutions in shaping forms of work on the border between employment and self-employment on both the national and also the industry level.

Chapter 3 argues that dependent self-employment has crucial implications for social and labour market policies. The employment status under which a person carries out his or her work matters because the access to employment rights depends on the employment status. Self-employed persons are widely excluded from employment protection and social security law. Most European countries face the problem of a high degree of uncertainty attached to the legal and social criteria by which workers are classified. This chapter shows that conventional classifications have become too rigid to deal effectively with the growth of non-standard forms of work. As a result, certain groups of workers are excluded from (parts of) the social security system as well as from the protection of labour law. This chapter contrasts those European countries that introduced a hybrid legal category to capture dependent forms of self-employment (i.e. Italy, Germany and Austria) with those who still apply a largely dichotomic approach (e.g. UK, France, Sweden) and discusses the effects of these different regulations and institutional set-ups. Finally, the legal set-up in European countries is contrasted with that of US framework.

Chapter 4 gives the supply-side picture of the story. It analyses workers on the border between employment and self-employment, asking – on the basis of both quantitative and qualitative methods – who these workers are and why they supply this kind of work. After the introduction of a theoretical framework of analysis, it presents original qualitative case study research in the UK, Italy and Austria as well as quantitative research using the British and Italian Labour Force Surveys. Results of the qualitative research show that supply-side measures (such as tax policy), the absence of opportunities for dependent employment, lower start-up costs and a simpler work process play a crucial role for individuals to work as dependent self-employed. Multivariate analysis of the British and Italian Labour Force Surveys show a very different picture of the two countries, highlighting the different labour market institutions. While dependent self-employment in the UK is a story of outsourcing the low-qualified and older staff, creating a flexible, secondary low-cost labour market, Italy's dependent self-employed workers are the young, highly qualified that struggle on a highly protected insider–outsider labour market.

Chapter 5 explores economic and sociological theories of the firm and argues that the sharp delineation of markets, hierarchies and hybrids used in conventional theories does not allow us to explain dependent forms of outsourcing. First, it is shown that dependent outsourcing consists of both hierarchical and (relational) market elements. Dependent long-term business relationships are based on relational contracts that are laced with elements of dependency and hierarchy. Second, firms simultaneously make, buy and cooperate, using different control mechanisms for the same function. On the basis of this finding, the key features of dependent outsourcing are discussed. Finally, this chapter explores relevant sociological theories of the firm that help to explain governance structures that use dependent forms of outsourcing. These insights assist in deriving relevant research questions for the empirical investigation of the driving factors of dependent outsourcing in the subsequent chapter.

Chapter 6 looks at the demand side, i.e. at firms that deploy dependent self-employed workers, applying an organisational theory framework. The main intention of this chapter is to investigate the reasons and effects for firms to deploy dependent self-employed workers and, especially, how they solve the control–flexibility dilemma. More specifically, it is shown by which formal and informal mechanisms dependency is created and which implications we find for commitment and trust. The key argument of this chapter is that firms have established governance structures based on markets, hierarchies and self-enforcing relational contracts so that they are able to keep a substantial amount of control despite of sourcing out labour. It is argued that these work relationships produce dependency. On the basis of original qualitative case study research in various industries (i.e. insurance, freight, business services) in the UK, Italy and Austria, it is demonstrated that dependency is created, firstly, by the contractual restriction of alternative uses of resources, secondly, by managerial support measures that bind the worker closely to the firm, thirdly, by relationship-specific investments made by the worker and fourthly, by authority elements. Temporal and network embeddedness plays a crucial role in creating 'calculative' trust and reducing opportunism of both parties.

The final chapter discusses the findings of the study in the light of relevant labour and social policy research and current social developments. It shows that the 'varieties of capitalism' literature is too rigid in the dualistic view of organising capitalism. In contrast, this study finds that within-system diversity [e.g. high (low) employment protection in combination with weak (strong) industrial regulation] is crucial in explaining recent developments of outcontracting labour. Thus, it puts forward the analytical combination of macro- and micro-level research. Further, it proposes policy recommendations that help to balance labour and social protection and the incentives for entrepreneurial activities.

2
Work on the Border Between Employment and Self-Employment

2.1 Recent trends of self-employment

Self-employment consistently increased in all European countries between the mid-1970s until the mid-1990s. The OECD (2000) (see Table 2.1) shows that most European countries saw a rise in self-employment between 1979 and 1997 – with a higher growth of women's self-employment than that of men (although the level of women's self-employment rates are in all the European countries still well below men's).[1]

Data on self-employment in the EU (see Table 2.2) show that self-employment has slightly decreased in most countries during the period between 1995 and 2005. Only the Czech Republic, Slovakia and Germany (modest) show a growing trend. In 2005, roughly 16 per cent of the EU labour force was self-employed (including, however, the agriculture sector). Strikingly, south European countries have a self-employment rate above the EU average, which is due to the small-scale business structure of these countries. Most post-socialist countries show a rapid emergence of self-employment which is also a consequence of public policies to foster the economic transition to capitalism (OECD 2000).

These data do not reveal the heterogeneity within the group of the self-employed, however. It consists not only of traditional craft producers and shop owners but increasingly also of unskilled self-employed and professionals working as freelancers or other semi-autonomous work arrangements. Comparing 11 OECD countries, Arum and Müller (2004: 7 and 430ff) point out that self-employment is increasingly

Table 2.1 Annual average growth rates of self-employment[a] and total civilian employment (in percentages)

	1979–90		1990–97	
	Self-employment	Civilian employment	Self-employment	Civilian employment
Austria[b]	−1.4	1.2	4.8	1.6
Belgium[c]	1.5	0.2	1.5	0.0
Denmark	−1.4	1.0	−0.7	0.4
Finland	4.8	1.5	0.4	−1.6
France	−0.5	0.6	−1.4	0.4
Germany[d]	0.3	0.8	2.4	−0.5
Greece	0.5	1.5	1.5	1.4
Ireland[e]	2.8	0.4	3.3	3.8
Italy	2.6	1.1	−0.2	−0.5
Luxembourg	−0.6	2.0	..	..
Netherlands[f]	1.5	2.4	5.7	2.2
Portugal	6.4	3.5	2.4	0.6
Spain	2.2	1.5	1.6	1.0
Sweden	5.3	0.8	1.4	−1.7
UK[c]	6.6	0.5	−0.9	0.0

.. Data not available.
[a] Excluding agricultural sector and unpaid family workers.
[b] Excluding some owner-managers of incorporated enterprises.
[c] 1990–96 instead of 1990–97.
[d] 1991–97 instead of 1990–97.
[e] Excluding owner-managers of incorporated enterprises.
[f] 1975–79 instead of 1973–79.
Source: OECD (2000).

heterogeneous within and between countries with a progressively stronger prevalence of professional/managerial occupations in corporatist and neoliberal states. Moreover, they highlight that societies with low levels of labour market regulation have a greater share of unskilled self-employment.

The increased heterogeneity of self-employment seems also to be associated with the rising instability due to the growth of short-term spells in this labour market status especially for unskilled occupations and women (Houseman and Polivka 2000; Arum and Müller 2004: 452; Hyytinen and Rouvinen 2006). Thus, although the overall self-employment rates have been pretty stable over the last 15 years, there is a greater number of individuals affected by self-employment over their life course.

Table 2.2 Self-employment in some EU countries, 1995–2005

	All			Men			Women		
	1995	2005	Change %points	1995	2005	Change %points	1995	2005	Change %points
Austria	20.2	19.9	−0.3	20.5	22.9	+2.4	19.9	16.3	−3.3
Belgium	18.3	16.2	−2.1	19.5	18.6	−0.9	16.4	13.0	−3.4
Czech Rep.	11.9	18.0	+6.1	17.2[a]	22.8	+5.6	9.1[a]	11.7	+2.6
Denmark	7.6	6.3	−1.3	9.9	8.5	−1.4	4.8	3.8	−1.0
Finland	13.7	11.6	−2.1	17.7	15.2	−2.5	9.3	7.8	−1.5
France	10.7	8.9	−1.8	12.6	11.3	−1.3	8.3	6.1	−2.2
Germany	10.0	11.2	+1.2	11.6	13.4	+1.8	7.8	8.6	+0.8
Greece	45.8	40.8	−5.0	47.0	43.7	−3.3	43.7	36.0	−7.7
Hungary	17.9	13.8	−4.1	21.1[b]	17.1	−4.0	12.4[b]	9.8	−2.6
Ireland	20.5	17.0	−3.5	27.2	24.2	−3.0	9.3	7.1	−2.2
Italy	26.9	24.5	−2.5	29.6	28.1	−1.5	22.1	18.9	−3.2
Netherlands	15.7	13.7	−2.0	17.0	16.1	−0.9	13.8	10.8	−3.0
Poland	36.5	28.8	−7.7	39.1[a]	31.2	−7.9	34.0[a]	25.8	−8.2
Portugal	25.2	24.1	−1.1	26.1	25.4	−0.7	24.1	22.6	−1.5
Slovakia	6.6	13.0	+6.4	9.5[a]	17.6	+8.1	4.2[a]	7.1	+2.9
Slovenia	18.8	17.1	−1.7	21.2[c]	19.5	−1.7	15.4[c]	14.3	−1.1
Spain	18.8	14.4	−4.4	19.5	16.3	−3.2	17.5	11.5	−6.0
Sweden	5.6	4.8	−0.8	8.1	6.8	−1.3	2.8	2.6	−0.2
UK	13.8	12.7	−0.5	18.4	17.1	−1.3	8.0	7.7	−0.3
EU25	16.7	15.6	−1.1	19.4	18.7	−0.7	12.9	11.6	−1.3
US	8.3[d]	7.2[e]	−1.1						

[a] 1998.
[b] 1997.
[c] 1999.
[d] 1996.
[e] 2002.
Self-employment in per cent of total employment.
Source: European Commission, Employment in Europe 2006.

2.2 Dependent forms of outsourcing and the development of self-employment

Recent changes in industrial organisation – such as greater stress on outsourcing and the rise in franchising activities – is a pivotal factor for the development of self-employment in Europe. Meager (1998), for instance, sees outsourcing as one of the main reasons for the rapid growth in self-employment in the UK during the 1980s. There is, however, empirical support for the thesis that a growing share of outsourcing is related to work relationships where the agent is strongly integrated into the business of the principal (Semlinger 1993; Dietrich 1996; Burchell et al. 1999; Eiro 2002). Although many governments have increased their efforts to foster self-employment, concerns about dependent self-employment have been raised in many European countries. Countries like Germany, Greece, Belgium, Italy and Austria have introduced special measures to control dependent self-employment.

The OECD (2000) suggests that it is likely that there has been an increase in forms of work in the grey zone between self-employment and normal employment, referring to contractors who work in a dependent relationship with just one enterprise and who have only little or no more autonomy than employees although they are classified as self-employed. Scarce knowledge about dependent forms of self-employment in terms of quantity and quality, however, makes it difficult for policymakers to impose focused measures. The limited research on this topic is a direct result of the difficulty of drawing a line between self-employment and normal employment, as discussed in the introductory chapter.

In 2002, the European Foundation for the Improvement of Living and Working Conditions published a report on 'Economically dependent workers, employment law and industrial relations', presenting not only legal developments in the EU countries but also some figures on dependent self-employment (Eiro 2002). However, due to the problem of defining dependent self-employment and the lack of legal regulations in most EU countries, Eiro (2002) only presents data for those countries where regulations exist that cover at least part of the group of dependent self-employed workers (i.e. Austria, Denmark, Germany, Greece, Italy, the Netherlands and Portugal). Although these data have to be treated with extreme caution as Eiro (2002) points out, there seems to be evidence that around 1 per cent of the work-force in these countries are dependent self-employed workers. They work predominantly in sectors where outsourcing and subcontracting is a common phenomenon: construction, road transport, hotels and catering, finance, maintenance, media and ICT.

For the UK, Burchell et al. (1999) find that 5 per cent of all those in employment are individuals who contract to supply their own personal services to an employer without having a contract of employment but who are to some degree economically dependent on the employer's business because they derive a substantial part of their income from this particular work. For Germany, Dietrich (1996) affirms that around 3 per cent of the labour force work in the grey zone between self-employment and employment. On the basis of Italian social security data, Berton et al. (2005) states that there were more than half a million 'parasubordinati' (i.e. self-employed without employees working for one company) in Italy in 1999, representing 2.5 per cent of those in employment. In Austria, there were around 1.1 per cent of the labour force working as self-employed for only one contractor and being bound by the instructions of the employer or contract partner (in terms of labour time and methods) in 2001 (Statistik Austria 2002). Further and even more important, these international surveys indicate a rapid growth of hierarchical forms of outsourcing (Eiro 2002; Chapter 4 in this book).

2.3 The special case of franchising

One important group in the grey zone between self-employment and normal employment are franchisees. Franchising, a special case of dependent self-employment,[2] describes types of contracts between franchisees and franchisors, where the franchisor owns a certain means of production such as land, buildings, machinery or trademarks. The crucial feature of franchising is that 'the contracts specify, to a significant extent, how the business is operated, and require the payment of part of total sales' (OECD 2000: 8). However, the degree of dependence of franchisees varies considerably according to the contract.[3] There is evidence that many franchisors seek inexperienced franchisees, so that they remain dependent on the franchisor (OECD 2000). Basically, the role of the franchisor is to place a certain means of production and a specific know-how at the franchisee's disposal. The franchisee, in turn, provides finance and labour. In that respect, franchising may represent an important 'port of entry' into self-employment since the franchisor delivers the necessary expertise to open and to run a business. The franchisee, however, must remunerate this expertise with a relatively high share of the turnover or profit. The franchisee is by definition dependent on the franchisor, whilst the degree of this dependence varies according to the contractual and actual situation.

Felstead (1993) analysed franchise contracts and stressed that only few franchisees are found to have significant levels of autonomy. He finds that franchisees are often dependent workers, being highly vulnerable to changes of rules and policy as well as priority and goals of the franchisors. Empirical research in the UK shows that franchisors often express a preference for franchisees without experience in the business so that they are 'more receptive to training and directions', and that they 'bring "no bad habits" or preconceptions with them' (Felstead 1993: 85). Looking at the Coca-Cola's franchise structure in Germany, Felstead

(1993: Chapter 6) finds two interdependent elements in the franchise relationship. Firstly, franchisees buy not only the main ingredient of the product they produce (i.e. the concentrate) but are also forced to buy other input factors (machines, cars, petrol, etc.) from specific suppliers and have to operate according to a standard formula. Secondly, not only the market exchange itself is controlled but also 'the use to which these purchases are put' are governed by 'a range of contractual clauses' (Felstead 1993: 186).

2.4 Evidence of independent contractors in the US

Using US establishment-level data, Davis-Blake and Uzzi (1993) explore why firms employ independent contractors. Without discussing the degree of (in)dependence these contractors face, they interpret independent contractors as self-employed individuals who have a contract of service with a subcontracting firm. Logistic regression results interestingly show that costs from fringe benefits and unionisation have no effect on the use of independent contractors. In contrast, factors such as variation in employment levels, establishment size and being part of a multiple-site firm have positive effects on the use of outside contractors. They see the use of independent contractors as a way of externalising administrative control since firms are unlikely to exercise such day-to-day control over independent contractors. Thus, independent contractors operate outside the normal administrative structure of the firm. It is predicted that firms with bureaucratic employment practices may use independent contractors as a way of gaining flexibility without disrupting the firm's routine practices. Indeed, results show a positive relationship between the level of bureaucratised employment practices in an establishment and the use of independent contractors. Further results reveal that the use of independent contractors is affected by industry. Firms in construction are more likely than firms in manufacturing to deploy independent contractors, and firms in service or trade proved less likely than firms in manufacturing to use independent contractors.

Harrison and Kelley (1993) explore management motivation for subcontracting and outsourcing by analysing a nationally representative sample of production managers in one thousand plants in the US metalwork sector. In this paper, outsourcing is characterised as a discrete choice between two existing alternatives: make versus buy. However, they argue that 'make' is only a meaningful alternative when the establishment already possesses the technology and the type of workforce capable of carrying out these activities within its own facilities. Consequently, their research focuses on the decision-making situation in which management still has in-house capability. Using logistic regression models, Harrison and Kelley (1993) find that plants with higher labour costs (in terms of average hourly wages) are more likely to source out than plants with lower wage costs. Firm size, further, has a significant effect on the likelihood of outsourcing, with larger firms tending to subcontract more. However, it is stressed that differences in the outsourcing practices of large and small companies cannot be credited to differences in the economic or technical characteristics of the manufacturing facilities these firms operate. Another interesting result is that the scope of production seems to play an important role in the decision to subcontract. Firms producing a greater variety of products are more likely to engage in outsourcing, while firms with a high degree of customisation in the production process seem to subcontract less. Finally, Harrison and Kelley (1993) find that when both a union and a joint problem-solving mechanism are present in the plant, the tendency to subcontract is reduced significantly. However, they find no support that the presence of joint labour-management problem-solving committees in non-unionised plants alone reduces the propensity for outsourcing.

Abraham and Taylor (1996) empirically examine three hypotheses about an employer's decision to contract out rather than to carry out a task in-house, using data from the US Industry Wage Survey in the manufacturing industry. The first hypothesis suggests that high-wage organisations contract out in order to take advantage of low market wage rates for certain types of low-skilled work. The second hypothesis looks at the relationship between peak period tasks and outsourcing, claiming that subcontracting is used to smooth the workload of regular staff. The third hypothesis claims that the decision to source out may not reflect considerations of the labour market and industrial relations at all but is based on the existence of scale economies accruing to specialised providers of particular services. Using ordered probit models, Abraham and Taylor (1996) find that a sketch of employers' motives for subcontracting is rather complex, reflecting a mixture of all three hypotheses. In more detail, their analysis suggests that the reason for outsourcing low-skill work in high-wage establishments is primarily to reduce hourly labour costs. The subcontracting of other tasks is mainly related with smaller establishment size or location. In turn, it is found that low-wage establishments are more likely to contract out certain types of high-skill services. These findings show that outsourcing behaviour is also based on internal equity considerations, which constrain the relative wage paid to employees within a single internal labour market. Moreover, they find support for the idea that the existence of economies of scale of the provided services is pivotal for the outsourcing decision. Additionally, their results suggest that firms in more cyclical industries only contract out specific tasks. For example, the data have shown that these firms are more likely to source out accounting services, while they are less likely to source out tasks like machine maintenance services. Thus, Abraham and Taylor (1996) conclude from these results that 'establishments may be discouraged from using outside contractors by the desire to reserve certain tasks to be performed by the regular work force during off-peak periods' (p. 417).

Kalleberg et al. (2000) analyse whether individuals with non-standard forms of work show more bad job characteristics (defined as low wages, lack of health insurance and/or pension) than individuals in standard employment in the US. For independent contractors (including both wage-and-salary and self-employed independent contractors) it is found that they are strongly associated with bad job characteristics also when controlling for age, education, occupation and industry. Not surprisingly, the results are even stronger for wage-and-salary than for self-employed contractors as well as stronger for women than for men (in both forms of contracting work).

Lautsch (2002) looks at contingent work (i.e. independent contracting and temporary work) in US firms and identifies systematic differences in issues such as job definition, wage rules and career development of contingent jobs across organisational contexts. She makes out different contingent work subsystems in the analysed firms that are either cost- or flexibility-focused or both. All of these contingent work subsystems generate trade-offs for both groups of workers (i.e. regular and contingent workers) as well as the firm. Thus, Lautsch (2002) opposes the view that contingent work has similar implications for firms and workers in all settings, stressing the heterogeneity of the effects of contingent work for both workers and firms and explaining these differences by performance objectives and production technologies.

Also Evans et al. (2004) and Kunda et al. (2002) criticise the dichotomic view in the literature – that is, on the one hand, the pessimistic view that contingent workers are mainly exploited and the optimistic view of the free agent (or sometimes also called 'portfolio worker') perspective that sees the agent as independent and entrepreneurial. One explanation for these two distinct views might be that the former empirically mainly focused on low-skilled workers, while the latter looked chiefly at high-skilled workers. Kunda et al. (2002) examined highly skilled technical professionals in a contingent labour market and point out that also high-skilled contractors reported feeling anxiety and estrangement although they are found to be better paid than permanent employees. Nevertheless, Kunda et al. (2002) reject the thesis that these workers are 'secondary sector' workers. In another paper based on the same empirical material, Evans et al. (2004) stress that the highly skilled contractors perceive themselves to have more flexibility than their employed counterparts, but do not use this gained opportunity to improve their work-life balance, but rather are found to work long hours and rarely schedule their time flexibly. Evans et al. (2004) put forward the argument that the contractors' time is strongly constraint by the cyclic structure of employment, the importance of reputation and the practice of billing by the hour and conclude that 'markets place more rather than fewer constraints on workers' time' (p. 1).

2.5 Evidence of dependent self-employment and dependent forms of outsourcing

Besides quantitative data on different forms of self-employment, sector-specific research provides evidence on dependent outsourcing and self-employment. The following presents a survey of three industries – i.e. the trucking, the construction and the media industry – in different countries where dependent self-employment is a common phenomenon.

The European and US trucking industries are characterised by a large fraction of owner-operators with just one truck (Fernández et al. 2000; Baker and Hubbard 2003, 2004; Arruñada et al. 2004; Chapter 6 of this book). Forwarders, whose main emphasis lies on planning and organising transport activities, do not necessarily carry out the actual physical transport. Instead, they source out these activities, either partly or as a whole. Thus, they either deploy both employees who use the asset of the employer and dependent self-employed workers who use their own trucks or they source out the whole fleet of trucks.

Baker and Hubbard (2003, 2004) analyse the explaining patterns of asset ownership in the US trucking industry. Drawing on Grossman and Hart (1986), they examine how contractibility affects asset ownership and the boundaries of the firm, focusing on the residual rights of control. They argue that ownership patterns (i.e. whether drivers own the trucks they drive or not) result from the non-contractibility of two sets of decision rights. The first set refers to rent-seeking activities like searching for orders other than those pre-arranged between forwarders and subcontractors, whilst the second set of non-contractible decision rights is linked to the way in which drivers operate trucks and, thus, maintain the trucks' value. The importance of each of these sets, so the argument goes, determines the optimal ownership of trucks. The results show that improved contracting through better control mechanisms (in this case through the use of on-board computers) leads to more integrated asset ownership and, thus, to larger firms. Improved contracting changes the set of decision rights through the allocation of residual control rights to the owner of the asset. Baker and Hubbard (2004) find that 'owner-operators are used for hauls where non-contractible decisions that affect trucks' value are important, but are used less once decisions become more contractible'. Hence, this empirical paper strongly supports the Grossman and Hart (1986) model of asset ownership, stressing the importance of residual control rights. They find that changes in contractibility affect firm boundaries or, more specifically, changes in monitoring technology tend to lead to less outsourcing. However, the analytic problem with this paper is that it is assumed that dependent forms of outsourcing are a legal fiction although the existence of such business relationships is not denied. In contrast, it is simply assumed that dependent outsourcing does not change the nature of incentive conflicts as described above.

Fernández et al. (1998, 2000) compare the European and US trucking industries and find that 'most of the owner-operators are quasi-integrated into larger organizations, which completely manages the work of the owner-operators' (Fernández et al. 2000: 304). They argue that this hybrid form of governance is generally more efficient than the vertical integration of trucks and drivers as it solves moral hazard problems related to the use of the trucks and simultaneously allows the quasi-integrated organisation to achieve economies of scale and density. It is argued that it is not these economies that lead to vertical integration but rather hold-up problems through specific assets. In a seminar paper, Klein et al. (1978) show that incomplete contracting and asset specificity can make vertical integration more efficient than outsourcing due to the existence of quasi-rents from specific assets. As a result, hold-up problems may arise when quasi-rents are exploitable. In order to circumvent hold-up problems, organisations vertically integrate. Drawing on Hart (1995), Fernández et al. (1998, 2000) argue that hold-up problems may also be (partly) solved by quasi-integration, that is by means of costly safeguards (e.g. implicit guarantees like non-exploitable specific investments in reputation) and the (necessarily incomplete) formalisation of contracts that allocates the residual control rights, thus ownership, to the driver (see also Arruñada et al. 2004). However, although Fernández et al. (1998, 2000) implicitly refer to dependent forms of outsourcing, they ignore that hold-up problems can be solved through relational contracts.

Moreover, as opposed to the US case (Baker and Hubbard 2003, 2004), Fernández et al. (2000) report that the vertical integration of trucks and the use of company drivers have not increased with the advances of ICT. Baker and Hubbard (2003, 2004), in contrast, argue that the ICT investments have led to a vertical integration of trucks and drivers as ICT facilitates control and monitor the behaviour of drivers as well as just-in-time delivery systems. Fernández et al. (2000), however, did not find an increase in vertical integration in Spain due to ICT investments and argue that this divergence is a result of institutional differences between the US and Spain. Firstly, they suggest that contrary to the US, the highly regulated Spanish labour law provides incentives to circumvent employment relationships. In a European comparison, they also provide evidence that vertical integration increases in those countries with less constraints on the labour relationship. Secondly, in contrast to the US, Spanish tax norms provide additional incentives for small firms, thus fostering vertical disintegration as well.

One of the first empirical papers on dependent self-employment analysed the US construction industry (Eccles 1981). It identifies the 'quasifirm' in the construction industry, which is based on a set of stable relationships between a general contractor and special trade subcontractors, the latter often being labour-only subcontractors. Drawing on Williamson's (1979) theoretical research on governance structures, Eccles' (1981) data reveal a governance structure with some market characteristics which falls somewhere between bilateral and unified structures. He concludes that the distinction between employees and subcontractors can be fuzzy in many cases, given the fact that many subcontractors work exclusively for one contractor. More specifically, Eccles (1981) finds that factors like better coordination and control, better quality of work, lower construction costs or economies of scale are important reasons as to why organisations integrate basic trades. More specialised tasks that are less critical to the progress of the project are more likely to be subcontracted to labour-only subcontractors.

In a more recent study, Nisbet (1997) compares the working conditions of employees and dependent self-employed workers in the British construction industry. The results of this case study show a multidimensional picture, with discrete advantages and disadvantages in both employment and self-employment for any level of skills. Firstly, there is evidence that the level of earnings of dependent self-employed workers seems to be higher than that of employees. Secondly, although self-employed subcontractors tend to perceive their job stability as being worse than for employees, they are, nevertheless, confident of finding another job in a short time.[4] Hence, most dependent self-employed workers claimed that job security was unproblematic. Thirdly, both employees and self-employed workers judged the tax system as being favourable for self-employment. Finally, job satisfaction and the ability to decide their own hours of work were highlighted as the main advantages for self-employed workers as compared to employees. In sum, those who prefer self-employment emphasised that independence in carrying out the job, job satisfaction, opportunities to earn higher than average wages and the advantages of the tax system were the main reasons for preferring self-employment over employment. Nisbet (1997) concludes that segmentation in the form of dualism is undermined by the existence of discrete advantages generally perceived to exist in both employment and dependent self-employment. It is argued that there is no simple dichotomy in respect of the key criteria of earnings and job security normally assumed to be indivisible in dualist studies. Moreover, Nisbet (1997) found no support for the dualist idea that labour-only subcontractors are a secondary labour force in comparison to 'entrepreneurial' sole proprietors. His research shows that the growth in self-employment in the construction industry is not necessarily indicative of the growth of a secondary labour force.

González-Díaz et al. (2000) analyse the causes of subcontracting in the Spanish construction industry using panel data of Spanish firms instead of the more common cross-sectional data and are, thus, able to control for unobserved firm-specific effects. However, their research focuses only on the outsourcing organisation without describing the characteristics of the subcontractors. Thus, we have no information on the frequency of labour-only subcontractors. Data show that 70 per cent of Spanish self-employed individuals are own-account workers. Consequently, we can assume that a substantial part of the subcontractors are labour-only subcontractors. González-Díaz et al. (2000) emphasise that a higher risk of hold-up reduces subcontracting because vertical integration is better for solving the quasi-rents expropriation problem. Moreover, they find that uncertainty has no statistically significant effect on subcontracting. Finally, they claim that subcontracting increases with the number of different products built by an organisation and its degree of specialisation in design and technical management. In another paper with the same empirical material,

González-Díaz et al. (1998) show that increases in the tax burden and the legal restriction in the variability of wages produce an incentive to source out workers in order to optimise labour under a new regulatory regime. Additional institutional constraints come from industry-specific regulations.

Bosch and Philips (2003) edited a book that compares the consequences of deregulation in the construction industry in nine countries in Europe, North America, Australia and Asia. They find that subcontracting – and thus, risk-shifting or risk-sharing – is in most countries a common response to the high financial risk faced in construction, although there are considerable differences across countries. Countries such as Denmark (Lubanski 2003), Germany (Bosch and Zühlke-Robinet 2003), the Netherlands (van der Meer 2003) and Australia (Underhill 2003) have created an environment where regulations and collective agreements lead to a highly skilled workforce and high-wage growth, creating an industry-specific labour market with a stable workforce. Other countries such as Spain (Byrne and van der Meer 2003), Korea (Yoon and Kang 2003) and especially the UK (Harvey 2003), however, have chosen the way of deregulation and the promotion of price and wage competition, resulting in a strongly fragmented subcontracting system, a high turnover of a low-skilled workforce and an underinvestment in new technology.[5] This international comparison shows that governmental policies (e.g. contractor licensing regulations, building codes, tax policies) play a pivotal role in the structure of subcontracting. Bosch and Philips (2003: 10) argue that subcontracting to individual workers 'is usually designed to evade regulations protecting wage workers rather than designed to extend specialization'. For the UK, for instance, Harvey (2003) argues that a shift of regulation in the British construction industry that reduced stable public demand and increased the incentives for more volatile private home ownership as well as the simultaneous promotion of self-employment during the 1980s and early 1990s, led to a strong increase in self-employment in the British construction industry (with 50 per cent of the construction workers being self-employed in 1999). Harvey (2003) claims that this shift towards self-employment means that, firstly, payments for these workers are outside any wage bargaining, secondly, they loose their entitlements such as holiday pay, sick pay, unemployment benefit and thirdly, they loose most employment protection for dismissal or discipline. These changes together with the removal of the employer's obligation to pay any national insurance contributions when outsourcing individual labour and workers reduced payments for national insurance lead to an overall reduction in labour costs through self-employment of roughly 20–30 per cent.

Storey et al. (2005), Dex et al. (2000) and Ursell (2000) analyse the changes in the competitive and regulative conditions for British television during the 1980s and the 1990s, which created an environment of increased uncertainty for those who work in the British media industry. Broadcasting legislation, increased competition and technological advances have changed both work practices and organisation. These changes have led to a workforce in which over 60 per cent are freelancers facing uncertainty (Ursell 2000).

Until the 1980s, the British television industry was structured as a vertically integrated public service broadcaster (BBC), together with a few integrated and heavily regulated private sector broadcasters. The regulative changes started with the launch of a new channel whose organisational structure deviated from the earlier vertically integrated structure, which created – together with further regulatory changes – a stimulus to the new independent production sector. Simultaneously, the changes in the organisational structure of the industry led to changes in work arrangements. Before the 1980s, the majority of television workers had long-term salaried labour contracts with broadcasters. However, industrial restructuring has meant that since the 1990s, the majority of workers in the industry have been either on fixed-term contracts or on freelance contracts on a self-employed basis. What followed is best termed as 'double outsourcing'. The broadcasters source many activities out to (in)dependent contractors who, in turn, only deploy a skeleton staff on short-term contracts and source a large part out again to self-employed freelancers. Thus, the distribution of risk has been changed dramatically. Dex et al. (2000: 285) conclude that 'many of the risks attached to television production have now been shifted away from programme controllers and broadcasters to the work force'.

Using both quantitative and qualitative data and methods, Dex et al. (2000) focus on the effects of deregulation and increasing uncertainty on the individuals' experiences in the labour market. Unsurprisingly, they find that uncertainty is indeed a problem for the majority of the media workers covered by the data because it causes stress. The group who struggles most with the new circumstances are those in their forties used to an earlier organisational form but too far away from retirement to feel unconcerned about the uncertainty they face. Further, it is found that self-employed freelance workers 'were substantially more vulnerable than staff to the problems of uncertainty and many appeared to be less able to adopt successful strategies to ameliorate some of the disadvantages of the uncertain environment'. Very small independent owners in particular feel as vulnerable as the freelance workers they deploy. Dex et al. (2000) also look at the strategies individuals adopt to respond to uncertainty. It is found that workers facing uncertainty start, firstly, to diversify their income portfolio to reduce risk and, secondly, try harder to collect information and to build informal contacts.

Similar results were found by Storey et al. (2005), who look at how freelancers in the British media industry incorporate an enterprise culture as a major element of their self-identities. They argue that freelancers use the notion of enterprise not only in reference to their individual success but also to failures. On the one hand, freelancers state to enjoy the independence and autonomy of their 'portfolio' work but also stress that the market often fails to work fairly and openly, pointing to existing power asymmetries in the labour market.

Baumann (2002) analyses the institutionalisation of training in the British and German media industries. Both the German and the British media industries are characterised by a high amount of freelance and subcontracting activity. Unlike to the situation in the 1980s, about a third of the entire workforce in both countries is now deployed either as a freelancer or on a short-term contract. This development has, of course, a strong impact on the training situation in the media industry since 'employers' are reluctant to invest in training highly mobile workers. This conflict has resulted in the practice of informal training on-the-job in both countries. Recognising the problem of free-riding and skills problems in the long run, industry actors have started to set up training institutions. However, Baumann (2002) finds that the institutional development took different roads in the two countries analysed due to the specificity of the societal embeddedness of the actors as well as the institutions. Nevertheless, it is shown that these institutional developments have not been created in a 'unidirectional' way, leaving enough room for the highly flexible needs of a permanently changing industry.

2.6 Conclusions

This chapter has presented an overview of empirical research on self-employment and employment in the grey zone between self-employment and employment. We have seen that self-employment has risen in most European countries, with women showing lower levels, but stronger increases in starting up their own business. However, there is evidence that various forms of outsourcing and subcontracting partly explain this increase in self-employment. The analysis of workers in the grey zone between self-employment and employment such as franchisees and outside contractors shows that these workers are often unable to exploit entrepreneurial possibilities due to a restricted alternative use of their resources. Empirical research in the trucking, construction and media industry provides evidence on dependent forms of outsourcing and the use of mixed control mechanisms. It has been shown that dependent outsourcing is generally more efficient than vertical integration as it solves moral hazard problems whilst simultaneously allowing to achieve economies of scale and partly solving hold-up problems. The increase in outsourcing was heavily driven by regulatory (media industry) and technological (trucking industry) developments.

3
The Institutional Factor: Labour Law and Regulations Across Europe

3.1 The legal uncertainty of dependent self-employment

Changes in the organisation of work over the last two decades have shown that the personal scope of labour law and parts of social security law in European countries, which have focused on permanent full-time employees, are too narrow. Thus, legal scientists have argued that the traditionally personal scope of labour law and parts of social security law no longer reflect the organisation of work in today's society (Sciarra 1991, 2004; Burchell et al. 1999; Supiot 2001; Engblom 2003; Freedland 2003; Perulli 2003). National legal discourses, however, are divided between the approach that a broader scope of labour law with a dominant role of contracts of employment would strengthen social justice, while the other approach sees labour law measures as a limit to economic efficiency and incentives, favouring the expansion of possible work arrangements governed by the principles of civil and commercial law (Freedland 2003: Chapter 1; Perulli 2003: 6; Sciarra 2004: 17).

In order to account for recent changes in work organisations, many European states as well as the European Union (EU) have introduced new laws and regulations. Atypical employees – such as part-time or fixed-term employees – have been given employment protection and social benefits similar to those of their colleagues who work on a permanent and full-time basis. Examples of this trend in Austria are the legal regulation of part-time work in 1992, which led to greater equality of treatment between full-time and part-time workers (Mühlberger 2000) or, more recently, the incorporation of parts of the dependent self-employed workforce into the social security system in 1997 and 1998. In the UK, the length of the continuous service part-time workers have to fulfil in order to be eligible to employment protection (such as redundancy and dismissal protection) was reduced from 5 to 2 years in 1995 (EIRR 1995). In 1999, the British Government reduced the threshold for the employer's contribution to marginal employment, leading to a subvention of low-paid work in the UK (Purcell et al. 1999). At the level of the EU, two directives focusing on part-time (1997)[1] and fixed-term employment (1999),[2] respectively, were introduced to improve the quality of these forms of work and to reduce the possibilities for using atypical work as a means of avoiding labour law and social security regulations (Engblom 2001, 2003; Freedland 2003). These two European directives show nicely the direction of EU law in regulating atypical work, indicating a binding principle to which national legislation must conform.

Both common law countries and continental legal systems distinguish a self-employed worker from an employee using criteria such as subordination, allocation of risk and dependence.[3] Yet as is shown, for instance, in Burchell et al. (1999) and in the empirical part of this book, this distinction is becoming increasingly difficult to apply. Freedland (2003: 18) argues that the dichotomist view of employees versus self-employed independent contractors is based on a 'false unity' of the two concepts, leading to a 'false duality'. The indirect assumption of this binary rationale is that labour law is based on the need to protect employees, which are regarded as the weak party in the employment contract. Self-employed persons, on the other hand, are seen as equal to the parties they contract with and are, thus, subject to market forces (Perulli 2003: 6f). However, new forms of work organisation prove that both concepts (i.e. employment versus self-employment) are fuzzy in reality, including a variety of work activities. The resulting 'grey zone' describes those types of work that show characteristics of both, employment and self-employment, which makes it difficult to fit them into the binary system. Additionally, the 'grey zone' refers to those types of work that appear to be self-employed, but which are, in fact, dependent or subordinate employed (often labelled 'false self-employment')[4] (Perulli 2003: 14f).

Dependent self-employment is a significant topic in current labour market research since the employment status under which a person carries out work matters. It matters because the access to employment rights depends on the employment status. More concretely, it matters because the application of rights and obligations concerning employment protection, social security and taxation varies across different employment statuses. We know, for instance, that self-employed persons are widely excluded from employment protection and employment security law. Thus, the classification of employment statuses is important not only from a legal perspective, but also from a social point of view.

However, most European countries face the problem of a high degree of uncertainty attached to the legal and social criteria by which workers are classified. As a result, certain groups of workers have been excluded from the social security system as well as from the protection of employment legislation. Legal scientists argue that dependent self-employed workers are definitely amongst those whose employment status is largely in doubt (Sciarra 1991, 2004; Burchell et al. 1999; Davies and Freedland 2000; Supiot 2001; Freedland 2003). Consequently, some countries have enacted, only partly successfully, laws to deal with those forms of work that are in this 'grey zone' between dependent employment and independent self-employment (OECD 2000).

In a study on dependent self-employed workers and employment law, the European Foundation for the Improvement of Living and Working Conditions (Eiro 2002) stresses that the difficulty of assessing dependent forms of self-employment are tackled in different ways throughout the EU. In countries with no statutory definition of dependent employment (Ireland, Sweden and the UK), case law is the most important source of assessment. Other countries (e.g. Austria, France, Portugal, Greece and Germany) have partly extended labour protection by legislative intervention either by the introduction of new laws for specific work relationships (Austria, France, Portugal, Greece and Germany) or by creating new legal employment statuses (Austria and Italy). Interestingly, Ireland is the only country to introduce 'soft regulation' by social dialogue, extending legal protection of workers in the grey zone.

In many European countries, the concept of employee has been redefined with a focus on criteria such as subordination, risk distribution and (in)dependence. European labour courts increasingly deploy these criteria within an indication clustering or mixed test, in an attempt to take all relevant circumstances into account without holding any as necessary or sufficient (Supiot 2001). This procedure gives courts a better understanding of the real circumstances of the employment or business relationship, regardless of the formal status of the worker, and allows the adjustment of the concept of employee to new forms of work and contracts. Furthermore, the personal scope of some labour law regulations in European countries has been expanded to include self-employed individuals as a separate category. For example, most national discrimination legislation in Europe as well as a recent EC directive on discrimination (2000)[5] do not only cover traditional employees but also individuals who personally perform work under a contract (Engblom 2001).

3.2 The scope of labour law in comparative perspective

In an empirical study on the operation of laws governing the classification of employment relationships in the UK, Burchell et al. (1999) find that elements of uncertainty characterise the employment status of a great part of those in employment. On the basis of a representative sample, they estimate that around 30 per cent of those in employment hold an unclear employment status. It is suggested that the use of the wider concept of 'worker' rather than that of 'employee' would increase the number of persons covered by employment rights by 5 per cent of all those in employment. Using a wider worker definition in labour law, argue Burchell et al. (1999), would include those individuals who contract to supply their own personal services to the employer without having a contract of employment but who are to some degree economically dependent on the employer's business because they derive a substantial part of their income from this particular 'employment'.

While British case law has provided enough legal material to draw the line between an employee and a self-employed person, there are few decisions on the distinction between a dependent worker and an independent self-employed person (Burchell et al. 1999).[6] Moreover, legal definitions of employment status differ across legislation fields. The employment status of a dependent self-employed worker may be different for employment protection legislation compared to tax purposes or social security legislation. For instance, a self-employed person under employment law may be classified as an employee under tax and social security law. The consequence of that particular case would be that this person would, on the one hand, not profit from potential tax advantages of the self-employed status and, on the other hand, would not qualify for employment protection measures such as unfair dismissal, redundancy compensation, statutory sick pay or statutory maternity pay (Burchell et al. 1999). In sum, the multi-level treatment of workers in the grey zone between dependent employment and independent self-employment brings additional difficulties for the assessment of dependent self-employment.

British legislation distinguishes between three different categories of the personal scope of labour law. First, an 'employee', as defined in the Employment Rights Act 1996, is an individual who works under a 'contract of employment'. Second, in the 1970s, British legislation expanded some employment protection acts to the newly created category of 'employed persons', introduced in the Equal Pay Act (1970), in parts of the Sex Discrimination Act 1975 and in the Race Relations Act 1976. 'Employed persons' are individuals with 'any other contract personally to execute any work or labour' (Freedland 2003: 23), going clearly beyond the definition of a 'contract of employment'. Third, recent British legislation has further accounted for the problem of classifying dependent self-employed workers to some extent, establishing the category of the 'worker' (Freedland 2003: 22ff).[7] For instance, legislation on working time,[8] minimum wage levels,[9] disability discrimination,[10] part-time work[11] and protection from unauthorised wage deductions[12] apply not only to traditional employees but to all contracts where an individual agrees to personally carry out work without running a genuine business[13] of their own (defined as 'workers') (Davies and Freedland 2000; Freedland 2003).

Although the idea of an employee-like category of workers has not historically been part of British labour law,[14] these recent attempts push forward the understanding that the employee-like category should (partly) receive the protection of labour law (Davies and Freedland 2000). However, as Burchell et al. (1999) point out, many aspects of the growing adoption in legislation of the concept of the 'worker' remain unclear, reflecting the fact that it is not yet clear which criteria the courts will apply in determining where the line between a dependent 'worker' and a genuinely independent self-employed individual is to be drawn. Freedland (2003: 13) also argues that British employment law has expanded into the category of 'contract for services',[15] but 'to an extent which is itself ill-defined and uncertain'. Consequently, it is still problematic to categorise specific sets of work activities in the grey zone in the British legal context.[16]

The legal tests, which are used by British courts to determine issues of status in employment cases, are not laid down in legislation but have mostly been developed through case law. These common law tests of employee status rely on four dimensions: 'control', 'integration', 'business reality' and 'mutuality of obligation' (Deakin and Morris 1998). The control tests focus on the discretion and autonomy a worker has. It looks at questions such as who determines what has to be done, how the work has to be carried out, when and where it has do be done. Due to the criticism that control is entirely consistent with both an employment contract and a business contract, British courts have begun to draw away from this test (Freedland 2003: 20). The integration test looks at the way the relationship between the worker and the employer (or contract partner) is organised and how bureaucratic rules (for instance, the inclusion in occupational benefit schemes) and disciplinary procedures are deployed. The basis of the business reality test is the allocation of risk and economic dependence. This test, which looks at where financial risk lies and how workers can profit from the performance of their task, has increasingly gained in importance. Examples of classification factors of the business reality test are the method of payment, the freedom to hire others or the provision of own equipment. Finally, the mutuality of obligation test, which is also increasingly used by British courts to decide about cases of employment status, focuses on formal evidence of subordination in the contract, although the existence of implicit contracts usually complicates the use of this test in court. This test checks whether there is a mutual obligation to provide work or to accept any work which is offered. A lack of this mutual obligation is an indicator that the relationship is not one of employer and employee. The mutuality of obligation test deploys factors such as the duration of employment, the regularity of employment or the right to refuse work (Deakin and Morris 1998; Burchell et al. 1999). Freedland (2003: 21) argues that there is still less agreement among labour lawyers and courts 'about how strongly a factor has to be present in order to characterize a work contract one way or the other'.

The classification of the employment status has, of course, severe effects on employment protection and social security. While (full-time, permanent) employees enjoy, for instance, the right of maternity leave, the right to take days off to care for sick family members, protection against unfair dismissal holiday and severance payments, their self-employed counterparts are not entitled to these employment protection measures.[17] Nevertheless, compared to Austria, employment protection through labour law is less regulated in the UK.

In contrast to the UK, Austrian labour courts are still much more focused on the criteria of personal rather than economic dependence, although Austrian courts increasingly deploy the criteria of economic dependence in cases where the 'real' employment status of an individual has to be investigated (Schwarz and Löschnigg 1997). Austrian labour law identifies personal dependency on the basis of five criteria. First, subordination under organisational rules such as working time, dress rules, acceptance of control or report of illness, which defines the degree of self-determination or subordination. Second, whether workers are subject to orders concerning how to use their labour and, third, control and disciplinary responsibility are further features of the authority of an employer and the dependency of the worker. Fourth, if not explicitly agreed otherwise, the personal duty of service is another way to characterise dependency.[18] Finally, the means of production are mostly provided by the employer (although this does not necessarily mean that all assets used by the worker must be the employer's).

Austrian labour law strictly distinguishes between personal and economic dependency. It is argued that economic dependency is not an appropriate criterion to identify a labour contract, since a wealthy employee may not necessarily be dependent on the income he or she earns. Consequently, labour courts routinely check for personal dependency if they want to prove whether someone works under a labour contract or not. However, in some cases, if the criteria of personal dependence is not sufficient for a judgement, labour courts additionally prove whether workers are economically dependent on their 'employer' (Schindler 2000).

Austrian commercial law characterises a self-employed person as someone who works on his or her own account and risk. Thus, bearing the entrepreneurial risk distinguishes a self-employed person from an employee. Interestingly, Austrian commercial law explicitly states that a certain degree of dependence and risk-taking does not necessarily mean that someone is not self-employed (Van Husen 2000). The legal consequence of being classified as self-employed according to Austrian commercial law is to be excluded from employment protection law.

Between the legal categories of 'employment' and 'self-employment', Austrian law knows different mixed forms, often commonly classified as 'employee-like' or 'arbeitnehmerähnliche' self-employed individuals. A 'freelancer' or 'freie DienstnehmerIn' is someone with no or only minor personal dependence (without a binding commitment in terms of time, place and how work is done) but who is economically dependent on the contractor. 'Freie DienstnehmerInnen' are treated as employees in some minor aspects of labour law such as legal liability. Yet the majority of employment protection measures do not apply to them.[19] A 'contractor for work and services' or WerkvertragvertragsnehmerIn is engaged to deliver a certain product or service at his or her own risk, with his or her own assets and without instructions from the contract partner. After delivering the product or service, the contract is terminated. Like 'freie DienstnehmerInnen', 'WerkvertragvertragsnehmerInnen' are excluded from major employment protection acts.[20] The same is true for a group of self-employed individuals, which was legally created in 1998 in order to prevent self-employed individuals escaping the social security system. This group, the so-called 'New Self-employed' or

'Neue Selbständige', is very heterogeneous and includes self-employed individuals such as scientists, artists, teachers, doctors, journalists and other types of freelancers. A widespread reform of the Austrian social security system between 1996 and 2000 has focused on the inclusion of the various kinds of self-employment in the social security system. As a result, self-employed workers earning over a certain (low) threshold, have hardly any possibility of escaping the statutory social security system. Nevertheless, only selected employment protection measures within labour law are applicable to these kinds of self-employment. Additional regulations of such 'business relationships' near the border of employment relationships come from commercial law. Recognising the difficulty of assessing dependent self-employment, the Austrian legislative introduced laws for specific work relationships to partly extend employment protection (e.g. sales representatives, pharmacists, sports people) (Eiro 2002).

It is important to note that the analysis in this section refers only to legal definitions, which are not necessarily equal to the economic and sociological concept of dependent self-employment. A dependent self-employed worker may appear on the market under various legal forms such as 'normal' self-employment, as a freie/r DienstnehmerIn, WerkvertragsnehmerIn or Neue/r Selbständige/r. The important point is that dependent self-employed workers are economically – and sometimes also personally – dependent on their contractor although they are self-employed (for instance, as a freie/r DienstnehmerIn or in the form of normal self-employment).

Whether a worker is classified as employee-like rather than being self-employed has to be investigated by labour courts. Of course, only cases where a party files a lawsuit will be investigated. Nagel (2002) reviews some legal cases where dependent self-employed workers appealed for employee status. For example, a self-employed carrier who worked for only one forwarder and who was obliged to permanently hold his lorry ready for orders by this forwarder was awarded an employee-like status which entitled him to protection of the insolvency protection act (Insolvenzentgeltsicherungsgesetz). However, another carrier with the same characteristics but with two additional employees, was not awarded to an employee-like status. A self-employed trade agent who sued for an employee-like status won the case for various reasons. First, his income nearly exclusively resulted from one business relationship; second, he was subject to orders by the contractor; third, he was obliged to report weekly about his turnover and fourth, he had to fulfil a certain minimum turnover. These cases show how labour courts operationalise and use the concepts of economic and personal dependence. However, as already stated above, only those business relationships where one party files a lawsuit will be investigated.[21]

In Italy, the 'genuine' self-employed workers ('lavoratori autonomi', i.e. autonomous workers) are those who perform a service or work without being subject to subordination, working with their own assets and without instructions. They are not salaried and are not subject to the social protection that is associated with salaried work (e.g. they are excluded from major employment protection acts). Additionally, Italian law knows the 'liberi professionisti' (i.e. free professionals) such as advocates, doctors, journalists and others, who have their own private, professional, social security funds and their own professional protection regarding maternity leave (though limited), illness and pension. They are, however, excluded from collective and firm agreements, working time regulation, protection in case of insolvency of the firm, holiday regulation and equal treatment regulation.

Similar to Austria, Italian law also knows a hybrid legal category to capture dependent forms of self-employment. These so-called 'contracts of continuous and coordinated collaboration' ('co.co.co.') and, more recently, 'contracts for a project' or 'co.pro.' have been increasingly used by Italian firms over the last decade. The aim of these work relationships is to have a more flexible contract both for the employer (promptness and simplicity in stipulating the contract) and for the employee (self-determination of timing and methods of the work). These contracts have, however, also been used by both the public and the private sector as a low-cost alternative to fixed-term and permanent contracts since they are not subject to substantial parts of employment protection and social security laws.

The first attempts to give a definition to contracts of continuous and coordinated collaboration can be found in the law 335/1995 (i.e. a reform of the pension system) which obliged these workers to contribute to a separate INPS (National Institute of Social Security) fund in order to obtain the right to a pension[22] and disability pension and in the 'Treu' law of 1997, which introduced a hybrid category between the legal categories of employment and self-employment, creating the contracts of continuous collaboration.

The collaborators are semi-independent contractors who sign fixed-term employment contracts to carry out a specific objective set by the employer. The work is performed in a regime of coordination, according to which the collaborator is free to decide the means, the place and the timing of his or her work and is theoretically allowed to work for more than one employer at the same time. Since 1998, collaborators get family allowance and an allowance during parental leave as well as during periods in hospital (but not for illness without hospitalisation). The legislative decree 38/2000 extended the obligatory insurance against accidents and professional diseases to collaborators. The fiscal law of 2000 obliged the employers to pay the collaborators on a monthly basis. The possibility to work on the basis of a contract of continuous collaboration was extended beyond professional and artistic activities, allowing also manual and non-professional workers to supply labour as collaborators.

It is only with the law 30/2003 ('Biagi Law') that the rules of collaboration were fixed and the cases in which it is possible to employ continuous and coordinated collaborators (co.co.co.) were limited.[23] In all other cases it is only possible to employ workers with a 'contract for a project' (co.pro.), meaning that they have to be limited to single projects. However, the possibility of control by the court is only formal and limited to the existence of a project, without any possibility of verifying the real working activity of the para-subordinate worker within the firm (CNEL 2004). Therefore, as a consequence of the Biagi Law, many co.co.co. jobs have been simply transformed into co.pro. jobs (IRES 2005).

Despite these recent laws, these work relationships still lack a coherent set of rules and collective agreements. As a consequence, collaborators do not have many of the rights and employment and social protection that are guaranteed to dependent workers. For instance, collaborators have less protection when they are temporarily unable to work (e.g. in case of illness or pregnancy). In particular, they provide the employer with the right to suspend the contract for up to 90 days in the event of illness, but they do not receive money in that period unless hospitalised (Fiscal Law 2000); in the case of maternity leave the suspension of the contract is only allowed for up to 5 months with 80 per cent of the previous wage. They are excluded from the minimum wage, Christmas bonus, severance payment, rules for holidays and leaves, the right for trade union action or equal opportunity and training rights (Regalia 2003). Moreover, the contribution to the separate INPS fund does not guarantee them a pension that is economically sufficient.[24]

In sum, it seems that the Italian legislation initially tried to extend the rights of employees to collaborators, but subsequently (with the Biagi law) attempted at limiting the use of co.co.co.[25] Similar to Austria, a dependent self-employed worker may legally appear on the market either as a genuine self-employed or as a worker on the basis of one of these hybrid forms. The important point is that dependent self-employed workers are economically – and sometimes also personally – dependent on their main or only contractor although they are not employees of the company they contract with.

While there is a tendency to broaden the personal scope of labour law in Europe to integrate also workers on the border between employment and self-employment, the personal scope of federal labour law in the US is almost without exemption[26] restricted to employees, strictly excluding self-employed independent contractors (Dunlop Commission 1994). To distinguish between an independent contractor and an employee, US labour courts use a economic realities test in cases concerning the Fair Labor Standard Act (FLSA) and the Equal Pay Act (EPA) and a more reduced control test for other labour law acts as well as social security and copyright law. While the control test refers to the issue of how the employer controls the manner and means by which a product or service is accomplished, the economic reality test focuses on the totality of circumstances, including issues of control, the workers' opportunities for profit or loss, investment in facilities, permanence of the relationship and the required skill level (Engblom 2003: 109ff). In sum, the use of the rather restricted control test for most issues of work relationships means that the labour law protection of dependent self-employed individuals is rather limited in the US. Linder (1999: 188) strongly criticises this restricted coverage, stressing the connected increase in 'pseudo self-employment' and a substantial deregulation of the US labour market.

Apart from strictly excluding independent contractors from labour law protection, some limitations to the personal scope of labour law also exclude certain groups of employees. For instance, the requirement of a certain period of employment duration, a minimum amount of hours per week or industry-specific regulations further excludes contingent workers from labour law protection (Engblom 2003: 110ff). Consequently, in comparison to labour law in European countries, where we observe a tendency to broaden the worker concept to at least partially include dependent self-employed workers, the US labour law applies a comparatively strict definition, leaving dependent self-employed workers uncovered by most labour protection measures.

3.3 Conclusions

We have argued that the employment status under which a worker carries out his or her work is crucially connected to employment rights and social security. However, this chapter has demonstrated that dependent self-employed workers are either totally beyond any employment protection or at least partly excluded. This is a consequence, firstly, of the difficulty of drawing the line between employment and self-employment and secondly, of policy measures to foster business start-ups and entrepreneurship.

While some countries have introduced a hybrid legal category, on the one hand, to facilitate outsourcing activities and, on the other hand, to simultaneously cover dependent self-employed workers with some legal rights that they would not have under the legal status of self-employment. Strikingly, the countries that have chosen this path are countries with a high level of labour regulation such as Germany, Italy and Austria. However, we have stressed that also in the countries with hybrid legal concepts, a part of dependent self-employed workers work as legally self-employed individuals as the case studies of the insurance and freight industry will demonstrate in Chapter 6.

Other countries such as the UK, in contrast, have opted for a partial extension of employment law to cover also those who work in the grey zone between employment and self-employment by extending some employment laws to the broader legal concept of the 'worker', also including a part of dependent self-employed workers. Finally, this chapter has put forward the argument that we see the tendency to partially cover dependent self-employed workers by employment protection laws and social security in Europe, while the US rather strictly excludes them.

4
The Supply Side: Identifying Workers on the Border Between Employment and Self-Employment

4.1 The determinants of self-employment

As already stressed in the introductory chapter of this study, the rise of self-employment is closely linked to the general restructuring process in industrial organisation observed since the 1970s. Research on the determinants of self-employment suggests that the greater stress on outsourcing and numerical flexibility is important explanation for the rise of self-employment (e.g. Rubery et al. 1993; Meager 1998; OECD 2000; Eiro 2002). These developments have, moreover, been intensified by governmental efforts to foster self-employment using various regulatory tools such as the tax system or supported direct credits. Both economists and sociologists have argued that new technologies and more specialised and variable patterns of consumer demand have influenced the re-emergence of small scale businesses and network forms of production (e.g. Piore and Sabel 1984; Powell 1990; Semlinger 1991; Zagler 2003).

Theoretical and empirical research on the determinants of self-employment shows that factors such as labour market and organisational changes, unemployment, the wealth of individuals, family background, immigration and the tax system are pivotal in influencing the development of self-employment. Although much research has been carried out on the business ventures of unemployed individuals, there is little consensus about the effects of unemployment on self-employment levels. On the one hand, the 'unemployment push theory' argues that high unemployment is connected to the absence of opportunities for paid employment, which provokes many individuals to move into self-employment in order to avoid or escape unemployment (Evans and

Leighton 1989; Bögenhold and Staber 1991; Acs et al. 1994). Comparing three different datasets in the UK, Smeaton (2003) argues that recent organisational restructuring has resulted in an increase of especially older self-employed workers that are pushed into self-employment due to a lack of other work opportunities. These workers report nevertheless high levels of work satisfaction because of the autonomy self-employment brings about despite of the existence of self-exploitation in the form of long working hours. On the other hand, the 'prosperity pull theory' stresses that individuals tend to become self-employed when unemployment is low since the chances for return to wage labour are higher (Taylor 1996). Meager (1992) argues that successful business start-ups and business survival are more likely at times of economic expansion, when unemployment is typically low. Analysing 23 OECD countries, Audretsch et al. (2005) found both effects at work but show particularly strong evidence for the argument that higher rates of self-employment means increased entrepreneurial activity, reducing unemployment in subsequent periods.

Several studies show that one possible barrier to becoming self-employed is lack of capital. Using US micro-data, Evans and Jovanovic (1989) and Evans and Leighton (1989) have analysed the liquidity constraints of self-employed individuals, and found that wealthier people are more likely to switch from employment to self-employment. Blanchflower and Oswald (1998) analysed British micro-data and found similar results, namely that the probability of self-employment correlates positively with whether an individual has received an inheritance or gift.

Taylor's (1996) analysis of the British Household Panel Study (BHPS) shows that both marital status and parent's employment status are significant determinants of self-employment. Data indicate that self-employed individuals are more likely to be married and to have parents (especially fathers) who are or were themselves self-employed. While the marital status seems to have an influence on the likelihood of being self-employed, the number of children has an ambiguous effect. Blanchflower (2000) finds no empirical evidence for the widespread assumption that number of children has a significant influence on the likelihood of self-employment. Indeed, he finds either no significant effect (e.g. in USA, Netherlands, Denmark or Spain) or instead a negative influence (e.g. in France, Germany, Italy and Greece), with the UK and Canada being the exceptions. For the latter two countries, Blanchflower (2000) finds a positive correlation between the number of children in a family and self-employment.

Self-employment among ethnic minorities and immigrants especially has been addressed using US and UK data. For example, Fairlie and Meyer (1996) analyse the data of the US census and find that the level of education and time since immigration are important determinants of self-employment. More specifically, data show that higher levels of education are associated with a higher probability of self-employment. The longer the period since immigration, the higher the chances of being self-employed. Interestingly, Fairlie and Meyer (1996) find that those groups with high self-employment rates do not come from countries with high self-employment rates. Furthermore, it is argued that an ethnic group's average self-employment earnings relative to average wage earning seems to be pivotal in determining the self-employment rate of that ethnic group. From their empirical analysis, the authors conclude that while they may be important for some groups, discrimination and language difficulties do not necessarily lead to self-employment, while high-relative returns from self-employment for many ethnic groups make this a preferable choice. Clarke and Drinkwater (2000) find similar results for the UK. They report that the difference between an individual's predicted return from paid and self-employment is an important predictor for self-employment. The authors suggest that 'the existence of discriminatory wages in the paid-employment sector may push minorities into entrepreneurship' (p. 626). Like Fairlie and Meyer (1996) for the US, Clarke and Drinkwater (2000) reveal that those with poor English language skills and more recent immigrants are less likely to be self-employed in the UK.

However, economic trends and individual characteristics or preferences are not sufficient to explain the international differences in self-employment rates. Consequently, it is necessary to consider the legal and institutional environment, which may be pivotal for understanding trends in self-employment. For instance, Robson (1998) explains the strong increase in self-employment in the UK in the 1980s with supply-side policy measures such as the reduction in the rate of income tax, which led to an 'entrepreneurial renaissance'. In a Canadian–US comparison, Schuetze (2000) analyses the effect of tax changes on male self-employment and finds that increases in income taxes have strong positive effects on the self-employment level. These results suggest that changes in the tax environment, rather than unemployment rates, explain to a considerable degree the trends in male non-primary sector self-employment in Canada and the US. In other words, Schuetze (2000) provides evidence that one of the motivations for becoming self-employed is the relative tax advantage. Thus, as already found in earlier research (e.g. Blau 1987; Evans and Leighton 1989), the tax environment is a strong predictor of self-employment.

International survey data indicate that a large share of working individuals would prefer to be self-employed. As reported in Blanchflower (2000), the International Social Survey Programme of 1989 asked random samples of individuals from 11 countries what kind of job they would prefer if they could choose between being an employee or being self-employed. Interestingly, a substantial part of all respondents as well as of those respondents who are employees reported that they would prefer self-employment. For instance, in the UK, 48 per cent of all respondents and 43 per cent of those respondents who are working as employees said that they would prefer self-employment. Similar results are provided by the survey on 'Employment Options of the Future' of the European Foundation for the Improvement of Living and Working Conditions, which focuses – among other issues – on attitudes towards self-employment in all 15 EU Member States and Norway (Atkinson 2000). This survey suggests that about 20 per cent of currently employed individuals would prefer self-employment. Moreover, great differences in attitudes towards self-employment are found between the two sexes, with men more likely to report that they would like to become self-employed than women.

This high theoretical potential for self-employment proves that there are some highly effective barriers for individuals to follow their apparent desire to run their own business. Examples of these barriers are credit market constraints or labour market regulation. Comparing 11 OECD countries, Arum and Müller (2004: 432) find that labour market regulation had strong effects on the level of self-employment. Especially for individuals in professional–managerial occupations it is shown that both low and high levels of labour market regulation create stronger incentives to become self-employed.

In the standard economic model of labour supply, the individual's decision to work is determined not only by wage rate and non-labour income but also by personal characteristics (such as age or gender) and individual preferences or tastes (e.g. motivation). Research on the individual's decision to supply labour in the form of self-employment strongly focuses on personal characteristics (e.g. personal wealth, family background) and individual preferences (e.g. human capital, motivation, management capabilities or taste for independence and flexibility). It is argued that individuals will choose to become self-employed if the value of the expected utilities is higher than in alternative arrangements. Utility is operationalised in different forms: earnings differentials between self-employed individuals and employees (e.g. Evans and Leighton 1989; Robson 1998) and/or utility in the form of increased independence and personal autonomy (Blanchflower and Oswald 1998).

Using these insights, Mühlberger (2002) develops an economic model of dependent self-employment. This model assumes that individuals can be either employed, self-employed or dependent self-employed. In addition to pecuniary utility from income, self-employed individuals enjoy non-pecuniary utility from independence. Dependent self-employed workers are assumed to have less non-pecuniary utility from being their own boss than 'normal' self-employed individuals due to the fact that they are in some way 'dependent' from their contractor. Furthermore, it is assumed that the different levels of human capital (e.g. management skills) lead to a different profitability of a single entrepreneurial project. Dependent self-employed workers are assumed to benefit from their contractors by obtaining support to increase profits by a certain premium, for which the contractors get a certain share. It is shown that in this model, dependent self-employment is more likely if the non-pecuniary return from self-employment compared to dependent self-employment is very low, the extra profits due to dependency are very high and if the contractor demands a low share of profits.

4.2 The motives to supply-dependent self-employed work: qualitative findings

Our case study research in the insurance industry (UK, Italy and Austria), in the business services industry (Italy and Austria) as well as in the Austrian freight industry shows the reasons to supply work in the form of dependent self-employment refer to the issues of time flexibility, increasing autonomy and simplifying the work process but also to rigid internal labour market structures and external pressures from the labour market.[1]

In all the three industries and countries, dependent self-employed workers stressed that despite of being tied to a principal, self-employment increases both their time flexibility and the autonomy. They state to have more control over the work process and how to do the job. We also find that moving to dependent self-employment is often not a voluntary decision. On the one hand, rigid internal labour market structures determine the possible labour market statuses within a firm and, on the other hand, tight labour markets increase the power of employers to source out labour. In all the three industries and countries we found companies that work exclusively with dependent self-employed workers without any employees (except in the management and back office area).

British and Austrian dependent self-employed insurance agents argue that compared to independent financial advisers or insurance brokers, the establishment of a tied agency is associated with considerably lower costs. Thus, insurance agents who wish to become self-employed without investing a high amount of money and/or effort prefer a tied business relationship. Tied agents underline the simplicity of their work, the possibility to determine the quantity of work and the reduced control in comparison to an employment relation. Further motives put forward are tax benefits and reduced legal liability.

> I just love what I do and I find it simple, the job itself is so simple. I totally agree with you that you would be able to sell more products as an IFA and that you have more security as an employed agent. The reason why I do what I do is that I like the freedom to write my own pay check.
>
> Tied agent of a British general insurance company that sells insurance products and additionally manages a team of 15 tied agents. Company A.

Being tied to only one insurance company facilitates business cooperation and the content of work considerably. Interviews reveal that in comparison with independent financial advisers, tied agents are clearly more risk avers, esteeming the support of the outsourcing insurance company. Although they wish to be self-employed, they appreciate, on the other hand, the support of their principles and the simplification of their work. Thus, they cannot be regarded as Schumpeterian entrepreneurs but as supported owner-operators.

> Compared to an independent business, tied agency is better because it is easier and cheaper to set up because facilities are provided. One has more security, more autonomy and more freedom.
>
> Tied agent of a British long-term insurance company. Company B.

In contrast to the British and Austrian case, Italian insurance companies do not employ their insurance agents but work exclusively with self-employed tied agents. Thus, the traditional labour market organisation of the industry determines the possible work forms for insurance agents.

Also in the Italian and Austrian business services industry we find that the main reasons to voluntary supply-dependent self-employed work are time flexibility and work autonomy but also the possibility to choose one's working team. Time flexibility was especially stressed by workers with children and by those who are still in education.

> I wanted to be able to work whenever I felt like it. As we have a child now, I also wanted to take the responsibility and take care of the kid, so that my wife can go to work. I thought working on my own account would enable us to share household and childcare duties fifty-fifty. (I 1)

> During my studies I thought self-employment gave me the maximum flexibility to manage studying and working at the same time. Moreover, I was interested in working for a company providing financial services and they only offer the job on an own account bases. (I 8)

Additionally, dependent self-employed workers in both the Italian and Austrian business services industry stress the desire to realise their own ideas and to get more appreciation for the work done. Especially in Austria, many former employees complained about the hierarchy within firms and the lack of possibilities to fulfil their ideas.

As in the insurance industry, also the financial dimension proofed to be of some importance for the decision to work on one's own account. Some interviewees stressed that they expected higher hourly wages, but also that self-employment would give them tax advantages and the possibility to work longer hours in order to achieve a higher total income.

> I had huge debts. I needed money and working on my own-account gives me the opportunity to earn more, if I work more. It also leaves more possibilities open in regard to the tax declaration. (I 14)

Those who state to involuntary work as dependent self-employed stress that there was either no employed job available or that the company they contract with only offered the specific job on the basis of a contract of subcontracting. As a consequence, most of these workers see their position as dependent self-employed workers as a temporary solution to avoid unemployment.

> I was fired and I needed some work very quickly. There were no real alternative jobs available. A friend of mine gave me the hint that the

company he is working for still is looking for subcontractors in the computer business. Working on my own account is not really 'my thing'. I see it as a kind of temporary solution. (I 11)

In the Austrian freight industry we found that mainly young and highly motivated drivers decide to become self-employed. These workers consider self-employment as a chance of higher job satisfaction and higher earnings as well as a possibility to have more flexible working time.

However, all of the interviewed drivers have become self-employed because their former employers decided to source out their fleet of trucks. Consequently, they had to choice to either switch to another employer or to become self-employed. The majority of the interviewed drivers admitted that they would not have taken this step if there had not been the decision of their former employer to outsource the fleet of trucks.

The main argument for becoming self-employed was the possibility to increase the income. However, we found that higher income resulted not from higher hourly wages but from longer working hours. Another motive for dependent self-employed drivers was the possibility to schedule working time more flexibly.

The incentives to voluntary move from employment to self-employment are strongly dependent on the social security and employment protection that is connected to the various labour market statuses. Austrian and Italian dependent self-employed workers claim that social security, fringe benefits and the compensation system for employed workers are the main advantages of employment. In contrast to the UK, the marginal benefits of employment compared to self-employment are higher in Italy and Austria.

> Yes [company K has already approached me regarding a tied agency], but I couldn't accept this offer, because opposed to employees, self-employed persons are disadvantaged regarding the social security net. [...] This starts already with the pension. [...] [Or] if I get ill, being self-employed, I don't have such a social security net compared to an employee.
> Employed insurance agent of an Austrian insurance company. Company K.

In sum, we found that dependent self-employment may also reflect the needs of workers. In contrast to the 'entrepreneurial' self-employed (i.e. those who work for different clients/firms), dependent self-employment

54 *Dependent Self-Employment*

is associated with lower start-up costs and a simpler work process (in terms of coordination). In comparison to employment, externalised workers face similar, yet less control, more flexibility, often a reduced legal liability and tax benefits. Finally, the absence of opportunities for employment following redundancies may push workers into such a labour market status.

4.3 Dependent self-employment in Austria

In June 2001, the Austrian statistic office introduced an ad hoc module on work organisation and working time into the micro-census, focusing also on dependent self-employed workers. Unfortunately, due to the huge number of respondents that refused to answer the ad hoc module, there are too few observations of dependent self-employed workers in the micro-data for a multivariate analysis along the lines of that carried out on the British Labour Force Survey (BLFS). Consequently, this data problem restricts our analysis to aggregated data published by the Austrian national statistics office.

Nevertheless, this survey still gives us quantitative information about dependent self-employment in Austria for the first time (Statistik Austria 2002). Table 4.1 shows the key facts of dependent self-employment in Austria. In this survey, dependent self-employment is operationalised as follows. A dependent self-employed worker is a person who claims to be self-employed, but who is bound by the instructions of an employer or contract partner in terms of labour time and labour methods and who is, furthermore, only deployed by one single contractor or customer and whose contract does not end with the completion of the product or the service.

Based on this definition, the survey indicates that about 40 000 individuals or 1.1 per cent of the labour force are dependent self-employed in Austria. Thus, we see that dependent self-employment is still an uncommon phenomenon in Austria. However, it is important to note that this survey uses a narrow definition of dependent self-employment. Thus, these data do not represent the entire grey zone between self-employment and normal employment but focuses on explicitly dependent forms of self-employment. Moreover, data concerning the recent development of employee-like persons (i.e. *Neue Selbständige, freie DienstnehmerInnen*) point towards a sharp increase in such forms of employment.[2]

The data show that two thirds of the dependent self-employed workers in Austria are men. A total of 1.3 per cent of the male labour force

Table 4.1 Dependent self-employment in Austria (2001)

	Distribution of dependent self-employed workers			% of the labour force		
	Men	Women	All	Men	Women	All
Age						
15–29	9.1	9.7	9.3	0.6	0.3	0.4
30–44	37.9	40.3	38.4	1.1	0.7	0.9
45–59	39.4	44.8	41.5	1.7	1.5	1.6
Over 60	13.6	4.5	10.6	6.0	2.1	4.7
Highest education						
ISCED 2 – Lower secondary level of education	4.6	14.2	7.8	0.4	0.5	0.5
ISCED 3b – Apprenticeship, secondary education (short duration)	40.9	40.3	40.7	1.0	0.8	0.9
ISCED 3a – Secondary education (long duration)	10.2	11.9	11.1	2.2	1.4	1.8
ISCED 4 – Post-secondary non-tertiary education	7.6	10.4	8.5	1.4	1.1	1.2
ISCED 5b – Tertiary education, non-university	37.1	20.9	31.7	2.7	1.1	2.0
ISCED 5a – University	–	1.5	0.5	–	3.8	2.3
Industry – ÖNACE classification						
Agriculture, fishing, mining, quarrying	–	–	–	–	–	–
Manufacturing	14.4	1.5	10.1	0.7	0.1	0.5
Electricity, gas and water supply	–	–	–	–	–	–
Construction	10.2	1.5	7.3	1.0	0.8	1.0
Wholesale, retail and repair of automobiles and consumer goods	28.8	31.3	29.6	2.9	1.3	2.1
Hotels and restaurants	8.7	13.4	10.6	3.3	1.4	2.1
Transport and communication	8.7	0.7	6.0	1.2	0.2	1.0
Financial intermediation	3.4	2.2	3.3	1.5	0.5	1.0
Real estate and business activities	15.5	9.0	13.3	2.8	0.8	1.8
Public administration and social security	–	–	–	–	–	–

Table 4.1 (Continued)

	Distribution of dependent self-employed workers			% of the labour force		
	Men	Women	All	Men	Women	All
Education	2.3	4.5	3.3	0.9	0.4	0.6
Health, veterinary and social work	5.3	14.9	8.5	1.9	0.9	1.1
Other community, social and personal work	2.3	20.1	8.3	0.9	3.2	2.2
Private households with employed persons	–	–	–	–	–	–
Occupation – ISCO-88 (COM)						
Legislators, senior officials and managers	55.7	32.1	47.7	6.9	4.5	6.2
Scientists	12.1	12.7	12.3	1.7	0.9	1.3
Technicians and associate professionals	18.6	19.9	22.1	1.7	1.6	1.7
Clerks	0.4	1.5	0.8	0.1	0.1	0.1
Service workers, shop and market sales workers	8.0	17.9	11.3	1.2	0.7	0.9
Skilled agricultural and fishery workers	–	–	–	–	–	–
Craft and related trades workers	4.6	–	3.0	0.2	–	0.2
Plant and machine operators and assemblers	1.5	–	1.0	0.2	–	0.1
Elementary occupations	–	6.0	2.0	–	0.4	0.2
Region						
Burgenland	2.3	2.2	2.3	0.9	0.6	0.8
Carinthia	11.7	15.7	13.1	0.8	0.7	0.8
Lower Austria	12.1	26.1	16.8	0.8	1.0	0.9
Upper Austria	9.9	7.5	9.0	2.0	1.0	1.6
Salzburg	13.6	16.4	14.6	1.2	1.0	1.2
Styria	15.2	6.7	12.6	1.1	0.4	0.8
Tyrol	14.4	10.4	13.1	2.8	1.2	2.1
Vorarlberg	13.3	9.7	12.1	2.0	1.1	1.6
Vienna	7.6	4.5	6.8	2.2	1.0	1.7
In per cent of the whole labour force				1.3	0.9	1.1
Number of observations (in thousands)	26.4	13.4	39.8			

Source: Statistik Austria (2002: 342).

and 0.9 per cent of the female labour force are found to be dependent self-employed. Dependent self-employment in Austria seems to increase in likelihood with age (up to the age of 60). The largest part of these workers are between 45 and 59 years old. In terms of the whole labour force 0.4 per cent of the 15–29 year olds, 0.9 per cent of the 30–44 year olds, 1.6 per cent of the 45–59 year olds and, finally, 4.7 per cent of the over 60 are dependent self-employed (Statistik Austria 2002: 342).

Moreover, education-related data specify that the majority of dependent self-employed workers have completed an apprenticeship or short-term secondary education (around 40 per cent). Interestingly, roughly a third of the dependent self-employed workers have a tertiary non-university education [this includes, for instance, workers with a master crafts(wo)man's diploma, 'Meisterprüfung'] – that is, the highest level of vocational education. Thus, there seems to be an M-shaped relationship between education and dependent self-employment with individuals with a lower (apprenticeship) and a higher level of applied education (master crafts(wo)man's diploma or 'Meisterprüfung') forming the peaks.

The variable industry shows once again that dependent self-employed work is segregated by gender. While men work predominantly in the industrial sector, women are over-represented in the service sector. However, the majority of both men and women are deployed in the sector 'Wholesale, retail and repair of automobiles and consumer goods.' This sector includes sales agents who are, of course, more likely to be dependent self-employed. The occupation group with the highest share of dependent self-employed workers is the group 'legislators, senior officials and managers'. However, it is assumed that self-employed persons tend to characterise themselves as managers, leading to artificial over-representation in this group. The regional variable shows that dependent self-employment is prevalent mainly in Lower Austria, Salzburg, Carinthia and Tyrol. The region of Burgenland and, surprisingly, Vienna shows the lowest share of dependent self-employment.

The data of the Austrian micro-census reveal another interesting result (see Table 4.2). More than two thirds of the dependent self-employed workers employ additional employees. This indicates that the definition used in the BLFS may be too narrow. However, due to a lack of the clear definition of subordination (as discussed above), the definition used may be a better approximation.

Interestingly, while 75 per cent of male self-employed workers deploy employees, only 55 per cent of female self-employed workers deploy

Table 4.2 Further characteristics of dependent self-employed workers in Austria (2001)

	Men	Women	All
Employees			
Self-employed with employees	75.0	55.2	68.3
Self-employed without employees	25.0	44.1	31.7
Normal working time			
Up to 35 hours	6.1	42.5	18.3
36 hours and more	93.9	57.5	81.7

Source: Statistik Austria (2002: 342).

employees. There is also a clear gender difference with respect to normal working hours. Whilst, the huge majority of men work more than 35 hours per week, many women work on a part-time basis.

4.4 Dependent self-employment in the UK

The BLFS of Spring 1999 was the first European survey that included variables permitting the identification of dependent self-employed workers. We use data from the more recent BLFS 2002 (Spring) for an analysis of the characteristics of dependent self-employed workers and define a dependent self-employed as a self-employed worker who has no employees and only one customer.[3] Applying this definition, we identify 527 dependent self-employed workers. The comparison groups are 32 925 employees and 5273 self-employed, who either have at least one employee or more than one customer, or both.

The sample characteristics, tabulated in Table 4.3, show that men are over-represented amongst the (independent) self-employed and, even more so, amongst the dependent self-employed workers. Roughly 78 per cent of the dependent self-employed workers in the sample are men. Dependent self-employed workers are, on average, older than employees but younger than the self-employed. The three groups do not differ much in their ethnic compositions, except that there are relatively more Asians among the self-employed than among the other two groups. The sample characteristics on gender and age are comparable to the study of Cowling and Taylor (2001) on the self-employed using the fifth wave (1995) of the BHPS. They divide the self-employed between those with and those without employees and find that men are more likely to be both self-employed with employees and self-employed

Table 4.3 Summary statistics by employment status (British Labour Force Survey)

	Employee		Self-employed		Dependent self-employed	
	Mean	SD	Mean	SD	Mean	SD
Male	0.574		0.738		0.778	
Age	38.908	11.826	44.814	10.391	42.725	11.785
Ethnicity						
White	0.951		0.942		0.953	
Mixed	0.004		0.003		0.004	
Asian	0.026		0.034		0.017	
Black	0.012		0.008		0.017	
Chinese	0.003		0.005		0.006	
Other	0.005		0.008		0.004	
Lives with spouse	0.557		0.705		0.632	
Kids under 19 years (#)	0.762	1.023	0.862	1.113	0.753	0.992
Kids under 5 years (#)	0.171	0.451	0.179	0.474	0.180	0.485
Kids 5–9 years (#)	0.201	0.490	0.238	0.537	0.203	0.480
Highest qualification						
Degree or equivalent	0.144		0.190		0.140	
Higher education	0.076		0.079		0.078	
GCE A-level or equivalent	0.274		0.331		0.362	
GCSE A–C level or equivalent	0.245		0.152		0.120	
Other qualification	0.143		0.118		0.148	
No qualification	0.119		0.129		0.152	
Residential tenure						
< 1 year	0.104		0.072		0.097	
1–2 years	0.102		0.082		0.093	
2–3 years	0.082		0.072		0.072	
3–5 years	0.127		0.122		0.123	
5–10 years	0.187		0.200		0.175	
$\geq$ 10 years	0.398		0.452		0.440	
Job characteristics						
Regular working hours[a]	33.747	11.955	41.151	18.085	36.573	18.668
Job tenure						
< 3 months	0.042		0.018		0.070	
3–6 months	0.037		0.021		0.061	
6–12 months	0.075		0.039		0.065	
1–2 years	0.149		0.084		0.118	
2–5 years	0.252		0.164		0.211	
5–10 years	0.159		0.165		0.157	
10–20 years	0.188		0.289		0.176	
$\geq$ 20 years	0.099		0.220		0.142	
Occupation						
Managers and sen. officials	0.175		0.193		0.042	

Table 4.3 (Continued)

	Employee		Self-employed		Dependent self-employed	
	Mean	SD	Mean	SD	Mean	SD
Professionals	0.075		0.124		0.135	
Associate prof. and techn.	0.107		0.142		0.131	
Clerical occupation	0.133		0.028		0.040	
Skilled trade	0.120		0.310		0.380	
Personal service	0.051		0.054		0.044	
Sales and customer services	0.102		0.029		0.011	
Operatives	0.113		0.081		0.129	
Elementary	0.123		0.038		0.089	
Same occupation as $t-1$	0.922		0.963		0.920	
Industry						
Agriculture	0.010		0.056		0.053	
Energy	0.018		0.003		0.009	
Manufacturing	0.241		0.061		0.089	
Construction	0.070		0.211		0.355	
Distribution	0.245		0.196		0.046	
Transport	0.087		0.070		0.093	
Banking and finance	0.201		0.193		0.184	
Public administration	0.084		0.098		0.076	
Other services	0.044		0.113		0.095	
Employment at $t-1$						
Self-employed w/o employees	0.011		0.657		0.784	
Part-time	0.208		0.182		0.209	
Supervisory	0.381		0.039		0.072	
Occupation						
Managers and sen. officials	0.172		0.191		0.059	
Professionals	0.076		0.123		0.121	
Associate prof. and techn.	0.106		0.143		0.131	
Clerical occupations	0.132		0.030		0.046	
Skilled trade	0.123		0.306		0.364	
Personal services	0.052		0.054		0.044	
Sales and customer services	0.103		0.031		0.017	
Operatives	0.113		0.082		0.131	
Elementary	0.124		0.039		0.087	
N	32 931		5273		527	

[a] # of observations: employee (32 925), self-employed (5273) and dependent self-employed (527).

without employees and that the self-employed without employees are younger than those with employees. In contrast to our results, however, they observe a low probability of non-whites being self-employed with employees and an over-representation of foreigners amongst the self-employed without employees.

The sample characteristics show that the self-employed are more likely to have a university degree than the other two groups and, in general, tend to be workers with more formal education. The dependent self-employed, in contrast, are about as likely to have higher education as employees but are more likely to have A-levels and are also more likely to have no qualification. The self-employed are more likely to be cohabiting with a spouse than the other two groups. The self-employed are also more likely to co-reside with a child under the age of 19. With respect to pre-school children, we do not find a difference between the three groups of workers. Residential tenure is highest among self-employed persons and lowest among employees, with dependent self-employed workers in the middle. However, there are, in sum, no big differences in residential tenure between the three groups. Looking at regular working hours, though, we see a rather strong difference between the groups. The self-employed work on average 41 hours per week, employees work 34 hours and dependent self-employed workers work 37 hours per week. Current job tenure is longest for the self-employed and it is shortest for the dependent self-employed. Most dependent self-employed workers are in a skilled trade, with comparatively few working in clerical occupations and in sales and other customer services. They are mainly working in the construction and the financial services industries, as also documented in Harvey (2003).

The cross-sectional nature of the data does not allow us to rigorously examine if the classification as dependent self-employed is caused by (short-term) fluctuations in employees or customers, or both. Workers were asked about their labour market status 1 year before the current interview, but unfortunately there is no information on the number of customers for the earlier data. We are however able to class self-dependent workers into two categories, those who had no employees and those who employed other workers. Table 4.4 provides a cross-tabulation of the employment statuses in Spring 2001 and 2002. We see that there is considerable persistence in the employment status: some 98 per cent of employees are employed at both dates; some 90 per cent of the self-employed are self-employed at both dates and 81 per cent of those who did not have employees in Spring 2001 did not have any 1 year later. While we are concerned about the missing

Table 4.4 Employment status, $t-1$ and t (row percentages)

	Employed, t	Self-employed, t			
		Employees, customers > 1	No employees, customers > 1	Employees, one customer	No employees, one customer
Employed, $t-1$	33 084	89	354	5	112
	98.34	0.26	1.05	0.01	0.33
Self-employed, $t-1$					
employees	54	1279	70	38	5
	3.73	88.45	4.84	2.63	0.35
no employees	211	148	3329	6	415
	5.14	3.60	81.02	0.15	10.10
Total	33 349	1516	3753	49	532
	85.08	3.87	9.57	0.13	1.36

information on the dependent self-employed's number of customers in Spring 2001, the table shows that of the 532 observations in 2002 we classify as dependent self-employed 415, or 78 per cent, were self-employed without employees in the previous year.

We estimate multinomial logit models to compare the three groups of workers. It estimates the odds of being a dependent self-employed worker versus the odds of being an employee and the odds of being a dependent self-employed worker versus being self-employed. Since we are mainly interested in comparing dependent self-employed worker with employees and self-employed individuals, respectively, we choose the group of dependent self-employed worker as the comparison group to identify the model.

All results are presented in relative risk ratios, RRR (the exponentiated coefficients). The RRRs give the odds of being in one group versus the odds of being an employee. A RRR greater (less) than one indicates that the risk of being in a group is greater (smaller) for higher values of a variable. The results are tabulated in Table 4.5.

The first of our models, which serves as a benchmark for the other specification below, uses only contemporaneous variables to the employment status. The estimation reveals that, in contrast to men, women have a greater risk of being employed than dependent self-employed, but if self-employed they face greater odds being dependent rather than independently self-employed. The odds for woman to be an employee rather than being dependent self-employed are more than twice than for a man. We also estimate that the odds for being

Table 4.5 Estimated risk of self-employment and dependent self-employment (multinomial logit)

	Model 1				Model 2			
	Employee		Self-employed		Employee		Self-employed	
	RRR	t-statistic	RRR	t-statistic	RRR	t-statistic	RRR	t-statistic
Personal characteristics								
Female	2.587	13.12	0.732	4.19	0.858	0.60	0.366	3.90
Age	0.899	35.16	1.063	21.33	0.872	48.05	1.075	25.85
Age squared/100	1.095	26.48	0.939	19.72	1.135	39.79	0.929	24.81
Kids under 5 years #	0.864	12.18	0.961	2.84	0.798	19.17	0.993	0.57
Female with kids under 5 years	0.787	5.11	1.132	2.65	0.900	2.01	1.058	1.07
Married or cohabiting	1.021	1.37	1.113	6.28	0.941	4.90	1.052	3.36
Married female					1.004	0.07	1.329	6.32
Non-white	1.199	2.11	1.502	5.30	1.308	2.93	1.481	5.16
Residential tenure								
1–2 years	0.993	0.11	1.058	0.59	0.983	0.23	1.054	0.53
2–3 years	1.041	0.80	1.010	0.16	1.015	0.26	1.004	0.06
More than 3 years	1.042	0.79	0.976	0.34	1.040	0.70	0.966	0.46
Education								
GCE A-level or equivalent	0.809	21.61	0.782	23.97	0.802	13.56	0.654	16.17
GCSE A–C level or equivalent	1.636	9.16	1.065	1.01	1.548	7.53	1.050	0.74
Other qualification	1.034	1.54	0.651	23.77	1.225	20.42	0.580	45.71
No formal qualification	0.902	9.44	0.683	82.88	1.055	2.73	0.680	13.22
Education*Female								
GCE A-level or equivalent					0.377	15.80	0.511	10.04
GCSE A–C level or equivalent					0.424	18.52	1.088	1.82

Table 4.5 (Continued)

	Model 1				Model 2			
	Employee		Self-employed		Employee		Self-employed	
	RRR	t-statistic	RRR	t-statistic	RRR	t-statistic	RRR	t-statistic
Other qualification	1.431	27.30			0.544	10.88	0.948	0.92
No formal qualification	1.601	31.70			0.459	12.84	1.580	7.28
Job tenure								
1–2 years	1.516	27.01	1.640	35.49	1.427	38.71	1.598	46.04
2–5 years	1.955	24.88	1.890	39.35	1.503	22.30	1.854	33.42
More than 5 years	1.614	6.39	3.131	83.53	1.259	10.67	3.127	65.36
Part-time			9.950	1.68	1.199	1.55	0.876	1.05
Part-time female			3.061	14.36	2.762	4.68	4.688	6.83
Labour market characteristics t − 1:								
Part-time					0.611	3.10	0.724	1.99
Part-time female					2.252	3.48	1.905	2.71
Supervisor					8.988	43.26	0.398	18.30

* Interaction variable.

Note: Estimation results from a multinomial logit regression, the comparison group consists of employees. Sample sizes are 38 213 employees, 5909 self-employed and 583 dependent self-employed for model 1 (model 2). Omitted categories are males with no child or children over the age of 5, males not married or cohabiting, white, residential tenure of more than 5 years, higher education, job tenure of 1 year or shorter, males working full-time, not a supervisor (at $t − 1$).
All models include 13 indicator variables for area of residence.

independent self-employed are greater, the older the worker is, but at a declining rate [RRRs of more (less) than one for age (age squared)]. On the other hand, when comparing the dependent self-employed with employees, we see that the odds for being dependent self-employed are smaller, the older the worker is with a slightly increasing rate. Workers with a pre-school-aged child are less likely to work either as employees or independent self-employed than dependent self-employed. Women with a pre-school-aged child are less likely being an employee than a dependent self-employed worker, but they are more likely to be independent self-employed. Workers who are married or cohabiting are more likely to be employed or independent self-employed, although the RRRs are statistically significant at conventional levels, the differences are rather small. The results from residential tenures do not show an easily interpretable pattern and are, moreover, not significant. It seems that longer residential tenure is estimated to be associated with greater odds of being employed. A novel result emerges from the analysis of ethnic background. We admit that the used dichotomy of white and non-white is a crude instrument, but the small number of observations forced our hands. Nevertheless, we estimate that workers from non-white ethnic backgrounds have lower odds of working as dependent self-employed than as employed. They are, however, more likely to work as independent self-employed, all other things being equal. When we consider formal education and the odds of being an employed worker or dependent self-employed, we find that workers with an A-level (or equivalent) education are less likely to be either employed or independent self-employed than dependent self-employed. The opposite, however, is true when looking at the next lower level of education. Those with no formal education have smaller odds being either employed and independent self-employed than dependent self-employed. The estimates show that dependent self-employment is associated with more labour market fluctuation, those with short job tenures are more likely to be working as dependent self-employed than as employees, in comparison to those with considerable longer job tenures. The same is true for the independent self-employed; workers with long job tenures are more likely to work independent self-employed than as dependent self-employed. Part-time workers have higher odds of being both employed (twice) and independent self-employed (ten times) rather than dependent self-employed; the same is true for part-time female workers although to a lesser degree.

How significant are these findings? We have performed a Wald test to test the differences between the dependent self-employed, the self-employed and the employed and are re-assured that the differences are, indeed, statistically significant (p-value of less than 0.00).

The BLFS also provides variables that gauge the respondent's labour market status 1 year ago. While such retrospective data may be afflicted with non-random error, we use them here as it comes closest to longitudinal data, which would allow the analysis of workers over time. We use these additional variables in Model Two, also tabulated in Table 4.5. These additional variables describe the job situation a year before the current interview in terms of whether the worker was working part- or full-time, whether he or she supervised other employees or not and the standard occupational category (SOC) of the job. We first note that most estimated odds do change little when we include the additional variables in our model. Changes occur for the association between gender and the work status and the civil status as well as the association between working part-time and self-employment. We see that those who were working part-time a year ago are more likely to work dependent self-employed rather than being employed or independent self-employed. However, part-time female workers have greater odds working as employees or independent self-employed than dependent self-employed. Those who had a job that included supervision of other workers in its duties are found to be much more likely to be employed than dependent self-employed, but the reverse is true when looking at independent self-employed individuals. Interestingly, those with supervision duties 1 year before are less likely being independent self-employed than dependent self-employed.

4.5 Dependent self-employment in Italy

Despite the active political debate on labour market flexibility and precariousness in Italy, there is little empirical evidence due to the lack of adequate datasets. One source of data on collaborators in Italy is the administrative INPS data, used by Berton et al. (2005), which contains information on workers in the private sector registered in the separate social security fund and are the actual contributors to the fund.[4] The creation of the separate INPS fund for collaborators showed that almost 1 million work relationships on the basis of a contract of continuous collaboration existed in 1995. Another source of data on collaborators is the Italian Labour Force Survey (ILFS)[5] by the National Institute of Statistics (ISTAT) which has included the category of collaborators since 2004.[6]

The two sources differ for various reasons. First, the ILFS is based on a questionnaire and it includes individuals working for both the private and the public sector, while the INPS data refer only to workers in the private sector, registered and contributing to the special social security fund reserved to collaborators. Secondly, in the INPS data the professional groups of administrators, syndics and auditors are included in the category of collaborators, while they are highly likely to define themselves as autonomous workers in the ILFS. More generally, the INPS includes all professionals in the category of collaborators, while ILFS does not. Finally, the questionnaire of the ILFS allows us to identify those collaborators who hold contracts of continuous and coordinated collaboration in their principal job, while the INPS special fund also counts those persons who are collaborators in their second job.[7]

For the empirical analysis we use the fourth quarter of the ILFS 2004. The dataset includes around 175 000 individuals belonging to 70 000 families and living in 1246 different municipalities. It contains information on personal, family and labour market characteristics. Thus, in comparison to the administrative INPS data used by Berton et al. (2005), this dataset contains more information on individuals interviewed (education, marital status, search for a new job, motivation for working part-time, etc.). Unfortunately, users are not provided with the personal identification code of the respondents, and therefore a panel analysis is not possible. However, the datasets contains information about the labour market status 1 year before, allowing at least an analysis on labour market transitions in the short run. Furthermore, it contains variables that allow to evaluate the effective degree of autonomy (or dependency) of collaborators with respect to the firm they contract with. Consequently, we investigate collaborators on the basis of three different definitions. The first definition looks at those collaborators who state that their principal main activity status is that of a collaborator (982 individuals). The second definition focuses at collaborators that additionally state that they work only for one agency (889 individuals, 90 per cent of all collaborators). The third definition reduces the group of the collaborators further to those who claim that they cannot decide autonomously over their working hours and their working location (508 individuals, 52 per cent of collaborators).

We reduced the sample to women between 20 and 59 and men between 20 and 64. Table 4.6 reports the descriptive statistics for employees, self-employed persons and collaborators (according to all three definitions). Contrary to employees and self-employed individuals,

Table 4.6 Descriptive statistics of the sample (Italian Labour Force Survey)

	Employee		Self-employed		Collaborators Definition One		Collaborators Definition Two		Collaborators Definition Three	
	Mean	SD	Mean	SD	Mean	SD	Mean	SD	Mean	SD
Personal characteristics										
Male (%)	55.9		74.9		40.5		40.1		36.9	
Female (%)	44.1		25.1		59.5		59.9		63.1	
Age	40.0	10.2	43.4	10.2	36.4	10.9	36.2	10.9	34.9	10.3
Married (%)	62.2		70.1		43.3		43.2		39.7	
Education (%)										
High education	13.7		14.4		30.3		29.2		27.8	
Medium education	45.8		37.4		50.2		50.4		51.1	
Low education	40.5		48.2		19.5		20.4		21.1	
Residence (%)										
North	51.1		54.5		49.8		53.4		48.9	
Centre	16.1		20.8		16.9		21.9		24.4	
South	32.8		24.7		33.3		24.7		26.7	
Job characteristics										
First job (%)	30.3		37.3		27.2		27.8		30.9	
Tenure (%)										
< 1year	13.2		6.3		32.8		33.4		34.6	
1–3 years	18.5		12.2		35.9		37.0		37.1	
3–5 years	11.2		9.1		11.4		11.4		12.8	
≥ 5years	57.1		72.4		19.9		18.2		15.5	
Sector (%)										
Agriculture	3.2		10.5		1.1		1.2		0.8	
Manufacturing	26.1		13.0		10.5		10.5		9.5	
Construction	7.3		13.2		1.9		1.9		1.7	
Commerce	10.7		25.8		9.7		9.5		9.9	
Tourism, Transport, Financial	19.8		27.0		41.7		42.1		37.9	
Public sector (including education and health)	27.8		4.2		25.3		25.5		29.4	
Other	5.1		6.3		9.8		9.3		10.8	
Working hours (week)	33.5	13.1	42.4	16.9	29.5	14.4	29.4	14.0	29.5	13.4
Part-time (%)	13.0		7.7		41.0		40.4		38.3	
Occupation (%)										
Managers	1.7		14.5		2.6		2.7		1.7	
Intellectuals and researcher	9.5		12.4		18.5		17.2		15.5	
Technicians	21.3		15.2		35.0		33.9		29.6	
White collars	14.9		–		19.9		20.7		22.6	
Qualified professionals	12.9		22.0		11.8		12.6		14.9	

Artisans and qualified blue collars	16.3	29.3	4.9	5.0	6.2
Low-qualified blue collars	11.8	3.1	2.4	2.6	3.5
Not qualified blue collars	11.6	3.5	4.9	5.3	6.0
Working 1 year before (%)	92.4	94.6	78.6	77.9	76.0
Number of observations	44913	12521	982	889	508

the share of women among collaborators is higher than that of men.[8] Around 50 per cent of the collaborators live in the Northern regions, and especially in the northwest (30 per cent). On average, collaborators are younger than their counterparts. A third of the collaborators is between 20 and 30, another third between 30 and 40, a fifth between 40 and 50 and the rest (15 per cent) is older than 50. The share of married people is lower among collaborators, probably because of the younger age, but also due to the effect of the precariousness of their position in the labour market (De La Rica and Iza 2005). Collaborators are more educated than employees and self-employed persons. Within the group of collaborators, women are, on average, more educated than men: a third of female collaborators are university graduates compared to only a quarter of male collaborators. Looking at job characteristics, we observe that the share of workers in the first job ever is not different among the three groups. However, job tenure is, on average, longer for employees and self-employed persons. Collaborators are mainly concentrated in the service sector (tourism, transport and financial) and in the public sector, followed by the manufacturing and commerce sectors. Using the INPS data, Altieri and Oteri (2004) found similar results: most of the enterprises deploying collaborators worked in the service sector. The incidence of part-time jobs is more than three times higher among collaborators than among employees, probably because an employed part-timer is more expensive for the firms[9] and therefore Italian firms hardly offer part-time jobs, which means that a contract of continuous collaboration might be a possibility for individuals to work part-time and for the firms to reduce the cost of part-time work. Berton et al. (2005) argue that contracts of continuous and coordinated collaboration can be considered as an instrument for women to find a part-time job. Our data shows that 72 per cent of collaborators working part-time are women (84 per cent among employees) that state that they work part-time because they have to take care of their children or of other relatives (43 per cent) or because they are studying (27 per cent). However, 47 per cent of female collaborators working part-time also declare that they could not find a full-time job (35 per cent among employees). We observe that collaborators are concentrated in the high- and medium-qualified occupations (technicians, white collars, intellectuals and researchers, qualified professionals). In particular, female collaborators seem to have more qualified jobs than men: 25 per cent are white-collar workers (13 per cent among men) and 16 per cent of female collaborators are qualified professionals (6 per cent for men). Data also show that most of the collaborators are not satisfied with their job and look for a more stable work position: 88 per cent of them would like to find a permanent job and 22 per cent are actually looking for a new job (the analogous figure among employees is only 7 per cent). The main reasons for searching a new job are that the contract is temporary (27 per cent), that the present job is considered as occasional (10 per cent), that they look for a more qualified (17 per cent) and better paid (28 per cent) job.

We estimate a multinomial logit model to compare three groups of workers: employees, self-employed individuals and collaborators (the latter according to the three definitions as described above). It estimates the odds of being a collaborator versus the odds of being an employee and the odds of being a collaborator versus being self-employed. Since we are mainly interested in comparing collaborators with employees and self-employed individuals, respectively, we choose the group of collaborators as the comparison group to identify the model. As above with the BLFS, the results are presented in RRR (i.e. the exponentiated coefficients). The RRR give the odds of being in one group versus the odds of being a collaborator with a RRR greater (less) than one indicates that the risk of being in the latter group is greater (smaller).

We estimate the model in three versions according to the three different definitions for collaborators which serve as the dependent variables. Firstly, we estimate the model with only strict exogenous characteristics (i.e. sex, age, marital status and education) in Table 4.7 and, secondly, with additional covariates (i.e. interaction affect between sex and part-time, first job, job tenure, regions and sectors) in Table 4.8. Both estimations have been clustered according to the household individuals who live in. The following interpretation of the results focuses on the second estimation (Table 4.8) and uses the collaborator status as the reference (thus it is the omitted category).

Table 4.7 Estimated risk of being self-employed or being an employee in comparison to being a collaborator

	Definition One				Definition Two				Definition Three			
	Employee		Self-employed		Employee		Self-employed		Employee		Self-employed	
	RRR	SE	RRR	SE	RRR	SE	RRR	SE	RRR	SE	RRR	SE
Personal characteristics												
Female	0.633**	0.042	0.282**	0.019	0.626**	0.044	0.279**	0.020	0.561**	0.053	0.250**	0.024
Age	1.178**	0.029	1.217**	0.031	1.180**	0.031	1.219**	0.033	1.149**	0.041	1.186**	0.043
Age squared/100	0.998**	0.000	0.998**	0.000	0.998**	0.000	0.998**	0.000	0.999**	0.000	0.999**	0.000
Married	1.477**	0.112	1.538**	0.121	1.445**	0.115	1.505**	0.123	1.549**	0.163	1.615**	0.173
Education												
Medium Education	0.526**	0.046	0.431**	0.039	0.550**	0.050	0.450**	0.042	0.607**	0.072	0.498**	0.060
High Education	0.228**	0.022	0.235**	0.023	0.246**	0.025	0.253**	0.026	0.281**	0.038	0.288**	0.039

Note: Estimation results from a multinomial logit regression, comparison group are collaborators.
Sample sizes: Definition One (Main activity status is collaborator): 44 913 employees, 982 collaborators, 12 521 self-employed. Definition Two (Main activity status is collaborator + work only for one agency): 44 913 employees, 889 collaborators, 12 521 self-employed. Definition Three (Main activity status is collaborator + work only for one agency + cannot decide upon working hours and working location): 44 913 employees, 508 collaborators, 12 521 self-employed.
Omitted categories are male, other civil status, low education.
Statistically significant (on a 5% error level) estimates are indicated by **.

Table 4.8 Estimated risk of being employed or self-employed in comparison to being a collaborator

	Definition One				Definition Two				Definition Three			
	Employees		Self-employed		Employees		Self-employed		Employees		Self-employed	
	RRR	SE	RRR	SE	RRR	SE	RRR	SE	RRR	SE	RRR	SE
Personal characteristics												
Female	1.058	0.088	0.638**	0.055	1.034	0.089§	0.624**	0.056	0.920	0.105	0.556**	0.065
Age	1.104**	0.028	1.155**	0.031	1.102**	0.029	1.153**	0.032	1.071*	0.039	1.119**	0.042
Age squared/100	0.998**	0.000	0.998**	0.000	0.999**	0.000	0.998**	0.000	0.999*	0.000	0.999**	0.000
Married	1.307**	0.103	1.398**	0.115	1.270**	0.104	1.358**	0.116	1.341**	0.145	1.437**	0.159
Education												
Medium education	0.482**	0.045	0.487**	0.047	0.509**	0.050	0.515**	0.052	0.598**	0.075	0.605**	0.077
High education	0.218**	0.024	0.539**	0.061	0.246**	0.028	0.611**	0.072	0.339**	0.050	0.841	0.126
Region												
North Italy	0.634**	0.065	0.783**	0.084	0.599**	0.064	0.738**	0.081	0.578**	0.078	0.714**	0.098
Central Italy	0.731**	0.063	0.865**	0.077	0.740**	0.067	0.875	0.082	0.845	0.101	1.001	0.122
First job	1.047	0.088	1.531**	0.133	0.994	0.088	1.452**	0.132	0.903	0.104	1.317**	0.155
Job tenure												
1–3 years	1.188**	1.100	1.725**	0.164	1.178*	0.102	1.708**	0.168	1.245*	0.144	1.806**	0.225
3–5 years	2.109**	0.250	3.736**	0.478	2.193**	0.273	3.885**	0.520	2.056**	0.327	3.642**	0.608
More than 5 years	6.212**	0.770	14.951**	1.953	7.024**	0.922	16.912**	2.330	7.928**	1.446	19.098**	3.580

Table 4.8 (Continued)

	Definition One				Definition Two				Definition Three			
	Employees		Self-employed		Employees		Self-employed		Employees		Self-employed	
	RRR	SE	RRR	SE	RRR	SE	RRR	SE	RRR	SE	RRR	SE
Sector												
Agriculture	3.191**	1.210	7.591**	2.882	3.004**	1.142	7.148**	2.721	3.559**	2.215	8.462**	5.275
Manufacturing	3.202**	0.377	1.157	0.141	3.216**	0.394	1.162	0.147	3.225**	0.551	1.166	0.203
Construction	4.633**	1.108	6.686**	1.612	4.887**	1.234	7.060**	1.796	4.812**	1.662	6.958**	2.414
Commerce	1.987**	0.249	4.361**	0.558	2.080**	0.276	4.570**	0.617	1.850**	0.326	4.071**	0.726
Tourism, finance, housing	1.919**	0.190	0.139**	0.015	1.844**	0.190	0.133**	0.015	1.268*	0.165	0.091**	0.013
Public administration	1.106	0.143	1.349**	0.184	1.207	0.166	1.475**	0.214	0.958	0.168	1.177	0.213
Female*part-time	0.402**	0.038	2.222**	0.024	0.425**	0.042	0.235**	0.026	0.515**	0.066	0.284**	0.039

Note: Estimation results from a multinomial logit regression, comparison group are collaborators. Sample sizes: Definition One (Main activity status is collaborator): 44 913 employees, 982 collaborators, 12 521 self-employed. Definition Two (Main activity status is collaborator + work only for one agency): 44 913 employees, 889 collaborators, 12 521 self-employed. Definition Three (Main activity status is collaborator + work only for one agency + cannot decide upon working hours and working location): 44 913 employees, 508 collaborators, 12 521 self-employed. Omitted categories are male, other civil status, job tenure less than 1 year, low education, male*part-time, not first job, other sectors, south Italy. Statistically significant (on a 5% error level) estimates are indicated by **, those on a 10% error level by *.

In comparison to men, women are slightly less likely to work as collaborators than as employees. However, this effect is not significant in either of the three definitions. Interestingly, we see that this chance is reversed in Definition Three. The latter shows that women are more likely to work as collaborators than as employees. In all three definitions, women have a greater risk of being a collaborator than being self-employed. The variable age is only measured in steps of 5 years in the dataset. Thus, we attributed each individual the median age of the respective age group. Results show that older workers have a smaller risk of being a collaborator than being employed (at a slightly increasing rate). The same is true when comparing collaborators with the self-employed: older workers are less likely to be collaborators than being self-employed. All the effects are more or less similar across the different definitions. In all three definitions, married workers have smaller odds of being collaborators than employed in comparison to non-married workers. Married workers are also less likely to work as collaborators than being self-employed. We find that highly educated workers are much more likely to work as collaborators then being employed. The same effect, but to a weaker degree, is found when looking at the self-employed versus collaborators. The odds of individuals with a university degree being a collaborator are roughly four times (twice) that of employees (self-employed). This effect is weaker in Definition Three than in Definition One and Two. In comparison to workers living in the South of Italy, workers of Central or North Italy are more likely to be collaborators than being employed. We do not find neither statistically significant nor strong effects for the variable whether this particular job is the first job ever when comparing employees with collaborators. Thus, there is no significant evidence that contracts of continuous and coordinated collaboration help individuals to enter the labour market. Interestingly, comparing self-employed and collaborators we find that individuals who work in their first job ever are more likely to work as self-employed than as a collaborator (statistically significant at a five per cent level for all definitions). Workers with longer job tenure are less likely to be collaborators than being employed. This effect increases with the length of the job tenure and also when comparing Definition One with Definition Two and Three. For instance, using Definition Three (Definition One) the risk of being an employee is roughly 8 (6) times higher than the risk of being a collaborator for those with job tenure of more than 5 years. The risk of being a collaborator compared to an employee is more than twice as high for those having a job tenure between 3 and 5 years (more or less equal across the different definitions). The effect is even stronger when comparing self-employed persons with collaborators: the odds of being self-employed instead of working as a collaborator as defined in Definition Three are 19 times higher for job tenures of 5 years. Individuals working in the omitted sector – i.e. other sectors – are more likely to work as collaborators than employees compared to the other sectors (i.e. 'agriculture', 'manufacturing', 'construction', 'commerce and public administration' and 'tourism, transport, finance and housing'). For instance, workers in the construction (manufacturing) industry are roughly 4(3) times as likely to work as employees than as collaborators. These results are even stronger when comparing collaborators with self-employed individuals. Finally, women working part-time are more than twice as likely working as collaborators than being employed. As above, this effect is slightly weaker in Definition Three than in the other two definitions. Similarly, women working part-time are more likely to be a collaborator than being self-employed.

Although the data do not allow a panel analysis, we nevertheless have information about the labour market status 1 year before. We are aware of the problem that such retrospective data may be afflicted with non-random error, but we use them here as they come closest to longitudinal data. Table 4.9 depicts the transitions between the different labour markets statuses from 1 year to the next. It is shown that around 79 per cent of the collaborators stay in the same group. A 10 per cent of the collaborators in the year 2003 became employees in 2004, 8 per cent became unemployed and only 4 per cent became self-employed.

In Table 4.10 we estimate a probit model with the labour market status 1 year before as an independent variable. Other independent variables are the strictly exogenous personal characteristics (i.e. sex, age, age squared, civil status and education). The dependent variable divides

Table 4.9 Transitions between three different labour market statuses

Labour Market Status in 2003	Labour Market Status in 2004								Total N
	Employee		Collaborators		Self-employed		Unemployed		
	n	%	n	%	n	%	n	%	
Employee	41842	95.7	93	0.2	347	0.8	1450	3.3	43732
Collaborator	82	9.5	682	78.7	30	3.5	72	8.3	866
Self-employed	115	0.8	7	0.1	13421	98.0	155	1.1	13698
Unemployed	1680	18.1	77	0.8	262	2.8	7237	78.2	9256
Total	43719		859		14060		8914		67552

Table 4.10 Probit estimation of the likelihood to work at time t (work = 1, unemployed = 0)

	Coefficient	SE
Female	−0.137**	0.022
Age	0.059**	0.008
Age squared/100	0.000**	0.000
Married	0.155**	0.026
Medium education	0.270**	0.024
High education	0.434**	0.041
Employee $t-1$	0.471**	0.064
Self-employed $t-1$	0.839**	0.070
Constant	−0.231	0.161

Note: Omitted categories are male, other civil status, low education and collaborator $t-1$. Sample size: 1677 did not work at time t and 56 466 worked at time t. Statistically significant (on a 5% error level) estimates are indicated by **.

those who worked in 2004 and those who were unemployed and/or in search for a job. The results show that those who were employees in 2003 are more likely to work in 2004 compared to those who were collaborators in 2003 (omitted category). Similarly, we find that those who were self-employed in 2003 are more likely to work in 2004 in contrast to the collaborators in 2003.

Finally, Table 4.11 presents a multinomial analysis of the effect of the labour market status in 2003 at the probabilities of being either an employee, collaborator, self-employed or unemployed in 2004. As above, the other independent variable is the strictly exogenous personal characteristics (i.e. sex, age, age squared, civil status and education). In order to avoid the problem of a high persistency, we only analyse those with a job tenure (or unemployment duration) of less than 12 months. We find that those who were employees in 2003 are much more likely to be an employee again a year later compared to collaborators (in 2003). Those who were self-employed in 2003 are more likely to be an employee in 2004 compared to collaborators (in 2003). Those who were employees in 2003 are more likely to be self-employed in 2004 compared to collaborators (in 2003). Those who were self-employed in 2003 are much more likely to be self-employed in 2003 compared to collaborators (in 2003). Also the unemployed have greater chances of becoming either employed or self-employed (or remain unemployed) than collaborators. In other terms, collaborators have a smaller risk of becoming unemployed 1 year later compared to the unemployed, but

Table 4.11 Estimated risk of being self-employed or being an employee in comparison to being a collaborator

	Employees		Self-employed		Unemployed	
	RRR	SE	RRR	SE	RRR	SE
Female	0.867	0.130	0.412**	0.070	1.121	0.210
Age	1.068	0.056	1.205**	0.072	0.992	0.064
Age squared/100	0.999*	0.001	0.997**	0.001	1.000	0.001
Married	1.533**	0.282	1.693**	0.346	1.300	0.297
Medium education	0.469**	0.091	0.578**	0.122	0.280**	0.065
High education	0.247**	0.054	0.357**	0.088	0.147**	0.043
Employee $t-1$	36.227**	7.800	7.925**	2.214	34.871**	35.716
Self-employed $t-1$	13.435**	5.831	60.018**	27.659	32.205**	37.643
Unemployed $t-1$	18.390**	4.046	6.638**	1.895	177.457**	180.698

Note: Omitted categories are male, other civil status, low education and collaborator $t-1$. Sample size: 3451 employees, 158 collaborators, 516 self-employed (only those who have changed job within the last 12 months). Statistically significant (on a 5% error level) estimates are indicated by **.

they are less likely to become both employed or self-employed compared to the unemployed.

4.6 Conclusions

Factors such as labour market and organisational changes, unemployment in an economy, the wealth of the individuals, the family background, immigration or the tax system are pivotal in influencing the development of self-employment in an economy. In the canonical model of labour supply, the individual's decision to work is determined not only by the wage rate and the non-labour income but also by personal characteristics (such as age or gender) and individual preferences or tastes (e.g. motivation). Research on the individual's decision to supply labour in the form of self-employment focuses very much on personal characteristics (e. g. personal wealth, family background) and individual preferences (e.g. human capital, motivation, management capabilities or taste for independence and flexibility). The stressed motives of the dependent self-employed workers we have interviewed in different industries are indeed around the issues of flexibility, independence, management (in)capabilities and motivation, but they also argued that rigid internal labour market structures and external pressures from the labour market forced them into dependent self-employment.

Using the BLFS and the ILFS, we analysed the characteristics of dependent self-employed workers in comparison with employees and self-employed individuals. We found that women have a smaller risk of being dependent self-employed compared to employees (not significant for Italy, however), but if self-employed they are more likely to be dependent rather than independent self-employed. For both countries we also estimated that married individuals have lower odds of being dependent self-employed than in the other two labour market statuses. In terms of age we see that in both countries, older workers are more likely to be independent self-employed rather than dependent self-employed. In Italy, the same is also true when comparing employees and dependent self-employed workers. Interestingly, in the UK we find that the older worker's odds for being dependent self-employed are smaller as those for employees. In Italy we found strong effects of the education level with workers having a university degree being much more likely to be dependent self-employed. We found the same result in the UK but to a considerable lesser degree. Looking at workers with low or no education, however, we observe that they are more likely to be dependent self-employment in the UK but not in Italy. Unsurprisingly, in both countries we find that workers with short job tenures are associated with being dependent self-employed. Italian women working part-time have a higher risk of being dependent self-employed than being employed or self-employed, suggesting that contracts of continuous collaboration give women the possibility to work part-time in Italy, an effect we did not find in the UK. This might be due to the fact that there are hardly part-time jobs offered in Italy due to high costs of part-time work in Italy for employers.

The analysis of the transitions shows that in both countries most dependent self-employed workers are also in the same labour market status 1 year later. In Italy, the probability of working in the year of observation is higher for those who have been employed or self-employed than for those who have been dependent self-employed 1 year before. We found that dependent self-employed workers have less chance than both employees and self-employed individuals to become either an employee or self-employed. Thus we find a high persistency of dependent self-employment in Italy and at the same time we find that these contracts are not a vehicle for more stable and better-protected jobs. Our results show that these contracts are not an instrument for young people to enter into the labour market, but many young and highly educated workers in Italy are forced to accept this type of contract that does not guarantee them neither flexibility nor job protection.

In comparison to the UK, dependent self-employed workers in Italy seem not to be used to increase the labour flexibility of low-qualified workers but as a low-cost alternative to deploy highly educated young professionals. In contrast to the UK, Italy has a strong insider–outsider labour market, with high protection for insiders and rather low protection for outsiders. These results suggest that Italian firms are trying to reduce the circle of insiders in the labour market and to find a way to circumvent labour market protection for incoming workers. This has effects on both human capital accumulation and family formation (specifically fertility). Neither the employer nor the dependent self-employed have enough incentives to invest in human capital (both general and firm-specific), which is especially problematic for young people in the transition from education to the labour market. As argued by De la Rica and Iza (2005) for fixed-term workers, precariousness in the labour market has the effect to postpone family formation and thus to reduce fertility.

5
The Organisational Governance of Dependent Forms of Self-Employment

5.1 The importance of informal structures

Research on dependent forms of outsourcing has to focus on both formal organisational structures and, even more importantly, on informal organisational structures. Analysing only formal structures and relations would not reveal the actual organisation of dependent long-term business relationships. We argue that business relationships based on dependent forms of outsourcing rely on relational contracts that are additionally strengthened by the dependent element of such business relationships. In this context, dependency basically means that the subcontractor (i.e. the upstream party) is restricted in his or her alternative actions by both formal and informal agreements.

Starting from Max Weber's investigation on formal organisational structures and processes (Weber 1922), organisational sociology has been enriched by research on the importance of informal structures and agreements in and between organisations (e.g. Blau and Scott 1962; Macaulay 1963; Dore 1983; Powell 1990). While sociologists have focused their research not only on relational contracts within firms but also between firms, economists have, until recently, looked mainly at formal contracts. Recent economic research on relational contracts draws heavily on the insights organisational sociology has provided. Nevertheless, this chapter will show that in economics relational contracts rely on reciprocity and quid pro quo logic, while in sociology relational contracts are based on social embeddedness (i.e. reputation, friendship, interdependence or altruism) and trust (Granovetter 1985; Powell 1990).

The sociological critique of economic theories of the firm focuses mainly on the elimination of social relations from economic analysis which leads to an undersocialised view. In a seminal paper, Granovetter (1985: 489) criticises Williamson's analysis of markets and hierarchies, as it does 'not allow for the extent to which concrete personal relations and the obligations inherent in them discourage malfeasance, quite apart from institutional arrangements'. Moreover, sociologists argue that social institutions and arrangements are viewed as efficient solutions to certain economic problems rather than as the results of historical, social or political forces (Fligstein and Freeland 1995; Grimshaw and Rubery 2005).

This theoretical chapter explores economic and sociological theories of the firm and claims that the sharp delineation of markets, hierarchies and hybrids used in conventional theories of the firm does not allow an explanation of dependent forms of outsourcing. It is argued, firstly, that dependent outsourcing shows elements of both hierarchy and (relational) markets and, secondly, that firms simultaneously make, buy and cooperate. On the basis of these findings, the key features of dependent outsourcing are discussed. Finally, this chapter explores relevant theories of the firm that help to explain governance structures that use dependent forms of outsourcing, deriving relevant research questions for empirical investigation in the subsequent chapter.

5.2 Markets, hierarchies and relational contracts

5.2.1 The market-versus-hierarchy approach

Research on organisational governance has been determined by a sharp delineation of markets and hierarchies. These two different modes of governance have long been seen as two alternative mechanisms for allocating resources. Starting from Coase's seminal publication 'The Nature of the Firm' in 1937, organisational theorists looked at the logic of the existence of firms and asked why the allocation of resources is not achieved through the price mechanism, thus by the market.[1] Coase indicates five reasons for the existence of firms: the costs of organising production through the price mechanism, contract costs (which are reduced within firms), the costs of sequential short-term contracts, regulation constraints (e.g. taxes) and, finally, the existence of 'marketing' costs (i.e. the costs of using the price mechanism). Coase identifies the costs of market transactions as the reason for the existence of firms. Firms, he argues, exist only where they perform better than markets could. In other words, the high costs of market transactions can make it more efficient to coordinate production within firms than through markets. Thus, the boundaries of the firm are explained by efficiency considerations.

Williamson (1975, 1985) carried out important research on the nature of transaction costs and their causes, drawing heavily on Coase's insights. More specifically, he looks at the conditions and reasons for which economic transactions are performed within the boundaries of hierarchical firms (i.e. in-house production) rather than by market transactions outside the firm. The underlying basic assumption in answering this question is that the adopted organisational form always represents the most efficient one in terms of costs of economic transactions, as already argued by Coase (1937). While market transactions refer to economic transactions between different firms (i.e. when products or services are bought from another firm), the notion 'hierarchies' relates to economic transactions within hierarchical firms (i.e. when products are traded between divisions of a single firm). Williamson sees modes of organisation as lying on a continuum between markets and hierarchies, suggesting that firms might do better than markets because they can rely on relational contracts as argued by Simon (1951), who sees an employment relationship as a relational contract.[2]

Williamson (1975) argues that it is not technology but transactions that are decisive in determining the efficacy of different modes of organisation. He bases his main argument, namely that firms (hierarchies) function better than markets in completing a related set of transactions, according to four subarguments. The first refers to the human inability to rationally assess the costs and benefits of every choice available on the market. Bounded rationality problems in uncertain and complex environments can be better solved within hierarchies than within markets. Contrary to the market, hierarchies can rely on adaptive, sequential decision processes and routines. Consequently, 'efficient codes' and 'convergent expectations', which economise on bounded rationality, are developed. Second, hierarchies are less vulnerable to the hazards of opportunism due to additional incentive and control structures, since hierarchies can be more effectively audited, and disputes within hierarchies are easier to settle than those within markets. The cause of the hazard of opportunism is that complementary labour specialisation creates vulnerabilities. Owners of highly specialised, complementary resources risk the danger of being 'held up' by their contract partner unless the initial agreement is (re)negotiated to obtain better terms. Third, hierarchies help to overcome information problems, which arise mainly because of uncertainty and opportunism. The cost of collecting and transferring information is minimised through intra-firm information channels. Additionally, hierarchies are apt to be superior to markets in reducing the problem of opportunistic behaviour in the communication process. Finally, it is claimed that market exchange tends to encourage calculative relations, whereas hierarchies are 'better able to make allowance for quasimoral involvements among the parties' (Williamson 1975: 38). Thus, he argues that trust is more easily developed within firms than between firms. To summarise, market transactions face the problem of incomplete contracts which may motivate firms to use hierarchical modes of organisation instead of these.

Williamson's argumentation was heavily criticised for its very narrow definition of the market, which he sees as only formal and incomplete contracts. The functioning of the market itself remains unclear in his analysis. The main point of critique is that problems of bounded rationality and uncertainty, opportunism and information can also be reduced within markets, as is elaborated in more detail below. Nonetheless, Williamson's conclusion reflected the actual organisational trend of vertical integration, which was observed during the 1960s and 1970s. The tendency to vertical disintegration has, since the 1980s, been followed by research on relational contracts between firms.

Formal contracts are indeed mostly imperfect, but firms use relational contracts for both inter-organisational and intra-organisational relationships to overcome this problem. Hence, it is not only firms that are riddled with relational contracts but also business relationships (Gibbons 2000a). Dependent outsourcing, joint ventures or business networks are the most obvious examples to underline this argument.

Responding to this line of critique, Williamson (1985) integrates the concept of relational contracts into his transaction costs approach. His book 'Economic Institutions of Capitalism' (1985) brings two major and important innovations. Firstly, relational contracts between firms are investigated, and secondly, the limits on efficacy of firms and hierarchies are discussed in more detail.[3] Williamson (1985) looks more closely at hybrid transactions, which are related to relational contracts. He argues that economic rationality determines the organisation of specific transactions, suggesting that three dimensions are critical for describing transactions: asset specificity, uncertainty and frequency. In this context, asset specificity means that durable investments have been made to support particular investments (ex ante investments) and that the opportunity costs of these investments are lower in best alternative use. Uncertainty is read as behavioural uncertainty, that is uncertainty which arises due to problems of human action (e.g. opportunism). Frequency is related to the number of transactions. The argument is that these three dimensions together determine the governance structure. The higher the degree of these three dimensions, the higher the probability of establishing a non-market governance system (i.e. vertical integration in contrast to external business relations). Transactions with a high level of uncertainty and a high degree of asset specificity require complex contracts and have, moreover, a greater need for ex post adjustments. High frequency of transactions reduces the fixed costs of a non-market governance system.

Based on these insights, Williamson (1985: 68ff) uses Macneil's (1978) categories of contracts to develop a classification of efficient governance options as shown in Table 5.1. Classical contracting refers to the 'ideal' market transaction whose nature of agreement is delimited to formal features which can be enforced in courts. Thus, classical contracting applies to non-specific transactions in both occasional and recurrent contracting (i.e. market governance). Neoclassical contracting relates to long-term business relationships with mixed and highly specific occasional transactions. This type of contracting recognises the incompleteness of agreements and relies, on the one hand, on confidence and, on the other, on third-party assistance in resolving possible disputes. Consequently, Williamson relates neoclassical contracting to trilateral governance. Relational contracting results from the pressure to sustain ongoing relations. Problems of increasing duration and the complexity of long-term business relations reveal the shortcomings of classical and neoclassical contracts. Relational contracts refer not to any singular transaction but to the 'entire relation as it has developed [through] time' (Macneil 1978: 890). Williamson matches two different types of governance to relational contracts, namely unified governance and

Table 5.1 Efficient governance of transactions

		Investment characteristics		
		Non-specific	Mixed	Idiosyncratic
Frequency	Occasional	Market governance (classical contracting)	Trilateral governance (neoclassical contracting)	
	Recurrent		Bilateral governance (relational contracting)	Unified governance

Source: Williamson (1985: 79).

bilateral governance. The fundamental difference between these two governance structures is that within bilateral governance the autonomy of the parties is maintained, whereas this is not the case within unified governance. Unified governance means that the transaction does not occur on the market, but is organised within the firm through hierarchies (i.e. vertical integration). Williamson sees the advantages of vertical integration in the 'adaptations [that] can be made in a sequential way without the need to consult, complete, or revise interfirm agreements' (1985: 78). He argues that vertical integration is the most efficient governance form where highly idiosyncratic transactions are concerned. Bilateral governance is applied to transactions that occur frequently at an intermediate level of asset specificity. One example of this application is a long-term business relationship between two independent firms which trade customised material.

In sum, Williamson's (1985) key argument is that every transaction can be linked to a most efficient organisational arrangement. The matching of transaction characteristics with governance structures is given in Table 5.1.

Transaction cost economics explores the inefficiencies of the market in conducting certain transactions. It assumes that agency problems (i.e. post-contractual opportunism with respect to relationship-specific investments) are mitigated when a transaction takes place within the firm. It does not, however, look closely at the inefficiencies of the firm in its internal organisation and performance. Also, in assuming that every contract that may occur within a firm can also be placed between firms, transaction cost economics fails to explain why firms do or do not merge, nor does it explain why agency problems are mitigated under integration. More generally, transaction cost economics focuses its analysis on the boundaries of the firm rather than inside the firm. Nevertheless, the analysis of transaction cost economics helps us to think about the role of imperfect contracts and specific investments and how they are related to the transactional efficiency of alternative governance structures such as vertical integration and relational contracts.

Recent organisational developments such as an increase in outsourcing activities, however, have shown that firms outsource even those transactions with high asset specificity. For instance, firms increasingly buy firm-specific software from outside contractors or, to give another example, car manufacturing firms source out major production steps. As discussed above, transaction cost economics argues that under certain conditions of high asset specificity, market transactions become subject to higher levels of opportunism and bounded rationality, making them more costly to govern. High asset specificity means that transaction-specific investments have been made, which then increases the opportunity costs of the alternative use (where possible). This, in turn, increases the likelihood of opportunism, which can, however, be reduced within firms through hierarchical power ('fiat'). This process explains vertical integration in terms of transaction cost economics. The crucial point within this chain of argumentation is that it is assumed that the firm can reduce the likelihood of opportunism through internal fiat.

5.2.2 Relational contracts, repeated games and reciprocity

More recent research on governance structures has accounted for the fact that business organisations have changed significantly since the 1970s, with relational contracts between firms having gained massively in importance. Firm boundaries have become blurred due to new forms of long-term, ongoing business cooperations which cannot be explained by the dichotomic view of arm's length market relationships ('buy') versus vertical integration ('make'). Consequently, this stream of research investigates the 'make or cooperate' decisions by firms, and analyses the functioning of stable and enduring contractual market relationships. The main point that this kind of work presents is that long-term business relationships based on relational contracts help firms to circumvent difficulties in formal contracting (Powell 1990; Baker et al. 1999; Helper et al. 2000).

Relational contracts refer to informal agreements, unwritten codes and understandings that powerfully affect the behaviour of individuals within firms and the behaviour of firms when cooperating with others (Powell 1990; Baker et al. 1999). Hence, relational contracts are assumed to be prevalent not only within firms but also between firms. Relational contracts between firms can be observed on both lines – the vertical (e.g. long-term supplier relationships) and the horizontal lines (e.g. business networks and joint ventures). The powerful influence of relational contracts in all cases – that is within and between firms and on vertical and horizontal lines – is due to the future pay-offs of the long-term relationship.

Departing from Macaulay (1963) – who was among the first to analyse the importance of non-contractual relations between businesses – sociologists have widely investigated the logic and consequences of relational contracts. Dore (1983) identifies relational contracts in the Japanese textile industry in which 'goodwill "give-and-take" is expected to temper the pursuit of self-interest' (p. 459). Dore argues that these supply relationships – in which activities are coordinated by a large number of family enterprises – are, firstly, based on the principle of mutuality and secondly, guided by the stability of the relationship. He finds that opportunism is less of a danger in these business relationships, which he calls 'moralised trading relationship of mutual goodwill (Dore 1983: 463).

Powell (1990: 271), in analysing network forms of organisations, describes relational contracts in networks as being based on 'reciprocal, preferential, mutually supportive actions'. Powell argues that the continuum view of economic exchange suggested by Williamson (1975, 1985), with discrete market transactions at the one end and the highly centralised firm at the other, intermediate or hybrid forms being between these two poles, is misleading because it 'blinds us to the role played by reciprocity and collaboration as alternative governance mechanisms' (Powell 1990: 267). Instead he sees business networks as a 'separate, different mode of exchange, one with its own logic' (p. 269) based on relational contracts. The logic behind forms of governance is their strong dependence on the nature of the relationship, mutual interest, reputational concerns and the norm of reciprocity.

Sociological interest in network forms of organisations has increased enormously over the last two decades. This intensive research interest has been triggered by recent developments in the structures of business organisations from the large hierarchical firm to networks of lateral and horizontal inter-linkages within and among firms (Nohria 1992; Castells 1996). Podolny and Page (1998: 57) stress that this stream of research has shown 'that network forms of organisation foster learning, represent a mechanism for the attainment of status or legitimacy, provide a variety of economic benefits, facilitate the management of resource dependencies, and provide considerable autonomy for employees'. Networks, it is assumed, are effective because they enable firms to gain quick access to goods and services as and when an immediate need arises due to rapidly changing market environments (Fligstein and Freeland 1995).

Podolny and Page (1998: 59) define a network form of organisation 'as any collection of actors ($N \geq 2$) that pursue repeated, enduring exchange relations with one another and, at the same time, lack a legitimate organizational authority to arbitrate and resolve disputes that may arise during the exchange'. Thus, network forms describe relational contracts between firms and include business relationships such as joint ventures, business alliances, business groups, franchising and outsourcing. For instance, in investigating business alliances and partnerships, Powell (2001: 59) finds that fixed contracts are ineffectual, and are thus replaced by relational contracts which are supported by 'reputation, friendship and interdependence'.

Sociological research on relational contracts shows that reciprocity is central to ongoing cooperation between businesses. Although reciprocity is only vaguely defined in the literature, it is certainly used in a different way when compared to economic research. The main difference between the economic and sociological views on reciprocity relates to the question of the equivalence of the exchange value. While economists tend to argue that reciprocity involves exchanges of more or less equivalent value in the long run, sociologists employ a fuzzy definition of equivalence, stressing normative standards, indebtedness and obligation. The long-term perspective of relational contracts, so the argument goes, promotes security and stability and generates trust (Powell 1990: 272f).

Relational contracts, then, are dependent on the functioning of social relations in and between firms. All the core features of relational contracts thus refer to the basic idea that organisations are socially embedded entities, meaning that economic actions in business relationships are affected by underlying social relations (Granovetter 1985). In his seminal paper 'Economic Action and Social Structure: The Problem of Embeddedness', Granovetter (1985) argues that sociologists have to analyse the overall structure of relationships in which organisations and their actors are embedded in order to understand the effects of social structures on economic life. The main claim of this paper is that economic action is embedded in social relations, which sometimes facilitate and at other times derail exchange. Granovetter (1985: 487) points out that 'actors do not behave or decide as atoms outside a social context, nor do they adhere slavishly to a script written for them by the particular intersection of social categories that they happen to occupy. Their attempts at purposive action are instead embedded in concrete, ongoing systems of social relations.' He suggests that the structure of these social relations plays a crucial role in generating trust and discouraging malfeasance. Thus, it is the underlying social relation rather than institutional arrangements or generalised morality, which produces trust and trustworthy behaviour in economic exchange relationships. In sum, Granovetter (1985: 493) sees the embeddedness approach to business relationships as a 'way between the oversocialised approach of generalised morality and the undersocialised one of impersonal, institutional arrangements by following and analyzing concrete patterns of social relations'.

Although Granovetter's paper provoked an enormous upsurge in interest on the role of networks in the economy, his concept of 'embeddedness' remains vague and rather programmatic. While it states that social relations shape economic action, it does not show how this process works (Uzzi 1996). Our main point of critique, however, is that Granovetter overemphasises the social content of ongoing economic relations, leading to 'strong expectations of trust and abstention from opportunism' (Granovetter 1985: 490). Instead, we argue that it is not the social content of an ongoing economic relation itself that may generate trust, but past experiences and – more importantly – the future pay-offs of the relationship.

The economic approach to relational contracts mainly analyses how the current behaviour of business partners influences their future relationship or how threats and promises concerning future behaviour may affect current behaviour (Gibbons 2000b). Methodologically, economists capture relational contracts with a repeated game model where the 'players' meet repeatedly (until a randomly chosen date). Of course, the outcome of this set-up differs dramatically from a one-shot market interaction where the business partners do not meet again after the business deal is completed. In short, in a one-shot market interaction 'betrayal' pays, whereas in a repeated game model 'trust' is rational behaviour. However, the outcome of the repeated game model depends on the value of the pay-off, which is determined not only by the time value of money but also by the probability that the business partners will meet again after the period in question. Using this set-up, Baker et al. (1999) find that cooperation is optimal if the business relationship is sufficiently likely to continue in the future. In other words, cooperating – or trust – pays-off in the long run.

The need for relational contracts arises from the problem of setting up complete contracts. Complete contracts must specify ex ante all aspects of the business deal which must be verifiable ex post by a third party such as a court. This may be possible for straightforward business deals on standardised products but not for more complex deals on customised products or services. Furthermore, in complex business relations it is usually too costly – if possible at all – to write complete contracts. Relational contracts also have the advantage in that they leave room for adapting to new information which arises during the business relation. The non-specificity of relational contracts, however, means that they are not enforceable by a third party. Consequently, relational contracts must be self-enforcing, meaning that 'the short-run value of reneging

Table 5.2 Combinations of ownership and governance regimes that define four organisational forms

Governance environment	Ownership environment	
	Non-integrated asset ownership	Integrated asset ownership
Spot	Spot outsourcing	Spot employment
Relational	Relational outsourcing	Relational employment

Source: Baker et al. (1999: 7).

must be less than the long-run value of the relationship' (Baker et al. 1999: 3).

Baker et al. (1999) look at ownership structures combined with governance regimes and define four organisational forms: spot outsourcing, spot employment, relational outsourcing and relational employment (see Table 5.2).

Transactions under non-integration refer to business relationships with independent contractors (the 'upstream party'), who own the asset used for production. Transactions under integration, on the other hand, are transactions within firms where the downstream party (the user) owns the asset, making the upstream party the employee. Under both ownership structures the downstream party is interested in getting high value goods from the upstream party. A 'high value' is assumed to be observable but non-contractible. The production of a high value, however, can be encouraged by promising to pay the upstream party a bonus. Thus, self-enforcing relational contracts can provide the necessary incentives to produce goods with an observable, but non-contractible, high value due to the long-term value of the relationship.

The fundamental difference between transactions under non-integration and integration is that under non-integration, the upstream party (i.e. the independent contractor) has an outside option because the produced good has an alternative-use value. Therefore, under non-integration, the upstream party can threaten to consign the good to its alternative use. Under integration, the firm still owns the good when the upstream party reneges on the bonus.[4] In this case, the downstream party can prevent the upstream party from dealing with other firms. Renegation on the bonus under non-integration means that the downstream party cannot use the good unless it pays, at least, the alternative-use value.

The governance environment refers to the frequency of business deals. Spot interactions are one-shot relationships, in which the parties will deal with one another only once. Relational interactions, on the other hand, are long-term business relationships where parties trade with each other on a regular basis.

Baker et al. (1999) compare the self-enforcing strength of a business deal under vertical integration versus non-integration. Their main proposition is that 'integration affects the parties' temptations to renege on a relational contract, and hence affects the best relational contract the parties can sustain' (Baker et al. 1999: 3). Thus, the incentive to betray a given relational contract depends on the governance environment the transactions are embedded in, or, in other words, whether the two parties are integrated or non-integrated.

Baker at al. (1999) derive three results related to this proposition. First, vertical integration can be an efficient response when supply prices vary widely. The reason for this is that under non-integration high supply prices create an incentive to renege on relational contracts. Second, they show that high-powered incentives produce a higher temptation to renege under integration than under non-integration. Due to missing alternative uses under integration, the temptation not to pay the bonus is smaller under non-integration than under integration. The upstream party under non-integration has an outside option because the produced good has an alternative-use value. Under integration, in contrast, the upstream party's good has no alternative use since the downstream party can prevent the upstream party from dealing with other firms. Third, they find that the temptation to renege will be too great if the surplus from relational employment only slightly exceeds the surplus from spot outsourcing. Thus, the relational contract is not self-enforcing in this case. In sum, Baker et al. (1999) provide a new answer to the question posed by Coase: 'Why are there firms?' According to their results, a firm arises only if a spot market performs sufficiently poorly.

5.3 Governing dependent forms of outsourcing

5.3.1 Relational contracts and dependent forms of outsourcing

As already argued above, the sharp delineation of markets and hierarchies offered in Coase (1937) as well as in Williamson (1985), that is continuum view including hybrids, cannot explain many of the business structures that have evolved since the 1980s. Research on relational contracts has aimed at theoretically explaining new forms of governance. The aim of this approach is to capture the organisational logic of business structures that rely on stable, long-term relationships between firms. Networks (e.g. Child 1987; Powell 1990; Uzzi 1996; Thompson 2003), alliances (e.g. Gulati 2004), joint ventures (e.g. Kogut 2004), business groups (e.g. Granovetter 1995) or outsourcing (e.g. Dore 1983; Helper et al. 2000) are some examples where the market-versus-hierarchy approach fails, and new analytical tools such as relational contract theory have been developed. In brief, this research on long-term relationships between firms documents that informal mechanisms (e.g. reciprocity) strengthen formal contracts, leading to a variety of advantages such as spreading risks, facilitating the management of resource dependencies, fostering learning, enhancing flexibility, gaining access to specific know-how, realising economies of scale, entering new markets and so on. However, we run into trouble explaining dependent forms of outsourcing with markets, hierarchies or relational contracts.

Relational contract theory has undoubtedly enriched research on organisational governance, allowing an 'embedded' view of the social structure of markets and hierarchies. Nevertheless, the distinction between markets and hierarchies – in both spot and relational perspectives – as mutually exclusive governance structures detracts from the fact that spot or relational markets and hierarchies often occur in combination with one another. For instance, modern multi-divisional firms often deploy mixed control mechanisms such as profit centres or transfer-pricing. In such cases a price control mechanism is mixed with a hierarchical governance structure (Bradach and Eccles 1989).

We hypothesise that the organisational structure of firms that use dependent forms of outsourcing shows two important characteristics. Firstly, dependent outsourcing shows elements of both hierarchy and (relational) markets. More specifically, dependent long-term business relationships are based on relational contracts that are laced with elements of hierarchy. The authority mechanism is primarily enforced by relational contracts since legal regulations hardly allow referring to authority in formal contracts. The price mechanism comes into play through asset ownership and governance structure competition. Asset ownership means that the dependent self-employed worker de facto owns the produced good or service, which has an implicit price and is, thus, tradable and marketable. Competition through other organisational structures – that is hierarchy (employees) and spot markets (occasional independent contractors) – further enhances the price mechanism by reducing the bargaining power of the dependent self-employed. The market mechanism, however, is laced by long-term relational contracts, producing (calculative) trust through reciprocity and mutual dependency.

Secondly, many firms that deploy dependent self-employed workers also have employees or spot business relationships which essentially do the same job. Thus, firms simultaneously make, buy *and* cooperate rather than of the classical make-or-buy decision. Transactions are not only embedded in the social context as suggested by Granovetter (1985) but also in the context of other transactions. Transactions that are controlled by one mechanism have an impact on transactions controlled by another mechanism (Bradach and Eccles 1989). For instance, analysing fast-food chains that use both company stores and franchise stores, Lewin-Solomons (1998) shows that such systems produce a dynamic efficiency. On the one hand, company stores can use the innovative ideas (such as management or technical innovations that lead to more efficient operating procedures) generated by their franchisees for the benefit of the company stores. On the other hand, franchisers can use the information about production their company stores generate to control the franchisees and reduce the uncertainty of opportunistic bargaining. Thus, it may be an efficient solution to simultaneously run company and franchise stores even if company stores are less efficient than franchise stores. Moreover, using various control mechanisms simultaneously fosters competition between the two, creating additional incentives for both in-house managers and outside contractors.

Grimshaw and Rubery (2005) offer a similar argument, stressing that the simultaneous use of different governance structures displaces risk and consolidates power. They argue that this corporate strategy is deployed to restructure internal organisation by using external threat to weaken the internal power of labour and circumvent internal constraints. For instance, if the institutionalisation of internal structures such as labour costs is too difficult to change, externalisation may be employed to indirectly alter the system. Thus, they argue that the external threat serves to increase internal competition and to reduce internal worker bargaining power.

In the introductory chapter to this study, we discussed the examples of the freight and insurance industries, showing that both carriers and insurance companies deploy employees, dependent self-employed workers and independent self-employed personnel. These examples accentuate the fact that distinct organisational control mechanisms are used simultaneously for the same function by the same firm. For instance, insurance companies sell their product via various distribution channels. First, the direct sales force which has an employment relationship with the insurance company. This is supervised or controlled using an authority mechanism and firm-specific routines. Conflicts between the employees and the employer are usually solved by administrative fiat and supervisory power. The relationship between the direct sales force and the insurance company is based on a formal and bureaucratic 'climate', producing a medium to a high level of commitment. Flexibility for the insurance company in this distribution channel is low due to various reasons, which will be discussed in more detail in the following chapter. Second, firms use independent financial advisers who are self-employed and sell products from various insurance companies on the basis of contracts. In this distribution channel, the control mechanism can only be executed through prices. Conflicts between the two parties are solved by third parties such as the courts. The tone or climate between the business partners relies on precision, or perhaps suspicion (depending on the frequency of business), which produces low commitment between the two parties. However, the degree of flexibility an insurance company gains by using this distribution channel is high, precisely due to this low level of commitment. Third, tied agents who are self-employed but sell insurance products from only one company are used. The key features of this channel are described below.

5.3.2 The key features of dependent business relationships

Drawing from Powell's (1990) analysis of the key features of markets, namely hierarchies and networks, Table 5.3 introduces the additional element of dependent outsourcing. It is shown that this governance structure uses elements from all three governance structures, thus representing a hybrid form. The following discusses the key features of dependent long-term business relationships and derives research questions to be examined in the empirical analysis in Chapter 5, where we test whether these hypothesised key features are indeed observable in dependent business relationships.

Dependent long-term business relationships are based on both formal contracts and informal agreements. A formal contract regulates the basics of the relationship, often forbidding the dependent self-employed worker to deal with other parties (exclusiveness). However, formal contracts do not reveal the actual organisation of the relationship. Informal agreements, unwritten codes of conduct and understandings – in short, relational contracts – determine the social structure of the business relationship. Relational contracts also regulate those parts of the relationship that are neither observable nor measurable. Furthermore,

Table 5.3 Key features of various governance structures

Key features	Governance structure			
	Market	Hierarchy	Relational market	Dependent outsourcing
Normative basis	Contract, property rights	Employment relationships	Complementary strengths	Formal and relational contracts, dependency
Control mechanism	Prices	Authority, routines	Relational, reciprocity	Authority, prices and relational
Methods of conflict resolution	Third party enforceability	Administrative fiat, supervision	Reciprocity, reputational concerns	Third party enforceability, administrative fiat and self-enforcing relational contracts
Tone or climate	Precision and/or suspicion	Formal, bureaucratic	Reciprocal, mutual benefits	Bureaucratic, mutual benefits
Amount of commitment	Low	Medium to high	Medium to high	(Medium to) High
Degree of flexibility	High	Low	Medium to high	Medium
Degree of dependency	Independent	Dependent	Interdependent	Dependent

Source: Adapted from Powell (1990).

dependency is created not only by formal contracts but also by informal agreements. Consequently, we pose the following research questions for empirical investigation in the following chapter:

> *Research Question A1: Which aspects of dependent long-term business relationships are regulated by formal and which by informal, relational contracts?*
> *Research Question A2: On what basis is dependency created?*

As discussed above, dependent forms of outsourcing use both authority and price control mechanisms to reduce opportunism. On the one hand, control is executed using authority structures similar to those in employment relationships. On the other hand, a price mechanism through asset ownership and competition by governance structures further enhances control. However, these two control mechanisms are embedded in a third mechanism, that is the power of relational contracts, that further reduces the threat of opportunism.

> *Research Question A3: How does the downstream party use authority and price mechanisms to control the upstream party?*
> *Research Question A4: What role do relational contracts play in controlling the upstream party?*

These two key features of the normative basis and the control mechanism also influence methods of conflict resolution. Measurable and, thus, contractible outcomes that are regulated by the formal contract are enforceable by a third party such as a court. However, it is argued that administrative fiat also plays a role in conflict resolution because firms often use the same administrative structure for both employees and dependent self-employed workers. Finally, those parts of the relationship that are not measurable – and sometimes not observable in the short run (e.g. quality of customer care) – are governed by relational contracts.

> *Research Question A5: Which conflicts are solved by courts, which by relational contracts and which by administrative fiat?*

The general climate of a dependent business relationship is, on the one hand, bureaucratic because of the authority elements, yet on the other, the mutual benefits of these long-term business relationships help to establish a specific kind of trust. It is argued that such business relationships are based on relational contracts that are fortified by authority elements.

> *Research Question A6: Which mode of trust is produced in dependent business relationships?*

Connected to the climate of business relationships is the amount of commitment the upstream party has to the downstream party. In contrast to spot markets, dependent business relationships are characterised by a higher level of commitment by the upstream party due to the close tie to the downstream party. However, commitment may also be the result of the dependent element of these business relationships.

Research Question A7: How is commitment generated in dependent business relationships?

The degree of flexibility the outsourcing firm may realise by deploying dependent self-employed workers is higher compared to employees because the mixture of a formal contract and a relational contract leaves room for manoeuvre. Of course, firms will not observe the same amount of flexibility as in spot markets due to the existence of a basic long-term contract. However, a medium amount of flexibility allows quick reactions to uncertain environments while simultaneously enabling basic stability.

Research Question A8: Does the downstream party gain flexibility by deploying dependent self-employed workers?

5.3.3 Explaining dependent outsourcing from an organisational sociology perspective

Dependent forms of outsourcing demonstrate that viewing transactions as being governed either by markets, hierarchy or relational contracts inaccurately reflects the complexity of business organisations. The economic approach to organisational governance, however, illustrates that deploying pure structural forms enables researchers to develop specific predictions within a rigid framework (e.g. Baker et al. 1999). The sociological approach, in contrast, departs from a broader framework that allows the incorporation of different explanatory factors without being restricted to pure structural forms.

A pure neoclassical economic model would predict that there is one optimal way of organising transactions in equilibrium. Thus, we should observe very similar – or even identical – organisational structures across economies. If the governance structure of firms is mainly a result of efficiency considerations, we should, according to this line of argument, observe convergence across firms since all firms have the same economic goal. The fact that we do not observe this means that economies are either never in equilibrium (or in one possible equilibrium of a multi-equilibrium model) – as argued by Nelson and Winter (1982) – or that the rigidity of economic models fail to explain actual differences in organisational structures. Organisational sociologists have produced a vast literature investigating the reasons for cross-country organisational diversity – although there is also evidence that organisational convergence has been increasing (Powell 2001; Supiot 2001; Crouch 2003). The following employs various sociological approaches that help to examine the pivotal factors influencing the existence of dependent forms of self-employment.[5] By looking at different sociological approaches, we can identify the various drives behind such complex forms of organisations without being bound to one specific perspective.

Until the 1960s, organisation theory mainly focused on internal organisational operations, leaving the organisations' environment aside. In the 1960s, structural contingency theory emerged, which began the conceptualisation of the importance of the environment in which an organisation acts (e.g. Lawrence and Lorsch 1967; Thompson 1967). The basic idea here is that different environments require different organisational structures, and consequently organisations with structures more closely matched to the requirements of their context will be more effective than others (Pfeffer 1982: 148).[6] Simply put, the most effective way to run a company is contingent upon its environment. For example, producing in a market with high cyclical fluctuations will mean that flexible organisation for determining the structure of labour management is optimal. This approach assumes that rational actors perceive these strategic contingencies and that they have the internal power to alter the firm's strategies and structures in order to adapt to environmental conditions (Fligstein and Freeland 1995).

One line of critique of the structural contingency theory emphasises that the source of this internal power remains vague. Newer theory thus focused on the firm's internal decision-making processes, arguing that actors' power within organisations depends on their ability to manage internal and external resource dependencies. Resource dependence theory (Pfeffer and Salancik 1978) perceives organisations as interdependent with those elements of the environment with which they interact, and, consequently, underlines that organisational behaviour is externally influenced. The basic argument is that organisations will be more likely to respond to those actors in the environment which control critical resources. Inter-organisational power[7] affects the activities of organisations, which means that the strategies of organisations and their managers to cope with external constraints result from resource interdependence (Pfeffer 1982: 192ff).[8] For instance, firms need resources such as raw materials, capital, labour or knowledge which renders then vulnerable in their environment.

One way of managing an organisation's external dependence is by introducing elements of authority into the market. 'Bridging', as resource dependence theorists label this strategy, leads to a pivotal modification of the organisation's boundaries through either formal or informal means (Nohria and Gulati 1994: 541). Common examples of this 'bridging' strategy to influence external dependency are mergers, acquisitions, business alliances, business networks or joint ventures. Pfeffer and Nowak (1976), for instance, look at joint ventures in the US oil and gas industry. They argue that firms undertake joint ventures – and hence introduce elements of authority into the market – not only to fulfil their internal need for a continuous source of supply, but also to reduce the uncertainties (e.g. varying supply prices) associated with dependency upon other organisations.

Dependent outsourcing is an even more powerful organisational strategy for managing resource dependencies. As argued above, dependent forms of outsourcing use mixed forms of governance structures. Authority mechanisms are written into formal contracts as well as implicitly implemented by informal contracts. Thus, while firms gain flexibility by outsourcing part of their operations, they still control their resources by tying them to the firm. Binding the upstream contractor to the firm through both a formal and an informal contract establishes a dependent outsourcing relationship and reduces the uncertainties associated with dependency upon other organisations. In other words, dependent outsourcing enables the firm to reduce business uncertainty through risk outsourcing and (human) capital insourcing.

Research Question B1: How does the authority mechanism in dependent long-term business relationships allow the downstream firm to control resources?

Research Question B2: Which kinds of uncertainties do the downstream firm mitigate through dependent outsourcing?

In contrast to resource dependence theory, population ecology (Hannan and Freeman 1977, 1989) does not focus explicitly on organisational adaptation to environmental contexts. It emphasises instead that the environment is the key mechanism in explaining organisational diversity. Thus, population ecologists stress that the environment 'selects' or determines an organisation's success or failure. The environment is defined as ecological niches, consisting of the resource pool upon which a group of competing organisations (population) depends. The firm-specific driving forces of adaptation result from constraints, which are both external (e.g. legal and financial barriers to market entry and exit, information availability, legitimacy considerations) and internal (for instance, the organisation's investment in plant and equipment or in sunk costs, information flows within organisations, internal political constraints, constraints from history and tradition). Consequently, the firm-specific external and internal constraints provoke diverse adaptation strategies across organisations. Population ecology divides environments between fine-grained environments in which there are many changes over time and coarse-grained environments in which there are more powerful changes in environmental conditions. The central argument of population ecology is that it is not the individual firm that finds the optimal form in its environmental context, but the other way around, that is the environment optimises conditions for and thus allows for the survival of certain organisations. As a result, organisational diversity arises due to different environmental constraints.

As we can see, population ecology builds on the biological ecologist approach of natural selection. Since organisational structure is determined by environmental constraints, no room is left for individual choice, and so this theory has widely been criticised for its extreme environmental determinism (Fligstein and Freeland 1995), its narrow definition of organisational forms and its limited theoretical causality 'which says little about the conditions under which new organizational forms are created and how that may in turn relate to their relative survival' (Nohria and Gulati 1994: 542).

Nonetheless, organisational ecology draws our attention to the firms' environment. The environment is identified as internal and external constraints, concluding that firm-specific external and internal constraints provoke different adaptation strategies across organisations. We argue that the emergence of dependent outsourcing was based in a coarse-grained environment with changes in the environment provoking innovation in organisational governance structures. Consequently, changing external and internal constraints have provoked dependent outsourcing.

Research Question B3: Was there a fundamental change in the environment in Austria and the UK that provoked dependent forms of outsourcing?

Both resource dependency theory and population ecology approaches define the environment of organisations mostly in terms of technological and economic constraints. However, firms face not only technological and economic environments but also institutional ones. The new institutional theory of organisations focuses on the impact of the social and cultural environment on organisations and how this environment shapes the goals and means of actors (e.g. Zucker 1987; Powell and DiMaggio 1991; Scott and Meyer 1994).[9]

Like other organisational theories of the firm, new institutional theory was developed as a reaction to economic approaches which see organisations as bounded, relatively autonomous and rational actors. New institutional theory, in contrast, argues that organisations are strongly embedded in wider institutional environments. Scott (1995: 33), for instance, gives the following definition of institutions: 'Institutions consist of cognitive, normative, and regulative structures and activities that provide stability and meaning to social behavior. Institutions are transported by various carriers – cultures, structures, and routines – and they operate at multiple levels of jurisdiction.' These institutions shape organisational activities as they become institutionalised by cognitive, normative and regulative means. Thus, institutions are based on repeated actions and shared conceptions of reality (Zucker 1987; Scott 1995).

Institutionalists emphasise that interaction within and between firms and their environment creates formal and informal rules, establishing organisational fields. Repetition and externalisation institutionalise these fields, which means that they take on an independent status with a strong normative effect on the governance of subsequent interactions. Hence, due to the institutionalisation of internal and external organisational interaction, changes in organisational forms are driven by considerations of legitimacy rather than by rationality and efficiency concerns (Zucker 1987; Scott 1995).

In their seminal paper on institutional homogenisation or 'isomorphism', DiMaggio and Powell (1983) argue that firms follow the actions of other organisations due to coercive pressures, legitimacy pressures or to reduce uncertainty. This adaptation process is labelled 'isomorphism'. Organisational actions are shaped, firstly, by governmental regulations or laws (coercive isomorphism), secondly, by norms, values and expectations (normative isomorphism) and, thirdly, by copying other organisations in order to reduce uncertainty (mimetic isomorphism). Responding to these institutional pressures describes the process of institutionalisation. DiMaggio and Powell (1983) claim that these institutional pressures help to explain why organisations become structurally similar but not necessarily more efficient. It is claimed that once organisational structures and practices are institutionalised, they take on an independent status, creating long-lasting effects.

Similar to the resource dependence theory and the population ecology approach, the new institutional approach to organisation helps us to identify the reasons for deploying dependent forms of outsourcing or, on the other hand, why firms do not deploy them. As argued above, political and legal pressures lead to similar organisational adaptation since laws and government regulations strictly determine room for manoeuvre. For example, if labour law broadly defines the concept of the worker so that this comprises dependent self-employed workers, then incentives for firms to deploy such workers are reduced. Additionally, industry regulation shapes organisational structure

> *Research Question B4: Do differences in the legal environment explain the different outcomes across investigated countries?*
> *Research Question B5: Do insurance companies adapt to laws and regulations in a similar way?*

Apart from legal rules on the macro- or meso-level, internal firm rules and structures create homogenised firm cultures across dependent firms. We argue that we will observe an influence on the governance structures of subsidiary companies, and that they are therefore likely to have similar organisational structures and methods. Consequently, we hypothesise that the decision to use dependent outsourcing is also determined by the strategy of the mother company.

> *Research Question B6: What influence do mother companies have on the set-up of organisational structures and governance?*

DiMaggio and Powell (1983) argue that uncertainty is a powerful force that encourages imitation. A famous example of mimetic behaviour is the US automobile industry. Observing that the Japanese automobile industry was an efficient producer on a lower cost basis, US automobile manufacturers began to copy parts of the organisational structure and working methods of the Japanese producers. Changes in the environment such as increased competition and changes in industry regulation in both the countries investigated here increased the uncertainty for business organisations, which may lead to mimetic processes. Moreover, mimetic behaviour can also be enhanced indirectly by employee transfer or directly by consulting companies and industry trade associations. In sum, organisations tend to imitate other firms that they perceive as being either more successful or more innovative than themselves.

> *Research Question B7: What role does imitative behaviour play in the use of dependent outsourcing?*
> *Research Question B8: Which are the 'leading' firms?*

Societal norms, values and expectations may be another source of isomorphic organisational change. As discussed above, the institutionalist approach stresses that institutionalised organisational fields are created by the repetition and externalisation of formal and informal rules ('routines') that govern interactions. If routines are seen either as successful in solving specific tasks or problems or simply considered as legitimate ways of solving problems, then they are gradually absorbed by other organisations. This externalisation detaches routines from their initial context and transforms them into general, shared social meanings beyond their point of origin (Tolbert and Zucker 1996). As argued previously, uncertainty within organisations or concerning the organisational environment may enhance the process of externalisation (DiMaggio and Powell 1983). Consequently, institutionalists see organisational operations as mainly based on incorporated routines and norms rather than on economic rationality.

DiMaggio and Powell (1983) stress that normative pressure is also shaped by the societal organisation of professionalisation. Firstly, formal education and professional training are important sources for the establishment of industrial norms. Secondly, professional and trade associations or consulting firms also produce normative rules about organisational behaviour. Thirdly, managers' social and professional networks facilitate the exchange of information and fortify commonly recognised routines and norms.

Research Question B9: What role have organisational routines and norms played in the emergence (or non-emergence) of dependent outsourcing?

The political–cultural approach identifies other important factors influencing organisational structures and practices which are not sufficiently considered in the theoretical approaches to organisations discussed so far, that is: the state, the culture of production and resulting power relations (Fligstein 1990, 1996, 2001; Campbell and Lindberg 1990).

Fligstein (1996: 657) argues that distinct state–firm interactions have produced 'unique cultures of production' across societies. Some examples of these interactions can be found in the production of market institutions such as property rights, governance structures, conceptions of control or the rules of exchange. All of the latter shape the business culture of a society (Campbell and Lindberg 1990).[10] Fligstein (1996: 657) argues that 'the social structures of markets and the internal organization of firms are best viewed as attempts to mitigate the effects of competition with other firms'. While firms try to create stable markets,[11] 'the politics of markets and the social organization of markets involve attempts to do so' (Fligstein 1996: 659). The state can play a pivotal role in the creation of these structures.[12] The enforcement of laws relating to property rights, governance structures and rules of exchange shape the conception of control, which can lead to stable markets (Fligstein 1990: Chapter 1).[13]

Fligstein (1996: 668f) hypothesises that the transformation of markets is caused either by a decrease in consumer demand, the entry of other firms which changes the conception of control and introduces procedures which force a re-organisation of the market or by the state changing the market rules. Hence, the transformation of markets is a result of exogenous forces. Moreover, Fligstein (1990, 1996) stresses that the construction of an organisational field and the creation of common understandings are based on political processes within and between firms. The most powerful group of actors develops a specific method for controlling an organisational field and imposes this on smaller groups (i.e. smaller firms or less powerful groups within firms). The legitimisation of these common understandings by the state establishes a specific conception of control.

Fligstein (1996) identifies three political processes which interact with each other: one within firms, one between firms and one of state actors. The first refers to power struggles within firms, the winners of which will impose their organisational culture and design upon the firm. The second creates a common understanding between firms, whereby the most powerful firms will have the largest impact on their formation. The third political process reflects the societal solution of the problem of property rights, governance structures, conception of control and rules of exchange. The political process within firms influences the political process between firms and this, in turn, is determined by the third political process at the state level.

In sum, the political–cultural approach introduces the state and thus provides a macro-level view combined with a micro-level view of political processes within and between firms. The basic argument is that the outcome of political processes between state actors, as well as within and between firms, creates a unique culture of production across different societies. The active formation of market institutions such as property rights, governance structures, conception of control or rules of exchange shapes the business culture of a society.

Research Question B10: What differences in the cultures of production exist between the two economies under investigation?
Research Question B11: Which market institutions set by the state help to develop dependent forms of outsourcing?
Research Question B12: Which power relations (within firms; between firms; between firms, the state and other institutions) can be identified that shape this specific form of organisational governance?

5.4 Conclusions

This chapter has presented the argument that long-term dependent business relationships cannot be explained by using the traditional market-versus-hierarchy approach. Instead, such business relationships rely on relational contracts that are additionally empowered by dependency (or the lack of alternative uses of resources) and hierarchical control elements. While the basics of the business relationship are written in formal contracts, their actual structure and organisation rely on unwritten, relational contracts. Consequently, relational contracts relate to the informal elements of long-term business relationships such as unwritten codes and understandings or informal agreements. Basically, relational contracts describe the social embeddedness of transactions and operations in a long-term business relationship.

Dependency in such business relationships is created, firstly, by the contractual restriction of alternative uses of resources ('exclusiveness'), secondly, by support measures that bind the upstream party to the downstream party (for instance through credits with special conditions as long as the business relationship goes on), thirdly, by relationship-specific investments made by the upstream party and fourthly, by authority elements of the business relationship (for instance, that the downstream party determines when, how and where work must be carried out). Thus, dependent long-term business relationships are based on relational contracts that are laced with elements of an hierarchical control mechanism. The market mechanism of such business relationships – which is enhanced by competition from other organisational structures – is, in turn, laced with elements of long-term relational contracts, producing commitment and trust.

This chapter furthermore analyses the pivotal determining factors for the existence of dependent outsourcing, with the help of relevant sociological theories of the firm, and formulates research questions for empirical investigation in the following chapters. Resource dependency theory argues that reducing the external dependence of an organisation upon other organisations may be achieved by introducing elements of an hierarchical control mechanism into the market thus modifying the boundaries of the firm. We suggest that this is exactly the process found in dependent outsourcing. The population-ecology approach draws our attention to the environments that create dependent outsourcing by determining internal and external constraints. New institutional theory focuses on the impact of cognitive, normative and regulative structures – in short, institutions – that provide stability and meaning to social behaviour. It is argued that organisational actions are shaped by governmental regulations, cultural norms and values and mimetic behaviour to reduce uncertainty. Thus, we ask how these institutions influence the creation of dependent self-employment. Finally, a political–cultural approach identifies the state, the culture of production and the resulting power relations as influencing factors on organisational structures. This view draws our empirical attention to a comparative investigation of the influence of the state in the creation of dependent self-employment.

6
The Creation of Dependent Self-Employment in Comparative Perspective

6.1 The research design

The following qualitative research aims at analysing dependent outsourcing and the creation of dependent self-employment in three industries in the UK, Italy and Austria. It does not aim at representativity but it will illustrate the logic of dependent outsourcing by looking at the mechanisms governing this special form of labour relations. Our main aim is to empirically demonstrate horizontal disintegration, the blurring of firm boundaries by mixing hierarchical and market elements in one distinct form of governance, namely dependent outsourcing. Moreover, we analyse how dependency is created and which role trust and power have in such business relations.

According to Yin (1993: 59), 'the case study method [...] is an empirical inquiry that investigates a contemporary phenomenon within its real-life context, addresses a situation in which the boundaries between phenomenon and context are not clearly evident, and uses multiple sources of evidence'. Consequently, the following case study analysis and data description aims at embedded fact description and interpretation in light of the theoretical issues discussed above. Moreover, this case study research is based not only on interviews but also draws on market research and social scientific literature. In order to draw coherent results, it is important to ask the same question of different sources of evidence (Yin 1993: 69).

The guiding research principle of this case study was to explore phenomena and build theory (Eisenhardt 1989). The first phase of data collection was to conduct semi-structured interviews with managers, employees, dependent self-employed workers and self-employed individuals. The second phase consisted of data evaluation in the context of existing theories and original theory construction, coding the interviews along the inter-related dimensions, formal/informal contracts (i.e. governance structures), dependency and control. In a third phase we conducted further interviews (only in the British and Austrian insurance industry) with officials from trade unions and professional associations to clarify observations and to discuss hierarchical forms of outsourcing and working relationships.

This empirical part is based on 27 interviews in the British, 19 in the Italian and 32 in the Austrian insurance industry, 40 interviews in the Italian and 14 in the Austrian business service industry and 15 interviews in the Austrian freight industry (i.e. 147 interviews in total). They were carried out between the end of the year 2000 and mid-2002. The interviews in the UK were conducted mainly in Central and Greater London, but also in Bristol, Cheltenham, Swindon and Yorkshire (Wakefield and Keighley), those in Italy in the northwest Italian region Piedmont and those in Austria in Vienna and in the provinces of Salzburg, Upper and Lower Austria.[1]

The research design, however, is not symmetrical as this book brings together various case studies. We present and discuss direct results from the British and Austrian insurance industry and the Austrian business service and freight industry. The results of the Italian interviews are not directly reported in the following, but we use Bertolini and Muehlberger (2006) as the informing reference. Sections 6.5–6.7 which present the results of the various case studies along the dimensions dependency, relational contracts and trust incorporate all case studies, those directly reported in this chapter and the results of Bertolini and Muehlberger (2006).

In the insurance industry, we interviewed not only managers from insurance companies but also salespeople representing different forms of work (i.e. dependent employment, dependent self-employment, independent self-employment): employees of the companies' direct sales force, tied agents, multi-tied agents and independent financial advisers (IFAs). In addition, officials from trade unions and professional associations were interviewed to discuss employment trends in the insurance industry. The duration of the semi-structured interviews varied between 20 minutes and 2 hours depending on the type of position of the respondents. While interviews with employees, dependent self-employed workers and self-employed individuals tended to last less than 45 minutes, those with managers were usually an hour at least. Interviews with insurance managers focused on the organisation of distribution, methods of recruitment, training and payment, differences in the working method and productivity of the different distribution channels, call centres, gender, all aspects of tied agency, the reason for multi-channel distribution and tied agency as well as cooperation with trade unions. Employed direct sales persons, tied agents and IFAs were asked about personal background, education, former occupation, training, payment, control, support, working hours and alternative working forms. With officials from interest organisations we discussed general (restructuring) trends in the industry, distribution strategies, level and intensity of the cooperation with insurance companies, (collective) bargaining issues, effects of tied agency as well as labour market and social policy issues.

In selecting the insurance companies in the UK and Austria, we focused especially on the distribution methods used by these companies. The companies covered by this case study represent approximately 43 per cent of the UK and 65 per cent of the Austrian market share. We were interested not only in companies that use the tied agent channel but also in companies that do not. In order to fully understand the logic behind the use of this form of dependent outsourcing it is equally important to understand the reasons for which some companies do not use it. In Italy the organisational structure is more uniform since all insurance companies work exclusively with tied agents (Bertolini and Muehlberger 2006).

The case study in the Austrian business service industry is based on 14 in-depth interviews with dependent self-employed persons (nine male, five female) working in the service sectors 'computer and related activities', 'research and development', 'consulting' and 'financial services'. Contacts with the interview-partners were established through the work@flex-network of the Austrian Trade Union of Salaried Private Sector Employees (GPA) and through personal contacts and references. Since the industry background is too diverse, we decided to interview only dependent self-employed workers that met the criteria of being self-employed with no employees, working only for one contractor. The case study in the Italian business service industry is based on 25 semi-structured interviews with dependent self-employed persons working in the sectors 'research and development', 'consulting' and 'education'. We interviewed also employers of the same sector (15 interviews). Contacts with the interview-partners were established through personal contacts and references. The interviews in both countries focused on the issues of the organisational governance of outsourcing, motives of both parties, firm-internal effects and consequences of outsourcing, contracts, daily routines, working methods and conditions, methods of recruitment, training and payment.

In the Austrian freight industry we interviewed nine managers, two employees of forwarding agents or carriers and three self-employed persons working as carriers, of which three described themselves as economically dependent. In total, nine forwarding agents and one carrier participated in the research. All of them have more than 100 employees. Six of the companies interviewed belong to an international group. The remaining four are independent Austrian companies, three of them family owned. The semi-structures interviews were focused on the following issues: characteristics of the process of outsourcing, motives for a forwarding agent to outsource physical transportation of the goods, effects of the outsourcing decision, specific advantages and drawbacks of dependent outsourcing for a forwarding agent, the daily cooperation of a forwarding agent and a subcontractor, characteristics of contracts between a forwarding agent and a (dependent) self-employed, reasons for a driver to become a (dependent) self-employed and the working condition of self-employed.

All interviews were conducted in a semi-structured way. Although we had a fixed list of issues we tried to cover in each interview, we never insisted on a special order, leaving room for the respondent to elaborate on issues he or she found important to discuss in more detail. If necessary we returned to old topics from a different point of view to make sure that we understood the respondent correctly and to check for biases caused by context.

It will be shown that important firm-internal decisions, such as the use of dependent self-employed workers, are based partly on manager's perceptions and beliefs since even high-level company managers do not represent the rational atomised actor with perfect information, being instead embedded in specific, ongoing systems of firm-internal social relations. This, however, does not mean that a manager's perceptions or beliefs are necessarily correct. The information pointed here is that they are pivotal in motivating decisions. Even incorrect perceptions and beliefs can provide the basis for managerial decisions (Bewley 1999).

6.2 Dependent self-employment in the British and Austrian insurance industry

6.2.1 Employment in the British and Austrian insurance industry

The 1980s were characterised by an expansion of financial services. Eventually, employment in the financial service sector increased substantially all over Europe. Deregulation, increased competition and organisational restructuring in the 1990s led to a decline in employment rates. The following gives an overview of both recent labour market trends and industrial relations in the Austrian and British insurance industries.

After a constant increase in employment rates during the 1970s and the 1980s (2.5 per cent per annum, on average), the Austrian insurance sector saw a slight decrease in employment rates during the late 1990s (Mesch 1998: 170). Although there has been a substantial rise in insurance business, product and process innovations due to IT investments and structural changes in organisational forms have led to a decline in employment rates. Between 1995 and 2001 employment in the insurance sector declined by 11.7 per cent (see Table 6.1). This decline of employment in the Austrian insurance industry is caused by both a reduction of the indoor office staff and also of the sales staff. While the indoor office staff was reduced by roughly 12 per cent between 1995 and 2002, the sales staff even declined by 28 per cent over the same period. The employed outbound sales force decreased not only due to the shift towards outsourcing but also due to the shift towards bancassurance (i.e. insurance products sold by banks).

Selling insurance is a strongly segregated business. Only 14 per cent of the outbound sales force are women. Within the group of the indoor staff, men and women are roughly equally represented. As in the outbound sales force, women are strongly under-represented at the management level. Part-time employment is interestingly still very low within the insurance industry compared to other industries within the service sector. The pattern of part-time employment, and especially the

Table 6.1 Number of employees in the Austrian insurance sector

Year	Number of employees	Change in %
1995	33 139	
1996	32 241	−2.7
1997	32 330	0.3
1998	32 024	−1.0
1999	31 036	−3.1
2000	30 675	−1.2
2001	29 276	−4.6

Source: Östat (2000: 165) and Statistik Austria (2003: 165).

strong over-representation of women, is, however, the same as in other industries. In sum, the labour market in the Austrian insurance industry is male dominated due to high over-representation within the sales force.

Industrial relations in the Austrian insurance industry are based on a multi-dimensional structure. Employees are represented by the Trade Union of Salaried Private Sector Employees, GPA (Gewerkschaft der Privatangestellten), which is a subdivision of the Austrian Trade Union Federation, ÖGB (Österreichischer Gewerkschaftsbund). Union density is traditionally high within the insurance sector: nearly 40 per cent of the employees are trade union members. This is, along with the banking sector, one of the highest density rates in private services (Blaschke 2001). However, not only the insurance sector, but the whole labour market is characterised by a steady decline in union membership in recent years (Ebbinghaus and Visser 2000).

Based on the comparatively strong trade union representation, income in financial services ranges among the highest in the service sector. Moreover, employment relationships in the insurance industry last significantly longer than the average industry employment duration (Mayerhuber and Url 1999: 700f). However, high protection mainly refers to indoor staff. The employed sales force has its own collective agreement, which is more incentive-oriented, linking pay closely to performance. Since the basic, fixed salary is very low, the main component of the salary is performance related.

Insurance companies are represented by the Central Employers' Association, the Federal Chamber of Business (WKÖ, Wirtschaftskammer Österreich), and by the Austrian Association of Insurance Companies (VVO, Versicherungsverband Österreich), which is a subunit of the WKÖ. Membership of the WKÖ is compulsory, and WKÖ members are also members of the VVO. The WKÖ has delegated its collective bargaining autonomy and its right to appraise draft legislation to the VVO. Activities in the VVO are coordinated by the WKÖ in order to harmonise the interests of different business groups. Insurance brokers and tied agents are represented by the Federal Committee of Insurance Brokers and by the Federal Committee of Insurance Agents, respectively. These two committees are also subunits of the WKÖ. However, they are not part of the unit 'Banking and Insurance' but of the unit 'Trade'. Thus, employees of insurance brokers or agents are subject to the collective agreement for the trade industry rather than the insurance industry. Furthermore, this organisational structure means that tied agents are represented by the same body as their contract partners, the insurance companies, namely by the Federal Chamber of Business (WKÖ), creating a new constellation of interest coordination (Muehlberger and Pernicka 2007). Since tied agents are self-employed they are compulsory members of the WKÖ, they are not allowed to join the trade union. However, the Trade Union of Salaried Private Sector Employees (GPA) has recently reacted to the increasing deployment of new forms of work, including dependent self-employed workers such as tied agents in the insurance industry. They started an initiative, introducing seven 'interest communities' (Interessengemeinschaften) – or platforms – to cover the interests of atypical workers and individuals working in specific occupations.[2] The platform 'work@flex', for example, includes individuals that work as freelancers or dependent self-employed workers regardless of the sector they work in. The network intends to increase communication among affected workers and to provide legal and training assistance with the aim of improving the current work situation of freelancers and dependent self-employed workers. Interaction is based on the Internet (www.interesse.at) and e-mail and regular meetings ('Flexforum'). Moreover, members of the network can take out an insurance policy covering loss of earnings due to illness with a private insurance company on special conditions. On a political level, the Austrian Trade Union Federation (ÖGB) is demanding a redefinition of the concept of employment and an extension of labour law to cover non-standard forms of employment and, especially, economically dependent self-employed workers. These platforms help the trade unions to mobilise individuals that are traditionally weakly organised. Additionally, this new structure allows freelance workers and dependent self-employed workers to join the platform without becoming a member of the trade union. Of course, increasing outsourcing undermines the coverage rate of collective bargaining and makes it difficult to organise the interests of outsourced workers.

In the UK insurance industry, employment levels are fairly volatile as shown in Table 6.2. Employment increased slightly from 1990 to 1991 but then strongly decreased between 1991 and 1995. This decline in the early 1990s was followed by a rise from 1995 to 1999.

Data from the British Annual Employment Survey and the Labour Force Survey give information about the gender distribution in the insurance labour market.[3] Table 6.3 shows that roughly half of all employees are women. Part-time employment is clearly lower than in other services. Although the share of women in part-time jobs increased from 13 per cent in 1996 to 17 per cent in 2000, it is still

Table 6.2 Number of employees in the UK insurance sector (Two digit SIC 1992: 66)

Year	Number of employees	Change in %
1990	240 300	
1991	246 900	+2.8
1992	234 200	−5.1
1993	222 000	−5.2
1994	219 700	−1.0
1995	213 200	−3.0
1996	213 600	+0.2
1997	228 500	+7.0
1998	230 800	+1.0
1999	231 200	+0.2
2000	225 700	−2.4
2001	226 900	+0.5

Source: ABI 2003a: 56.

Table 6.3 Number of employees in the UK insurance sector (Microcensus, two digit SIC 1992: 66)

Year	Men			Women			All
	Full-time	Part-time	All	Full-time	Part-time	All	
1996	108.3	2.2	110.5	87.0	13.5	100.5	210.9
1997	110.7	2.0	112.7	94.6	14.8	109.3	222.0
1998	116.8	2.2	118.9	103.2	17.6	120.8	239.8
1999	109.8	1.6	111.4	98.5	18.7	117.2	228.5
2000	108.9	1.7	110.6	99.1	19.9	119.0	229.6

In thousands; 1996–1999: Annual Employment Survey, 1999–2000: Labour Force Survey.
Source: 1996–1998: ONS 1997; 1999; 2000b. 1999–2000: ONS 2001a.

substantially lower than in the service sector as a whole in which nearly half of all women employed work part-time (ONS 2001a). Interviews in the British insurance industry demonstrate that women are mainly deployed as indoor staff. The outbound sales force, on the contrary, is heavily male dominated. Average earnings in the financial intermediation sector have risen strongly compared to most other industries (ONS 2001b: 108).

Industrial relations in the UK differ dramatically from those in Austria.[4] As in Austria, trade union membership has declined considerably. However, in the UK this decline is accompanied by a sharp decline in the coverage of collective agreements. Together with the declining coverage rate of collective bargaining is the move away from multi-employer bargaining to single-employer bargaining. Consequently, there is no collective bargaining on the sectoral level in the British insurance industry. Many, but not all, insurance companies fix pay thresholds at the company level. While some insurance companies recognise trade unions, others do not and, thus, negotiate pay and working conditions directly with employees. Nevertheless, 45 per cent of employees in the financial intermediation sector were covered by collective bargaining in 1997. This is by far the highest coverage rate in the private service sector (ONS 1998: 361). Union density is, at 33 per cent, among the highest in the private service sector (ONS 1998: 360).

Over the last years, the British trade union landscape was characterised by mergers. The two former major trade unions within the insurance industry, UNIFI and MSF, are now part of Amicus, Britain's second-largest trade union. Amicus organises workers in various industries, predominantly in the private sector. At the 2005 TUC Congress it was reported that Amicus had 1 200 000 members of whom 78 per cent were male.

6.2.2 The creation of dependent self-employment in the insurance industry

Most insurance companies sell their products through different distribution channels. The main distribution channel in the UK and in Austria is still the employed direct sales force, while tied agency is prevalent in Italy. In the continental European insurance industry we observe a shift towards the outsourced tied agent. Although there are different types of tied agents, we are primarily interested in the agent who is tied to one insurance company only. These tied agents carry out the same work as the employed direct sales force, namely selling the company's insurance products. However, they are not employees but self-employed and work on a private business contract.

Distribution channels represent an inter- and intra-firm network that manages the sales transactions (and connected services) of insurance products. While insurance companies focused their attention on the re-engineering process of internal operations in the 1980s, recent years have been preoccupied by distribution channel management. Eventually, this led to major strategic shifts in the ways in which insurance products are sold and how customers are serviced (Datamonitor 1999: 7). Historically, insurance companies distributed their products via a network of employed insurance salespeople. Today, insurance companies use different channels to sell, or distribute, insurance

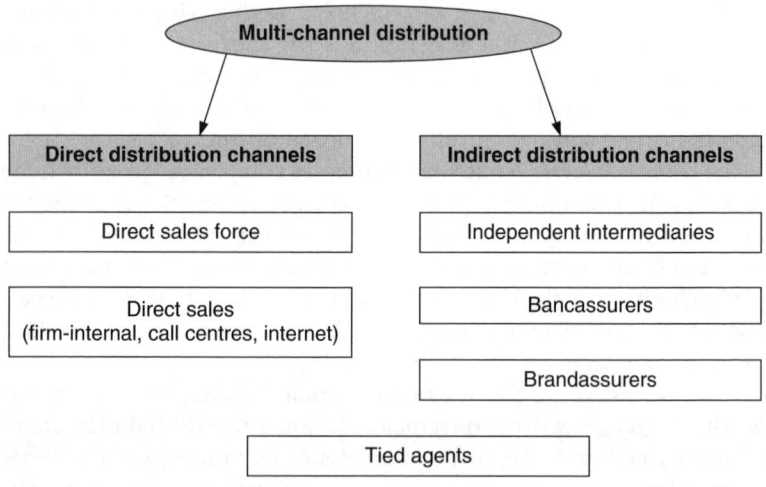

Figure 6.1 Multi-channel distribution

products. In principle, we can distinguish between direct and indirect distribution channels (Figure 6.1).

Direct distribution refers to both the direct sales force and the direct sale. The main difference between these two direct distribution channels is that the direct sales force personally approaches potential customers ('out-going'), whereas the direct sale channel approaches them via mailing and advertisements to which they can respond by telephoning the company or returning a form ('in-going'). The direct sales force is employed by the insurance company, working under a labour contract. They earn a basic salary plus a commission, which is related to the insurance products they sell. In both countries, the direct sales force has been reduced considerably. In the UK, the number of direct sales staff fell from 190 000 in 1991 to fewer than 37 000 in 2000 (FSA 2002).[5] Many British insurance companies have closed or sold off their direct sales force (primarily to Independent Financial Advisors). According to the Financial Services Authority (FSA), the direct sales force has been reduced due to a number of factors. The main factors are the high direct costs (of complying with a tougher regulatory regime), consumer demand for independent advice (due to the pension mis-selling scandal)[6] and the stronger need for advice due to greater product differentiation.

The number of Austrian direct sales force was stable between 1995 and 2001 but reduced by roughly 13 per cent between 2001 and 2002.

Results of the case study below demonstrate that insurance companies plan to cut this distribution channel further in order to increase the number of tied agents. As a result, the share of new business attracted by the direct sales force has decreased from roughly 46 per cent in 1997 to 30 per cent in 2001.

This move away from an employed direct sales force has substantially intensified the working pressure. For instance, an interviewee who changed to tied agency because he was dismissed as an employed insurance agent underlines how intensive the work environment had become:

> Companies have dramatically reduced their employed direct sales force. Those who remain are being squeezed out. It is a very tough environment. Control becomes stronger through new IT equipment. IT equipment is, on the one hand additional support, but, on the other hand, it also means that there is much more control since company managers know exactly what the direct sales force does (in fact, every hour). Realistically, one can only justify the basic income because it is hard to earn any bonus on top of that. Being in a direct sales force used to be very comfortable, one had a provided client base, fixed payment, a car, administrative support and so on. But this situation has changed very much. It is very, very pushy now. They push, push, push.
>
> Tied agent of a British long-term insurance company.
> Company B. Interview UK7.

The direct sales force's reward system is usually of mixed form. They get, on the one hand, a basic salary and, on the other hand, commission for the products sold (or for contracts that are renewed or prolonged). Thus, insurance companies deploy an incentive pay system to enhance performance and minimise shirking. In contrast to Austrian companies, British insurers have significantly reduced performance-related pay over the last years because they recognised that aggressive selling can severely damage customer relationships and, consequently, the brand.

A newer development within the direct sale channel is the emergence of Internet sale and the use of call centres. Many insurance companies heavily invested in call centres and information technology during the 1990s. Call centres are attractive for insurers because of their low-infrastructure costs (once the initial investments have been made) and their relatively simple operation, which is based around staff recruitment, training and the installation of the relevant software (Tufft

1998: 80). Moreover, in terms of labour organisation, call centres offer the possibility of flexible work organisation since there is no face-to-face interaction with customers. The main focus is not personal face-to-face interaction but easy access even at unusual hours. In other words, this direct distribution channel shifts the attention from the selling skills of insurance salespersons to easy and long-hour access for customers.

While Austrian insurance companies use call centres mostly for information and service purposes, British insurance companies sell insurance products through call centres. Call centres have been introduced to fulfil various functions. In most companies, they are separated according to their functions. Call centres are used as a tool for a first point of contact with customers, for dealing with on-going customer service and, finally, as sale points. The industry uses call centres as an initial contact point to take the customer's basic data and connect them to the competent division of the company. With instant access to customer files, the call centre staff are trained to deal with customer problems immediately. Call centres that sell insurance products usually sell very standardised products, requiring expertise in only a small range of products. Call centre staff usually work from a script, which produces a very standardised work process. For this reason, insurance companies tend not to use call centres to sell more complex products. Accordingly, this direct distribution channel is especially successful in standardised general insurance business such as the motor insurance market.

The share of sales made via the Internet is still low although most insurance companies have started to sell insurance policies on-line, some having even set up separate '.com' companies. To make this channel more attractive, most companies give discounts on Internet products. Although the Internet is the most cost-efficient means of distribution, most insurers that use the Internet for selling still face heavy losses due to high initial costs. So far, industry experience has shown that only simple products are sold successfully over the telephone or Internet. More complex, advice-dependent products which require lengthy fact-finding are seen as unlikely to succeed (Tufft 1998: 125). However, especially in the UK, high product regulation forces the insurers to provide simple and easily accessible long-term products at low costs which will eventually boost the direct distribution channel.

In our sample five British companies out of nine use the Internet and the telephone for selling insurance products. In Austria, six offer products on the Internet, and four out of the eight companies interviewed sell insurance contracts over the telephone (see Table 6.6). Although the majority of the companies included in this case study operate through these distribution channels, they bring, according to the companies' managers, little business. Nevertheless, the Internet and call centres are increasingly used for service and information purposes.

Both British and Austrian managers stress that call-centre staff tend to be younger than the direct sales force and their turnover is higher. While most British managers report a mixed gender environment in the call centres, Austrian managers disclose a female bias. Furthermore, call-centre staff is in most companies are salaried plus a bonus, but the bonus is normally only a small proportion of the salary. Due to the long opening hours of call centres and varieties in the volume of business, they usually work on flexible contracts.

British as well as Austrian managers emphasise that they sell few insurance products over the telephone. Especially in the UK, many long-term insurance companies have stopped telephone sales since turnover was too low to make it worthwhile as stressed by the following manager:

> We tried to do life insurances over the phone, we couldn't make it worth. Nobody has made it worth properly in the UK. [...] You can't make it worth. People want to look at someone, they want to look in someone's eyes, and, 'hey trust me'.
> Corporate Planning Manager of a British Bancassurer.
> Company G. Interview UK15.

Products sold over the Internet are mainly standardised products. Unsurprisingly, more complex products, which require face-to-face consultation, are either not offered over the Internet or, if offered, do not sell well. However, most British insurance managers expect the Internet to gain in importance since the government has launched standardised, straightforward products such as the CAT standard ISA[7] or the stakeholder pension. Regulation demands that these standardised products be offered at very low-administration costs. As a result, insurance companies are looking for cost-efficient ways to offer these regulated products. The Internet may be particularly suitable for this requirement, as some British managers stress.

The indirect distribution channel relates mainly to independent intermediaries. Newer methods of indirect selling are bancassurance and brandassurance. These methods rely on strategic alliances between insurance companies and banks or retailers. Numerous mergers and acquisitions in the British financial services industry have, moreover, created a tight network of ownership between the insurance and banking industries. Although there is also inner-ownership interlacements between insurance companies and banks in Austria, the organisation of the two sectors is still more separate than in the UK.

Independent intermediaries are able to sell insurance policies from any insurance company. In the UK, they are the strongest single distribution channel in both the long-term and the general insurance business (ABI 2000). Independent intermediaries in the long-term insurance market are called independent financial advisers (IFAs). The growing importance of IFAs is due not only to their success but to the relative failure of other channels (Tufft 1998: 116). The pension mis-selling scandal, which was mostly produced by direct sales forces and tied agents, increased the demand for independent financial advice. The main problem for the channel is the growing costs stemming from sales process regulations combined with falling margins through product regulation (e.g. CAT standard, stakeholder pensions). Standardised products which are easy to access and, more importantly, easy to compare do not require sophisticated financial advice. For these reasons, IFAs mainly concentrate on specific markets such as group and executive pensions or medium and high net worth individuals (Tufft 1998: 116f). In Austria, independent intermediaries play an increasing but less important role than in the UK. Almost a fifth of the premium income of the Austrian insurance industry was generated by independent intermediaries in 1999 (VVO 2000).

While tied agents only work with one insurance company, IFAs or insurance brokers in theory contract with many companies. However, most IFAs and brokers do not have sufficient resources to work with more than a couple of insurers. Additionally, in Austria, the insurance market is highly concentrated, which thus reduces the number of possible contract partners. In order to reduce transaction costs and additionally to increase bargaining power in negotiating contracts with insurance companies, many British IFAs and insurance brokers form part of an association. These associations provide training, research, competence requirements of the IFA and are responsible for compliance with rules. Moreover, some insurance companies have established their own IFA or broker firms. In Austria, the broker market is slightly different. Unlike to the UK, the Austrian insurance broker is allowed to sell both general and long-term insurance products. Broker and multi-tied agent associations do not have the same penetration as in the UK, but they are growing in importance. Associations in Austria are relatively smaller and have a different kind of organisation. Most Austrian broker and multi-tied agent associations offer their members not only training and service but also offices and secretarial staff. Moreover, they help their members to negotiate contracts with insurers. These associations offer self-employed brokers various kinds of support for which they pay a part of the commission they get from the insurers to the association. Thus, they are legally a firm, selling services to other firms.

Like in the UK, some Austrian insurance companies have established their own broker and multi-tied agent firms where they deploy self-employed agents. However, as opposed to the UK, these brokers or multi-tied agent firms usually sell in-house products. The goal of these broker channels is to generate new business for the insurance company and to transfer employed insurance agents to self-employment in order to circumvent labour law. These self-employed brokers are more or less tied to the insurance company their broker firm belongs to because they are required to sell mainly products from this very company. However, these brokers and multi-tied agents are not directly tied to the insurance company but to the broker arm of the insurer. These multi-tied agent associations provide secretarial staff, entrepreneurial knowledge; they do the accounting for the agents and support them in all administrative concerns. For their assistance, the associations – which are legally independent firms – take a part of the commission their members earn. The result that these entrepreneurial assistance associations provide is the creation of a hybrid form of self-employment. Although association members are self-employed, their actual working environment is similar to that of the employed direct sales force and tied agents. However, since they work for different insurance companies, their degree of dependency differs considerably from that of tied agents.

In both countries, many brokers and IFAs became self-employed because of the pressures on the direct sales force and redundancies in the insurance industry. Insurance companies sell more competitive products not via the direct sales force or tied agents but via intermediary and direct channels. Consequently, selling products becomes difficult for the employed and the tied agents as the following British IFA highlights:

> It was becoming horrible to work there to be honest with you. The products they offered got less and less. That leaves less choice for the clients. We couldn't offer a proper service for the clients. And the actual pressure was too much. The targets were unachievable most of the time. So, I found it personally the best time to leave and I went as an IFA because I feel this is the way people should be treated.
> British IFA who was an employed insurance agent for 22 years.
> Interview UK23.

According to British and Austrian insurance law, in contrast to tied agents, brokers and IFAs bear the full legal liability for mis-selling. This fact, the loss of social benefits and the pressure to cover overheads are seen as the most significant disadvantages of being an IFA. Additionally, both British IFAs and Austrian brokers argue that compared to tied agency or employment, the broker or IFA business is much more demanding since they do not have a (business or employment) relationship with only one company but with many. Thus, they have to transact their business (e.g. to solicit a quotation, to handle claims and to balance accounts) with several companies which causes considerably higher transaction costs compared to tied agency.

> When you are an IFA you are very much self-employed. You have a certain protection when you are a tied agent [...] what you haven't got as an IFA. You have the support of a big company behind you, just one big company. And the other thing is of course that you have got only a limited amount of products which is quite easy to get your head around. But as an IFA, you've got to do a lot of research because you've got the whole market to choose from and then you've got to make sure that that particular product is suitable for your client.
> British IFA who was a self-employed tied agent for 6 years.
> Interview UK24.

The interviews with IFAs and brokers on the one hand, and tied agents on the other, reveal that these two groups indeed have different preferences concerning risk, support and the multitudinousness of work. Compared to IFAs and brokers, tied agents appreciate the security and support of the insurance company they contract with and the simplicity such a business relationship offers.

Due to industrial restructuring in the UK, employment security has been dramatically reduced and therefore, the incentives to become self-employed have increased (push effect). For instance, a British IFA, who was an employed insurance agent for 22 years, argues that being self-employed does not necessarily mean less employment and financial security.

> When you are with a company like [the one I was at] you get this sort of cocoon around. It is safe and everything is ok and outside is real danger. But it is not like that when you actually get out of that. It took me 22 years to find out but now, once you've find it out – it is probably a bit late for me – you actually realise that there is not less

security outside than when you are in that company. I mean they are getting rid of people, so the security is not there. It is just an illusion, the company syndrome.

> British IFA (No. 2) who was an employed insurance agent for 22 years. Interview UK23.

Brandassurance refers to strategic partnerships between an insurer and a retail company (e.g. supermarkets). Although the retailer distributes product information under the insurer's name or sometimes also under its own name, advice and service is given over the telephone. In some cases, the administration of insurance policies is carried out mainly by the retailer, which means that the insurance company provides more or less only the financial background. Partnership marketing or brandassurance marketing are increasing particularly in the British general insurance sector. The standardisation of long-term insurance products has also established the sale of these products in the retail market (Tufft 1998: 122). The advantage for the insurer is the broad access to customers or specific customer groups due to an existing store network with regular customer contact, and, in the case that the retail company sells under its own name, brandassurance means that the insurer can build market share apart from its own brand. While brandassurance is increasingly common in the UK, it hardly exists in Austria.

As already mentioned above, bancassurers have steadily gained on the British long-term insurance market. Their most important advantage – compared to the traditional insurance company – is that they have access to a large customer base which also includes many (young) customers who have never bought insurance products before. Long-term insurance products such as life assurance or pensions are, moreover, alternative forms of investment, which allow bancassurers to innovate and provide a wider range of investment products. Finally, some banking transactions are legally linked to insurance, giving bancassurers the opportunity to cross-sell.[8] The existing customer base and the possibility for cross-selling implies a comparative advantage of bancassurance over other distribution methods, imposing great pressure on other channels. Nevertheless, bancassurance still has a relatively small sector share in the British long-term insurance market. Contrary to the UK, Austrian banks sell insurance products quite successfully. However, only a very few banks have set up their own insurance subsidiary. Most banks have strategic alliances with insurance companies, selling their insurance products.

Tied agents – which are the focus of our analysis – occupy a hybrid position between the direct and indirect distribution channels. In the

UK, tied agents (or appointed representatives) are only able to sell the products of one life (or long-term) insurer or of up to six non-life insurers (these are sometimes called company agents).[9] Although they are tied to a particular life insurance company, they are organisationally separated since they are (formally) self-employed. Both Austrian and British insurance law states that tied agents are representative of the insurance company they are tied to, whereas insurance brokers act – at least in theory – on behalf of the client. Both tied and the independent agents receive a commission for each policy they sell and a further commission at each subsequent renewal of the policy. The amount of commission is an agreed percentage of the total premium paid by the policyholder. Austrian insurance companies deploy both tied agents (*'Generalagenten'* or *'Ausschließlichkeitsagenten'*) and multi-tied agents (*'Mehrfachagenten'*). Whereas tied agents are only allowed to sell insurance products from one company, multi-tied agents can sell insurance products from any number of insurance companies. Unfortunately, available data does not distinguish between those tied agents that work only for one insurance company (tied agents) and those that work for more than one company (multi-tied agents). Nevertheless we observe a considerable increase in tied agency in Austria. Between 1995 and 2002 the number of active single- and multi-tied agents has risen by more than 600 per cent (from 1143 to 7460 in absolute numbers).

Although tied agents are closely linked to their insurance companies, they are self-employed. Thus, a tied agent who sells insurance products from only one company has a hybrid status between the direct and the indirect channel. The direct sales force and tied agents perform exactly the same kind of work, namely selling insurance products from one company to clients. The direct sales force, the tied agents and the independent agents are exemplary representatives of three forms of work: the employee status, dependent self-employment and independent self-employment, respectively.

As shown in Table 6.6, the most striking difference in the organisation of distribution channels between Austrian and British insurance companies is the use of the tied agent channel. Tied agents are self-employed insurance agents who have an exclusive business contract with one specific insurance company. Although they work on a self-employed basis from their own premises, they nevertheless access the market under the logo and name of the insurance company they work with. Most tied agencies are very small firms where the tied agent works either alone or with one or two employees.

Although the British insurance law allows tied agency, only few companies actually deploy tied agents. In Austria, on the contrary, tied agency is so far not regulated by law, leading to a problematic legal void. This reason may also have contributed to most Austrian insurance companies' recent creation of tied agent systems. As depicted in Table 6.6, while only three out of nine British companies work with tied agents, all Austrian insurance companies included in this study use the tied agent channel. Most of these Austrian companies have established tied agency only very recently as an integral part of the restructuring process since the 1990s.

The degree of dependence, however, varies considerably between the three British companies that use tied agents. Company A has until recently worked exclusively with tied agents that are only allowed to sell insurance products from this company and who work from offices owned by the tied agents. This company has also started to employ insurance agents on labour contracts. While tied agents from Company A are only allowed to sell a quite restricted range of products (i.e. health insurance products) of the company, tied agents from Company B are able to sell a wider range of insurance products from the different companies of the insurance group that stands behind Company B. However, a manager of this company stresses that tied agents only have access to a restricted product range:

> Tied agents don't have access to all of the products we sell through the independent market and vice versa which means actually we can sell more profitable products through the tied market. Whereas necessarily our products need to be more competitive in the IFA market to actually get on the lists at all. So, our product mix is actually much more profitable in the tied market.
> CEO Assistant of a British long-term insurance company that deploys 5000 tied agents. Company B. Interview UK4.

Hence, this insurance company uses the tied agent channel to sell a specific product mix, creating a competitive disadvantage for tied agents as compared to independent IFAs. Company B has, furthermore, an interesting arrangement that differs from the other companies. Most tied agents from Company B do not work from their own premises but from offices that are owned by Company B. Within these premises Company B employs a management and administrative staff that work for the self-employed tied agents.

In Austria, all insurance companies that participated in this study deploy tied agents. Austrian tied agents usually work from their own premises, selling general and life insurance products only from the company they are tied to. While most of these companies have built up a comprehensive tied agent system over the last years, two of the eight companies (i.e. Company N and Company Q) only deploy a couple of tied agents mainly due to mobility reasons (see further below). Company K is the only company that works mainly with tied agents; the other companies have only recently started to work with tied agents. Thus, these companies still employ significantly more insurance agents in their direct sales force than in tied agency.

In sum, there is no clear pattern of specific distribution strategies in the British and Austrian insurance market. Both market research literature (Reithofer 1997; Glancy 1998; Hunte 1998; MAPS 1998; Tufft 1998; ABI 1999; VVO 2000) and our own empirical research (see below) shows that, firstly, no single distribution channel dominates the industry and, secondly, there is a wide divergence of opinion across the industry regarding the dynamics of distribution. Accordingly, the focus of the distribution strategies varies significantly across firms.

Available data show that the main business in the British long-term insurance industry is raised by the IFAs and the direct sales force and that tied agents and other distribution channels play a minor role (see Table 6.4). Unfortunately, this data does not correspond properly with the distribution channels we have discussed above. The category 'direct sales force' includes any sales person who works for a life insurer, either on an employed or a self-employed basis transacting business face-to-face. The category 'tied agents' include any intermediary, except those included in the categories 'IFAs' and 'direct sales force', authorised to sell

Table 6.4 Sources of new regular premiums in the British long-term insurance business (total individual regular premiums)

Year	IFAs	Direct sales force	Tied agents	Direct marketing	Telesales	Other
1997	42.0	46.6	8.5	2.9	0	0
1998	37.0	51.4	6.9	3.6	0.8	0.2
1999	39.2	48.2	7.3	4.2	0.7	0.4
2000	44.2	44.4	4.9	3.5	1.4	1.6
2001	57.2	31.2	3.9	3.8	2.0	2.0
2002	57.5	33.7		5.9	0	2.8

From 2002 onwards the direct sales force and the tied agents are grouped together.
Source: 1997–1999: ABI 2001: 23; 2000–2002: ABI 2003b: 39.

the products of only one life insurer. Thus, the tied agents according to our definition are not shown in the category 'tied agents', but strangely enough in the category 'direct sales force'. Furthermore, bancassurers are also included in the category 'direct sales force'.

Data from the British FSA specify that roughly 36 000 IFAs, 22 500 direct sales force and around 8500 tied agents (appointed representatives) are registered as active advisers in the UK (FSA 2002: 43).

Austrian data, on the other hand, correspond quite closely to our definitions as discussed above. We see that banks play a major role in selling insurance products. However, this category includes bancassurers as well as banks selling products from other insurance companies. Furthermore, the data show that the business of the direct sales force has been reduced considerably. While nearly 46 per cent of new premiums were generated by the direct sales force in 1997, this number was reduced to 30 per cent 4 years later. The importance of other distribution channels – including tied agents, but excluding direct marketing – has risen during this period (see Table 6.5).

Arguably, the use of the different distribution channels is based not only on consumer rationality, but also on consumer lifestyles and 'learned' behaviour. Consumers do not necessarily choose the cost minimising method of buying an insurance product, but often buy the way their parents did or the way that those in their social environment buy insurance products. Taking this into account, most insurers try to reach potential customers through manifold channels. Thus, multi-channel distribution increases the chance for insurers to reach the relatively fragmented (potential) customer base. Finally, the huge range of product designs demands various ways of distribution since some products are inevitably better suited to some channels rather than others (Tufft 1998: 96).

Table 6.5 Sources of new premiums in the Austrian insurance business

Year	IFAs	Direct sales force	Tied agents	Multi-tied agents	Banks	Direct marketing	Other
1997	17.8	45.8	1.9	0.3	30.5	1.0	2.7
1998	18.5	40.2	2.2	0.5	35.4	0.8	2.3
1999	18.8	36.4	2.6	0.9	38.8	0.4	2.1
2000	19.8	34.2	2.8	1.4	38.3	0.6	2.9
2001	19.8	30.4	3.6	2.0	39.5	1.1	3.4

Source: Austrian Association of Insurance Companies (VVO).

Nevertheless, there are some clear common tendencies across the British and Austrian insurance industries. It is evident that, first, a direct sales force tends to be associated with high direct costs, whereas independent brokers and bancassurers tend to have lower costs (Tufft 1998: 95f). As a result, most insurance companies have dramatically reduced the number of their direct sales force and increased other distribution methods. While British insurance companies have constantly reduced the use of a tied agent channel over the last years, Austrian insurance companies increasingly deploy tied agents. Most insurance companies in Austria have recently established or enlarged their tied agent channel.

A survey of European insurance companies points to the willingness to outsource distribution (Parry 2000: 28). While most European insurers believe that their core activities, i.e. underwriting and claims management, are strategically important and should be kept in-house, they do not see any strategic need to keep distribution and customer service in-house. The driving elements behind outsourcing activities are cost reduction, redistribution of costs, flexibility to meet short-term needs and the focus on core activities. The survey identifies the loss of control over business activities as the main disincentive to outsource. Other problems involve the risk of losing sensitive company information, low internal skill development and the danger of following an overly short-term business approach. Parry (2000: 30) argues that while outsourcing is a tool for companies to expand, their need to outsource decreases after a certain point of expansion due to economies of scale. Having reached the size optimal for profiting from economies of scale, companies seek to take back control of their operations.

Multi-channel distribution represents, moreover, a possibility to diversify risk. By using different channels, insurance companies try to reduce dependency on a single distribution channel. Related to this is the influence of changes in regulation. Multi-channel distribution allows the insurer to react quickly to changes in regulation as highlighted by the following interviewee:

> There are two reasons. One, because it is there and people end up coming in a different fashion. Therefore we have got production from different sources that we wouldn't otherwise get if we used only one channel. [...] That's the first thing and the second thing is that you don't put all the eggs in one basket. If one channel like the IFA channel decides to offer products we don't have or that we don't meet their requirements, then we still got production

coming in from a different source. Those are the two strategic reasons.
Marketing Director of a British long-term insurance company that deploys tied agents (i.e. appointed representatives). Company E. Interview UK12.

In the UK especially, the logic of multi-channel distribution is closely linked to regulation. Products such as the CAT standard ISA or the stakeholder pension with low margins due to regulation force the insurer to find more economic methods of product distribution. A manager of a British long-term insurer, for example, stresses that the introduction of tightly regulated products leads to a standardisation of products:

> The government is launching [...] the stakeholder pension scheme – which has a charge of no more than one per cent, which means that the amount of money to pay agents and distribution structures is reduced dramatically, which is going to put pressure on workside models [...] into more remote business.
> Business Planning Manager of a British long-term insurer. Company I. Interview UK18.

Of course, this has direct effect on the organisation of work in the British insurance industry. Insurance companies have to redesign their products in order to make them appropriate to be sold by a non-authorised, strictly controlled and regulated staff who is only narrowly trained to sell specific products.

When discussing the logic of multi-channel distribution, many respondents – especially in Austria – emphasised the influence of culture. Interestingly, British managers mainly stressed customers' financial rationale when buying insurance products. Austrian managers and agents, in contrast, emphasise the importance of trust between insurance agents and their customers. However, this difference in perception of the customer–agent relation might also be the result of different degrees of competition, market concentration and, thus, marketing efforts. A manager of a British general insurance company illustrates the difference between the British and the continental model when comparing the German and British insurance markets:

> Well, I think it is a cultural thing as well. Because I looked at this myself. I went to visit a German insurance company and they were heavily tied-agent driven. And it is a history and tradition thing.

> There is a tied agent almost in every town. And for generations, people have bought from the tied agent. And the tied agency has existed within the same family for generations. And therefore it is a very strong cultural bond. It is not about the financial bond. It is an emotional, cultural, attitudinal thing. It is not just about the money. In the UK it seems to be more about the money. There is not the same local culture [that] has developed. There seems to be more willingness to go somewhere else because it is cheaper. I suppose the question is [whether] the UK moves to a more emotional culture or [whether] those markets in Europe move towards a more economic, financially driven culture. We operate in many countries of the world with tied agents propositions and when we look at them – as we are thinking about what we can learn to apply in the UK – what you keep coming back to is the culture of that community is different. The history and tradition is different.
> Manager of a British general insurance company. Company H. Interview UK16.

Indeed, a representative survey in Austria effected by Company O shows that Austrian consumers strongly value service. It was found that consumers are not as interested in buying the cheapest product as in finding an adviser whom they can trust.

> The main point was that it is not at all important for the customers to get the cheapest product on the market. They are willing to pay more when they can rely on the service, when they have an adviser whom they trust. We had big discussions about that. We had a completely different picture.
> Managing Director (direct sales force and tied agency operations) of an Austrian insurance company. Company O. Interview A 17.

Channel innovation is clearly influenced by new market entrants. In both countries, the success of new entrants was followed by changes in the distribution method of the major players. In Austria, a French insurer entered the market by acquiring a middle-ranking Austrian insurance company in the early 1990s and was the first to establish a comprehensive tied agency system.[10] Eventually, all major insurance companies followed this example, introducing their own tied agency system. In the UK, the success of an insurance company that initially sold insurance products exclusively over the telephones induced other companies to sell over the telephone. However, some have closed this channel again because of a lack of success. Both this case study and market research (e.g. Datamonitor 1999) show that the introduction of new distribution methods is very often based on imitation and unreflected herd behaviour, lacking a clear strategic agenda in accordance with the company's culture and existing social and employment relations.

Table 6.6 shows the anonymously encoded insurance companies included in this case study and their modes of distribution as of June 2001.[11] It clearly reflects the main differences in the distribution methods between Austrian and British insurance companies. First, Austrian companies use a wider variety of distribution channels and, second, unlike Austria, only a few British insurers use tied agency.

Excluding the British insurance companies that principally manage institutional pension funds, the companies covered by this case study

Table 6.6 Multi-channel distribution of the insurance companies included in the case study (Status: June 2001)

Company	Tied agents	Direct sales force	Brokers, IFAs	Internet sale	Telephone sale	Type of insurer
A (UK)	Yes	Yes	No	No	No	General insurer
B (UK)	Yes	No	Yes	No	No	Long-term insurer
C (UK)	No	Yes	No	No	Yes	Long-term insurer; stopped writing new business in 2000
D (UK)	No	Yes	No	Yes	No	Long-term insurer, membership organisation
E (UK)	Yes	Yes	Yes	Yes	Yes	Long-term insurer
F (UK)	No	No	Yes	Yes	Yes	Long-term insurer; intensive reorganisation in 2000
G (UK)	No	Yes	No	No	No	Long-term insurer; Bancassurer
H (UK)	No	No	Yes	Yes	Yes	General insurer
I (UK)	No	Yes	Yes	Yes	Yes	Long-term insurer
J (A)	Yes	Yes	Yes	Yes	No	Composite insurer
K (A)	Yes	Yes	Yes	No	No	Composite insurer; was acquired by Company O in 2002
L (A)	Yes	Yes	Yes	Yes	Yes	Composite insurer
M (A)	Yes	Yes	Yes	Yes	No	Composite insurer
N (A)	Yes	Yes	Yes	No	No	Composite, regional insurer
O (A)	Yes	Yes	Yes	Yes	Yes	Composite insurer
P (A)	Yes	Yes	Yes	Yes	Yes	Composite insurer
Q (A)	Yes	Yes	Yes	Yes	Yes	Composite insurer

represent approximately 42.8 per cent of the UK market share in 2000. Due to the high market concentration in Austria, it was possible to cover 64.7 per cent of this country's market share as of 2001.

6.2.3 The organisational logic of tied agency

Although British insurance companies have also reduced their direct sales force, UK managers claim that issues such as control, risk exposure, turnover cost, loyalty, brand values and company culture prevent them from introducing tied agency. Also, industry regulation demands close monitoring of the sales process, making outsourcing more costly. Finally, a deregulated labour law reduces the incentives for outsourcing. Austrian companies, in contrast, are confronted with less regulation of the sales process but with tighter regulation in labour law, thus increasing the incentives for outsourcing.

6.2.3.1 The effects of labour law and the cost structure

In Austria, industrial restructuring in the insurance industry has induced corporate strategies to increase productivity and reduce costs. To fulfil these goals, most insurance companies, on the one hand, considerably reduced their direct sales force, and introduced, on the other hand, the tied agent model. Both Austrian and British managers stress that working with tied agents brings two important advantages on the cost side. First, they seem to reduce overhead costs and second, they transform fixed costs into variable costs.

A direct sales force, so the argument goes, is expensive to operate due to the fact that it requires continuous support. If an insurance company pays its direct sales force a basic salary and provides back-office support (e.g. office space, secretarial staff, computers and so on), they have to make sure that their employed agents constantly see clients, which entails control costs. Tied agents, on the other hand, work entirely on commission with less back-office support, meaning that costs are directly related to production. Thus, insurance companies try to reduce their overhead costs by using tied agents.

> We pay the tied agent in such a way that we should not have higher costs than with employed insurance agents. This is definitely the direction, because otherwise it would not make any sense.
> Sales Director of an Austrian insurance company. Company M.
> Interview A9.

The conversion of fixed costs into variable costs is, moreover, closely connected to labour law, social security contributions, taxes on labour and collective bargaining agreements. In contrast to tied agents, the direct sales force is subject to labour law regulations, social security contributions to be paid not only by the employees but also by the employers, and their wages and working conditions are subject to collective bargaining. Due to tighter labour regulations in Austria, the costs of these are higher in Austria than in the UK. For this reason, the importance of these regulation costs was often highlighted by Austrian managers, as shown in the following quote:

> The one is employed and subject to the whole regulation of the labour law for employees, labour constitutional law, collective agreement and all these things. And the tied agent is self-employed. This is a major distinction for us from a business point of view. The direct sales force causes high fixed costs. [...] The tied agent only produces variable costs. [...] Being a tied agent, being self-employed, however, also means to bear the economic risk. For instance, illness: In this case, the tied agent has no security at all if she does not do anything by herself. This is different for the employed direct sales force. Of course, this produces fixed costs for the company.
> Managing Director (Sales and Marketing) of an Austrian insurance company. Company P. Interview A20.

As this insurance manager stresses, the conversion of fixed costs into variable cost by deploying tied agents means, in turn, that the tied agents have to bear the economic risk. For instance, tied agents are not protected in case of illness, do not earn any income when they take days off, have full (financial) liability for their production means (e.g. computers, cars, office) and are dependent on the competitiveness of the company's products. Moreover, working time or labour protection regulations do not come into effect. On the other hand, they do not have the entrepreneurial possibilities of IFAs because they are tied to only one insurance company.

Thus, outsourcing the sales force by setting up tied agency is a managerial strategy to source out economic risk and circumvent labour protection measures. Asked why tied agency was introduced in a large Austrian insurance company, a managing director of a tied agent association that is part of this company, for example, openly addresses the issue of circumventing labour law.

One has tried to find an alternative distribution channel, firstly, to generate new business and simultaneously dispose of the problem of labour law of the direct sales force.
>> Managing Director of an IFA and (multi-)tied agent association that is fully owned by Company O. Interview A19.

Another important factor is that the effects of costs are closely linked to the size of the companies due to scale effects. This gives us another explanation for the fact that tied agents are more prevalent in Austria than in the UK. British insurance companies are, on average, significantly larger than their Austrian counterparts, which allow them to profit from scale effects by using a direct sales force. As argued by some managers, fixed costs are not only caused by factors such as basic salary, social security contributions or fringe benefits but also by the amount of support the direct sales force needs for selling insurance products. Consequently, there is a certain threshold in company size for employing a direct sales force in order to be able to benefit from economies of scale.

Insurance companies are, however, also interested in gross costs (including costs from claims) and contract duration. A managing director of an Austrian insurance company, for example, reports that their tied agents and their employed sales force bring clients with a longer contract duration and with considerably less claims compared to the indirect channel which makes the tied agent and the direct sales force channels more profitable. Short contract duration seems to be the major disadvantage of working with IFAs since they often transfer business to other insurance companies when prices change. Thus, deploying tied agents allows insurance companies to benefit from the advantages of outsourcing without risking a weak business relationship where business is often transferred and claims are more prevalent.

6.2.3.2 Managerial control, risk exposure and industrial regulation

The reason why [...] we don't have a tied agency is that – even though they are directly related and regulated by the insurer – you don't have total control over their activities. Whereas if you've got a direct sales force, you do. They are deployed by you, in terms of conditions, you can be very, very clear on what the requirement on this job was; you pay them accordingly.
>> Business Planning Manager of a British long-term insurer, Company I. Interview UK18.

The issue of managerial control is one of the most important reasons why most British insurance companies do not work with tied agents. Managers of these companies stress emphatically the problem of control. The main arguments British managers emphasise are that managerial control is essential, firstly, for securing the value of the brand[12] and secondly, for meeting the requirements of industry regulation. For instance, when asked about the meaning and consequences of managerial control, a British manager stresses the importance of the brand and the problems of regulation:

> The control in terms of their activities. How they operate, what they do with your product, what they do with your brand and how they sell your products. We are in a very highly regulated market place. We had, in particular, many problems with regulation in the past. So that's why we wouldn't in particular want to sort of reduce the control in this area.
> Business Planning Manager of a British long-term insurer,
> Company I. Interview UK18.

Company F, a British long-term insurance company with a US parent company, serves as a good example of the British market since it experienced the direct consequences of less managerial control over tied agents in the pension mis-selling scandal. Heavily implicated in this scandal, the company decided, firstly, to reduce its product range and, secondly, to intensively re-organise and strongly revise this distribution strategy. More concretely, they transferred their direct sales force and their tied agents to an independent financial advisory company. Eventually, this insurance company extended its telephone and Internet sales services by enlarging their call centre in terms of size and range of service options offered. According to a manager of this company, tied agents were heavily involved in the pension mis-selling scandal. According to British insurance law, the insurance company bears the legal liability if a tied agent sells the wrong product. Having learned from this costly experience with commission-driven tied agents, the new sales staff in the call centres is not paid commission but a fixed salary only. The interviewee admitted that tied agents were less expensive for the company than their employed direct sales force, but it has also proven that tied agents are associated with higher risk exposure for the insurer. Since the insurer cannot control tied agents in the same way as the direct sales force (in terms of how they sell and what they recommend), the risk exposure is substantially higher. As an in-house function, the direct sales force is easier to control. Moreover, since the direct sales force is at least partly salaried, they have less pressure to sell than tied agents who work exclusively on commission. Consequently, the reduction of risk exposure after the involvement in the pension mis-selling scandal was the main reason for Company F to downscale the organisation. The company aims at reducing the overhead costs for remaining in business by focusing on a tighter operation and economic means of distribution which excludes an employed direct sales force and self-employed tied agents.

Company G, a British bancassurer, exclusively uses an employed direct sales force, also stressing the problem of controlling tied agents. When asked for the reason why they do not work with tied agents which induce lower overhead costs, a manager of company G emphatically stresses the difficulty of controlling tied agents. More concretely, this manager sees tied agents as mercenaries without loyalty to the company they are tied to.

> What we found with tied agents is, and the industry as a whole has found, is that tied agents are a bit like mercenaries. They are going to whoever is offering them the biggest commission. And if you read where lots of the big fines have taken place, where companies have been found for not having controlled the tied agents. That's where the problems were. I used to work for a company that had an appointed representative network – very difficult to control them. Because they have no loyalty except for themselves.
> Corporate Planning Manager of a British Bancassurer.
> Company G. Interview UK15.

The example of Company A, a British general insurance company with a US parent company, nicely documents the problem of a high turnover rate due to commission-driven tied agents is also stressed by the manager of company G. Company A worked entirely with tied agents until recently. However, due to severe and costly problems with a high turnover rate, the company decided to employ their agents.

> The reason why we have done it was because the turnover of the sales force is very high because they are self-employed. [...] So, we've decided that we will employ people so they have a basic income and then they would get bonuses and commission on top. So, we've decided that rather we keep spending money on recruiting

and training people, it would be better to pay people that income in the hope that we can keep them. So we can retain them longer.
> UK Sales Director of a general insurance company that deploys 250 tied agents and has just started to employ a direct sales force. Company A. Interview UK1.

This example of Company A shows, moreover, a distinctive trend in the British insurance industry, i.e. to reduce commission and increase the fixed part of agents' income. While the majority of Austrian employed agents' income consists of performance-related commission, British insurance companies increasingly pay their employed advisers a high fixed salary and only a small part based on commission. British managers argue that a high fixed salary enables more managerial control over the adviser and increases the quality of customer services.

The other reason is that by paying a salary you also have a greater control over an adviser. If you are paying a salary [...] that salary is not only for selling, it is also for looking after customers. And also by paying a salary you are making sure that that person does not have to sell to eat. That's the reason we do it.
> Managing Director of a British long-term insurance company with a membership organisation. Company D. Interview UK11.

By changing the incentive scheme, British insurance companies have attempted to make the sales process less aggressive in order to comply with regulations and protect brand value. Many British managers accentuate the importance of the brand. When using tied agents, it is apparently impossible to control how they treat the brand and the customer relationship.

No, we would never consider it [i.e. tied agency]. Never consider it! Because the brand is the most important thing, the customer relationship, the brand and the belief in the brand values. That's the important thing. And someone selling [Company B's] products last year, how can she be passionate about [our] products this year?
> Corporate Planning Manager of a British Bancassurer. Company G. Interview UK15.

Interestingly, the value of the brand as an explanation for why insurance companies use direct sales forces was mainly stressed by British managers. Austrian managers, on the other hand, did not directly point to this issue. It can be argued that this is a consequence of different market conditions and/or levels of competition. While the British insurance market, which was traditionally less regulated than the Austrian, was strongly liberalised in the late 1970s and early 1980s, the Austrian insurance market was only deregulated in the early 1990s, just before joining the EU.

Although most British managers see the employed direct sales force as the most cost-intensive channel, it is nevertheless seen as crucial for the insurer since it gives direct access to clients. Theoretically, the insurance company owns the client bank (i.e. the files of customers) used by both the direct sales force and tied agents. However, it is not the insurance company but the tied agents that have personal contact with customers. Thus, when tied agents change the insurance company they work with, the company faces a high risk of losing their customers. For instance, a manager of Company D, a British long-term insurance company with a membership organisation, points out, that 'owning' the customers is one of the most important reasons why this company works with a direct sales force.

> The main reason for relying on the channel of the direct sales force is [...] that if we would also distribute through IFAs, then the IFA owned that customer. And they would like that too much. [...] So, distributing through an IFA we wouldn't own that customer in the same way. And likewise if we tied somebody else to us, you know a tied broker [...], one wouldn't have the same control necessarily. And secondly, three years later they could tie to another organisation. What happens to those [our] members? [...] So that's why we sole-distribute our own products at the present time.
>
> Managing Director of a British long-term insurance company with a membership organisation. Company D. Interview UK11.

Finally, managerial control is crucial since it is directly linked to profit. Some managers report that although the employed direct sales force is ostensibly the most expensive distribution channel, it is at the end of the day the most profitable one. An Austrian manager, for instance, argues that the direct sales force is the most profitable distribution channel because the company has more managerial control over the agents. More concretely, companies have more influence over products that are sold, customer selection or damage adjustment, to give but a few examples. Another Austrian manager underlines that direct access to customers is an important explanation for the profitability of the direct sales force.

Nevertheless, most Austrian insurance companies struggle with the low productivity of the employed direct sales force. This is, furthermore, a reason why most of the companies have recently introduced a tied agent channel.

6.2.3.3 The effect of company culture

Having discussed the reasons why British insurance companies hesitate to contract out their sales forces, outsourcing is, nevertheless, an issue for British managers too. In addition to the arguments above, the history of a company and the resulting company culture are seen as reasons why some companies have not outsourced their direct sales force as yet.

> Yes, we constantly review that [i.e. outsourcing the direct sales force]. And it [i.e. costs] is one of the reasons why the direct sales force has been reduced considerably. [This company] goes back into 18 something, so it is a very old established company. And the direct sales force and visiting the customer at home is what [this company] started off doing – for the first hundred years it did nothing else. So, we are very reluctant of getting rid of that although in the hard business terms we would have to.
> Sales Operations Support Manager of a British long-term insurer. Company I. Interview UK17.

Nonetheless, the potential possibility of sourcing out labour is used to put pressure on the direct sales force. Consequently, employed insurance agents report a strong increase in work intensification due to industrial restructuring.

> The talk we hear all the time within the [company] is that one day, they franchise us off. [...] The rumour that goes around is they won't have to pay you a salary, they won't have to pay you a car, they won't have to do anything at all. That has been on the cards for some time now.
> Employed insurance agent of a British long-term insurance company. Company I. Interview UK19.

> I don't think that it [the use of tied agents] is necessarily something we have discounted forever and there are continuous thoughts that we might do it. So, it is not something we have completely discounted.
> Sales Operations Support Manager of a British long-term insurer. Company I. Interview UK17.

Another point is that the company culture of foreign subsidies is heavily influenced by the mother company. Insurance companies that are part of foreign holding companies which deploy a (successful) tied agent system in their country of origin are exposed to powerful pressure to introduce tied agency. For instance, two of the three British companies that work with tied agents are subsidies of foreign holding companies which explicitly determined the outsourcing strategy of their British subsidiaries. In Austria, a foreign insurer who entered the Austrian market in the mid-1990s was the first to introduce a tied agent system. Eventually, all major Austrian insurance companies started to deploy tied agents as already discussed. Those insurance companies with a foreign tied-agent-deploying mother company experienced the strongest pressure to source their agents out and were the first companies to do so as explicitly stressed (among other motives) by a manager of Company J.

> There are three essential motives [for outsourcing]. First, we are part of an international holding company. In the majority of the countries, especially in Europe, [Company J] has a very successful tied agent system. Germany is a prime example, or Italy. We here in Austria did not have this system as yet. [...] Thus, this is the first point, international experiences. Point two, the international experiences are not like this just because this is the way it works in one country, but because the sales people that work as [tied] agents, have significantly better performance. [...] The third point [...] are the costs.
> Head of Sales of an Austrian insurance company. Company J.
> Interview A1.

This manager also addresses the issue of motivation. Tied agents, argue most Austrian managers, are more motivated and are, thus, more productive than employed sales agents. The next section takes up these arguments in more detail.

6.2.3.4 Motivation and productivity

Some insurance managers argue that their employed direct sales force is, on average, characterised by low productivity. As pointed out earlier, insurance companies try to increase their productivity by using the tied agent channel. Especially in Austria, tied agency is an important part of the restructuring process in the insurance industry.

Of course, the observed higher productivity in the tied agent channel as reported by some managers is closely connected to the cost issues raised at the beginning of this section. If costs per insurance contract sold are lower due to factors such as risk transfer to the tied agents or the lack of labour regulations, the productivity of tied agents is likely to be higher when compared to the direct sales force.

Moreover, in both countries, several managers describe motivation as a key characteristic of tied agents. Tied agents are those who were successful in the direct sales force. Thus, assuming self-selection, those who are more motivated and less risk-averse seem to be more likely to switch from the direct sales force to tied agency as is shown, for example, in the following quote.

> [...] the nature of the tied agent is self-employment and, connected with that, perhaps higher motivation. Tied agents are those who were already successful in the direct sales force. The typical agent is a former, extremely successful, member of the direct sales force who became self-employed and who is rather a soloist.
>
> Head of Human Resource Management of an Austrian insurance company. Company O. Interview A16.

Additionally, insurance companies use the structure of commission payments, bonuses and rewards as a tool to explicitly attract volume-driven sales agents. Most insurance companies pay their tied agents a higher acquisition commission than their employed sales agents. The goal of this structure is obvious: a high acquisition commission induces self-selection.

However, the argument of higher productivity due to motivation loses its explanatory power if employed insurance agents are forced into tied agency as observed in some companies. In such cases, the insurance company also sources out the risk of low productivity.

> The goal [of outsourcing] is simply to use the underlying potential optimally. These entrepreneurs are more productive than the classical employee. This is the experience we have made. However, there is a very big trap – and some in our industry have fallen into this trap – [...] [other companies] have exclusively deployed tied agents and have simply forced all employed agents to become tied agents. In these cases, the productivity is a very different one, definitely lower than the one we have. [...] I prefer the non-entrepreneurial type to stay in the employed channel, where I can guide, control, support and develop him [her].
>
> Managing Director (direct sales force and tied agency operations) of an Austrian insurance company. Company O. Interview A7.

6.3 Dependent self-employment in the Austrian service sector

6.3.1 Employment trends in the Austrian service sector

During the last few decades, there has been one clear trend in the composition of the labour market: the shift from the primary (agriculture, mining) and secondary sector (manufacturing) to the tertiary sector (private and public services). The service sector itself is a heterogeneous sector with various subgroups and trends ranging from the low-skilled, low-paid 'trade' to the highly skilled and well-paid 'legal advice' subgroup.

Like in other European countries, the size of the service sector has risen continuously in Austria since the 1970s. However, the employment share of the service sector in Austria is still below the European average (in 2005, Austria: 66 per cent, EU15: 73 per cent). Since the 1980s, the service sector has been the only sector with increasing employment rates, even when total employment was stagnating or falling. The increase was, to a large extent, due to the entrance of newcomers and returnees into the labour market such as young workers, immigrant workers or previously non-participating women (Blaschke 2001: 268).

The highest increases of employment have been in the legal and business services as well as in health and social work between 1980 and 1994. Since 1995 growth rates have been slowing down, except in the categories 'other community, social and personal services' and 'health and social work' where we can still see some growth in employment. Since 1995, a decrease in employment can be observed in financial services, transport and communication due to semi-privatisation and deregulation of railways, postal and telecommunication services, leading to an increased competition, rationalisation and outsourcing.

The share of self-employment in the Austrian service sector is also clearly below the European average. Across service industries, the highest shares can be found in hotels and restaurants, business services and other community, social and personal service activities. During the early 1980s, the share of self-employment declined, increasing again in the early 1990s in most service industries, but particularly in the growing business services. However, there is evidence that the number of dependent self-employed workers increased steadily over the years (Blaschke 2001: 276).

Reasons for the overall growth of the service sector are manifold (Mesch 1998; Dolvik 2001;). Technical progress that led to the automation and specialisation of production processes is a major reason for a steep increase of productivity in manufacturing. Other factors influencing the shift towards the tertiary sector, and between branches of the tertiary sector, are changes in the wage structure, income and price elasticities of private demand for goods and services, increase of female participation in the labour market, demographic changes, a change in the structure of production processes and, therefore, a change in the demand for input factors, changes in tax and welfare systems as well as branch-specific regulations. Compared to manufacturing, productivity in the service sector did increase to a lower extent. This is mainly due to the fact that personal services can hardly be sped up because of a personal interaction with the customer. As a result, the relative share of employment in the tertiary sector rose steadily (Baumol's theory of 'cost-disease') (Dolvik 2001: 19).

Furthermore, the increase in the female participation rate had two effects: an increasing supply of labour, especially in the service sector (and to a large extent on a part-time basis), and at the same time, an increasing demand for services such as childcare, cleaning, taking care of the elderly, catering, housework and so on. Moreover, factors such as the increasing life expectancy and changes in lifestyle towards a more 'leisure-time-orientated' society lead to an increase of demands for entertainment, health care, beauty services and cultural and gastronomic services.

The Austrian service sector is predominated by female employees (in 2006: 56 per cent in service, 222 per cent in industry). However, we observe high segregation rates. High shares of female employment can be found in distributive trades, hotels and restaurants, education and in health and social work. In transport and communication the female share of dependent employment has been traditionally low. Throughout the 1990s, the share of female employment fell in the strongly expanding business service branch, mainly reflecting the relative increase of subsectors with a lower share of women such as 'computer and related activities' (Blaschke 2001: 272; Dolvik 2001: 541). Additionally we observe vertical segregation within the Austrian service industry. Men and women are not equally distributed across jobs with respect to hierarchical positions, skill levels and payment. The high-skilled, business-orientated branches of the expanding service sectors, often associated with high wages, are dominated by men, while women dominate in the low-skilled, badly paid and fluid jobs in precarious working conditions and weak organisations (Rubery 1999; Dolvik 2001). Both, low-skilled (and thus poorly paid) work and part-time employment can be found to a large extent in service sectors dominated by women such as hotels and restaurants, private households, social and personal service activities (low-skilled) and distributive trade, health and social services (part-time).

Another important factor of the growth of the service sector is the intermediary services, particularly the business services. Recent industrial restructuring processes have led to a trend of outsourcing of non-core activities, leading to a fundamental change in the demand for input factors. The intermediary (business to business) demand for business services (e.g. real estate, legal advice, insurance, auditing, consulting, financial services as well as technical services such as architects, research and development, design, advertisement, security, translation, software engineering, system administration) has been rising steadily due to increasing demand spurred by technological innovation, changes in markets and increased complexity (Mesch 1998: 65ff).

The trend towards project-oriented work and working on one's own account is on the rise in the business service industry. The trend towards outsourcing of services to self-employed workers can be observed, especially in knowledge-intensive business services, where non-standard employment is most likely to occur in the form of dependent self-employment, as the self-employed mostly specialise in the specific requests of one contractor (Mesch 1998: 175; Blaschke 2001: 278).

Changes in the industrial organisation towards smaller business units, a shift from the secondary to the tertiary sector, deregulation and privatisation, increasing international competition and increasing unemployment have affected industrial relations and have weakened the social partnership in Austria (Gstöttner-Hofer 1997; Mühlberger 2000; Eiro 2002). Union density is declining and consequently also the bargaining power. Firstly, this is due to a growth in the service sector, where union density traditionally is lower than in the public sector. Secondly, despite the increase of non-standard employment such as freelancing and dependent self-employment, these workers are still excluded from regular union membership. However, trade unions are well aware of the growing importance and specific problems of non-standard workers. Only recently, the Trade Union of Salaried Private Sector Employees (GPA) started an initiative, introducing seven 'interest communities' (Interessengemeinschaften) including various forms of atypical employment. The platform 'work@flex', for example, focuses at individuals working on the basis of a 'free service' contract (including freelancers and dependent self-employed workers), independent of the branch in which they are active. The network intends to increase communication and exchange of information and ideas among workers affected, aiming at the improvement of the current situation of freelancers and dependent self-employed workers. The interaction takes place in the Internet (http://www.interesse.at) and via e-mails and in regular meetings ('Flexforum'). Moreover, the GPA arranges private insurance contracts in case of illness and loss of earnings with a private insurance company for the members of the network at lower costs. Regarding dependent self-employment, the trade union (ÖGB) demands a redefinition of the concept of employment and an extension of labour law to cover non-standard forms of employment, especially economically dependent self-employed workers. The employers' association (WKÖ), on the other hand, advocates more flexibility and less regulation and collective bargaining. Interestingly, the WKÖ faces dramatic changes because very small businesses, one-person-companies and dependent self-employed workers are difficult to incorporate. This newer development results in the unusual situation where 'employers' and their 'workers' are both within the employers' association because it is mandatory for self-employed individuals to be a member of the WKÖ (Muehlberger and Pernicka 2007).

6.3.2 The dependent self-employed workers in the Austrian service industry

The following presents the conditions of work of dependent self-employed individuals in the Austrian service industry. Since the organisational background of these workers is highly diverse, we concentrate not on the outsourcing firms but rather on the dependent self-employed workers. The 14 workers included in this case study are deployed in consulting, research, software production, book keeping and in financial services. They are all self-employed or work on the basis of a hybrid legal category (see Chapter 3), but work only for one company in close cooperation.

This cooperation between the contractor and the subcontractor is usually based on written contracts, setting the framework of the rights and duties, but also strongly on informal agreements and unwritten rules. In general, the service or product that has to be delivered, the time of delivery and the price for the service or product is agreed on within a written contract. Most workers negotiate a 'package' once a year, fixing the hours of work and the hourly wage. Some workers in the computer service industry also report that due to delays in the company's planning and budgeting process, they did not yet get a renewal of their contract, but have worked without any contract for some time.

Workers in the consultancy and financial service sector do not have agreements on 'hour-packages', but on provisions and hourly wage. Thus, their income is strongly performance-related, with an increase in total income when they work longer hours. The compensation structure of some of these companies is rather sophisticated, but in general they are all based on a minimum wage (corresponding to a minimum amount of activities), the revenue of the project (or the sum of the company's financial package) and a deduction for back-office support and office rent. In some cases, the subcontractor has to return money or loses benefits, if she does not reach a certain minimum turnover.

> Once a year I go to the one in charge of human resources and negotiate the hours and the price. Usually the company buys a package for the whole year. This year I still have nothing written. But my boss told me that there will be a budget for our project. I trust him. (I 6)

> They expect a minimum turnover per month. If you cannot deliver that for a while, they ask you to pay back the loan or the money for the training. (I 1)

Most contracts also include restrictions to direct competition, consequently leading to penalties that the subcontractor has to pay to the contractual partner if they misuse company information.

> In case I asked colleagues to work for my own business or if I would tell a competitor company secrets, there are penalties written down in the contract. I think it's around one million Euro. But I don't think that this would ever be executed. (I 2)

Besides these written agreements, many additional unwritten rules exist. As the workers report, they are – if that they are not at their contractor's premises anyway – in constant contact through e-mail and telephone. Timetables have to be written and handed over to the project coordinator and of course it is inevitable for a team to come together for meetings. In most cases, there is a certain amount of control of the work to do (usually the project coordinator distributes the tasks) and even of the working time (in respect of office hours). However, there are also respondents who state that they are free in terms of how to do their work and when they fulfil it as long as it is delivered in time and satisfactory.

If I tell them [i.e. the contractor] I want to do my work from home, they would accept it once. But not showing up at the office three days a week would be too much. They expect me to be present in the firm. (I 1)

Team work, regular meetings, the support with marketing and management tools, training courses and research results enable the contractor to influence the way the work is done and presented. This close relationship between the subcontractor and contractor and the asymmetry in terms of information and resources produces dependency of the subcontractor on the (only) contractor. However, in some cases there is evidence that the dependency is a mutual one.

Some companies operate only with dependent self-employed workers and subcontractors. This implies a loss of direct contact to the client and a loss of knowledge and skills, which are all in the hands of the subcontractors. Moreover, as the dependent self-employed workers represent the contractor in the market and to the clients, their appearance and success is highly important for the brand and the reputation of the company. Some interview partners even mentioned the fact that their work relationship might be a case of 'hidden employment'. In case of an audit by the social security organisation, their contractual working agreements (on a self-employment basis) could not be upheld, a risk the outsourcing firm has to take.

Moreover, a large number of interviewees reported that they actually do not want to have more contractual partners. Either because they are fully engaged working for one company or because they benefit from the support given by their sole contracting partner. Being tied to only one contractor and getting support also means that they are not directly subject to market forces in a competitive environment. The workers interviewed (especially in the consultancy, computer and financial services) receive support through low-interest loans, payments in advance, office room, management know-how, back-office support and training. In sum, the dependency is in some cases definitely a mutual one and not always a disadvantage for the smaller subcontractor.

I'm not interested in setting up my own business. It would be too complicated. They have already set up a good infrastructure and a huge network I can use. I prefer the co-operation with this company. (I 12)

All respondents have a workplace or an office at their contractual partner's firm and carry out their work from there. Most of them additionally have a workplace at home, using it mainly for administrative work in the evenings or at weekends. Those working for a consultancy company or providing financial services also spend a lot of time at the clients' offices. All companies offer their subcontractors an office, back-office support (secretariat, laboratory, infrastructure) and in some cases even the working equipment (e.g. laptops).

> I have a workplace at home, but actually I work at my client's office. They want to keep the receipts and invoices in-house. Moreover, they have the bookkeeping-program on their computer. I do not have this software at home, this would be too expensive. (I 10)

> I spent most of the time in the company like an employee, although I have a workplace at home. But they have a faster, better computer. Moreover it's easier to work on the project if I sit face-to-face with my colleagues in the office. I get more information when I'm there. (I 2)

Those people working for a consultancy company or for a company providing financial services have to pay a certain amount of their income for this infrastructure and back-office support, some of them even when they do not use it because they work at home.

> We have to pay a certain amount of our income for the office and the back-office support like the phone, the secretary, the copy-machine and all the working material. Training and marketing is also provided by the company. (I 4)

The relationship between the dependent self-employed workers at the workplace (most of the time they share an office or the laboratory as they are working on one task or project) is reported to be good. They feel like colleagues working together for a certain project. Besides their specific tasks (e.g. programming, development of software, implementing a new organisational structure [consultants], conducting psychological tests, keeping the books), some of the respondents also reported that they have to support and train new 'colleagues' (normally also dependent self-employed workers).

> We are in daily contact, supporting each other regarding difficult clients or if somebody had a problem. Actually, it is kind of untypical for self-employed people, the way we are co-operating. (I 1)

Especially in the computer and related services, work is usually organised in projects. Whole departments are sourced out to small subcontractors, except the project coordinator. Coordinators usually have a permanent employment contract, being a mediator between the subcontractors and the companies. They are concerned with supervising and training the dependent self-employed workers, who typically have a higher fluctuation than employees.

> The whole team consists of freelancers. In the past there were more employees, but now there is not a single one in my department. Except the boss. The project co-ordinator is full-time employed. He is co-ordinating the team, distributes the work and is the communicator and mediator for the [contractor's] clients.(I 2)

The dependent self-employed workers describe their relationship to the 'core' workers (employees) overall as good. Regarding the task and the work that has to be done, there seems to be no difference between employees and dependent self-employed workers. In departments with mixed staff, employees and dependent self-employed workers work together regardless of the status of employment.

> The difference between us [i.e. dependent self-employed workers] and them [i.e. employees] is only the flexibility of time. They have certain core-times when to be in the office, we can do our work whenever we want – except for the meetings, then we have to be there. However, we all have to develop software. We are all on the same level. (I 2)

However, the different treatment of employees and dependent self-employed workers from the company's side also leads to tensions between the two groups, especially when the dependent self-employed workers are strongly integrated into the organisational structure of the firm, spending most of their time there and having intensive contact with the employees. Critical issues are, for example, the fact that employees have privileges dependent self-employed workers have not (e.g. use company canteen, internal information, invitation to social events such as Christmas dinner or company trips) and the missing career opportunities within the company.

> We are a great team and do a good job – nevertheless we are seen as outsiders and the management treats us like that. We don't get

any training courses and we have not even been invited to the yearly Christmas party. This is not ok. (I 7)

With respect to working time, we found three major groups. Firstly, those who are not completely dependent on the income they derive from the job in dependent self-employment (either because they have another job or because they have childcare responsibilities and regard the income as a contribution to the total household income). Their average weekly working hours are between 20 and 30 hours. The second group includes people who set a certain limit for themselves as to how many hours they want to work. This is partly because they want to finish their studies or because they are not willing to work more than an average employee (around 40 hours per week). The third group consists of those who work more than 50 hours per week. Not surprisingly, this group coincides almost totally with those who give more individualistic reasons for their decision to become dependent self-employed (self-realisation, appreciation, flexibility, self-determination) and are in general more satisfied with their current situation.

In comparison to my former job there was no big change concerning the hours I worked. I was always doing overtime. The only difference is that there is now a shift towards weekends and evening hours. (I 4)

All respondents reported that it is necessary to work in the evenings and at weekends, either to meet the client's deadlines or to complete the administrative work for their own business (e.g. bookkeeping, tax reports, time schedule, planning). Of course, this is especially the case with the third group and to a smaller extent with the first two groups. Most interview partners said that they do not go on holidays either because they cannot afford it (have debts to pay back or do not want to 'loose two or three weeks' without making money) or because they do not dare not to be available for their client. In sum, the overall working time of dependent self-employed workers is higher than that of employees, as the interviews confirmed.

As the company expects me to be there for him mainly in the core working time [9 a.m. to 6 p.m.] and I have to do all the administrative stuff by myself, it is clear that I have to work on weekends and in the evenings. In the beginning, I didn't even go on holidays, because

> I had no time and no money – and I did not dare not to be available for my company. (I 9)

6.3.3 Effects and consequences of dependent self-employment

For most workers flexibility is an advantage of self-employment, giving them the possibility to manage business and family responsibilities or leisure-time preferences. However, some also reported that this 'freedom' to work whenever one wants to, can potentially lead to work long hours, especially to work in the evenings and on weekends. The lack of holidays and the permanent pressure can cause burn-out-syndromes and exhaustion. In addition, the flexibility of working time is also restricted by the company's core working hours. For some interview partners the lack of continuous and stable working times is problematic and hard to manage.

> I thought the time management part would be easier. It is hard to allocate my time resources optimal – sometimes there is a lot to do at the same time, sometimes it's less, that's difficult to coordinate and find a 'golden middle way'. (I 3)

It seems that some individuals (especially in the consultancy and computer services) earn more money than employees due to higher gross hourly wages, longer weekly working hours and tax benefits. They admit that the higher income mostly derives from working longer hours. If they compared the net hourly wage with that of a normal employee, it would not be higher.

> If you work 40-hours per week like an employee, you do not earn more. You can earn more, but then you also work longer hours. (I 11)

Those interview partners that are not voluntarily dependent self-employed stated that their income is less than that of an employee in a comparable position, due to the deduction of social security and tax payments.

> As self-employed worker, you only have an income if you actually work. Normally the hourly rates should be higher to be able to pay the social security and tax duties, but this is not the case. For me, it would financially be better to have a fixed full-time employment. (I 7)

Most interviewees reported to have a tax consultant, completing the bookkeeping and the tax reports, or they are specifically educated themselves (i.e. bookkeeping courses or studies of business administration). Nevertheless, not all of the people interviewed have a perfect overview of their net income, but only a rough idea of how much they can spend and how much they have to pay for social security and tax duties.

Effects on the private situation are reported to be manifold. Most interviewees do not involve friends and family at all. Others get help from family members, especially for bookkeeping, typing or other 'back-office jobs'. Furthermore, the family status also seems to be of some importance for the people interviewed as they regard unstable income, long working hours, almost no holidays and no sick pay as too risky when having family responsibilities.

> Due to a severe illness of my wife, I had to stay at home and could not work. Consequently, I had no income for a while and I had to take up credits to meet my regular expenditures. Working on own-account is risky, and with family and children it's even a greater risk, as you are responsible not only for yourself. (I 1)

> If I had family, I would prefer a full-time employment. Risk is good, as long as you only have to take care for yourself. (I 6)

Table 6.7 shows some characteristics and findings regarding satisfaction, average weekly working hours, the existence of an office/ work place at the contractor's company, the financial situation and the existence of control (regarding the content and the working time).

Basically, those interview partners who became dependent self-employed on a voluntary basis are more satisfied with their job situation. In almost all cases, the desire and expectation of self-determination and self-realisation, higher earnings and flexibility have been fulfilled and the situation of dependency on one contractual partner is not regarded as a disadvantage. Most interviewees consider it convenient to have a close relationship to only one big client, supporting them with management services and knowledge, providing back-office services, a brand and marketing services to support the acquisition of new clients. Consequently, this group of dependent self-employed workers wants to keep up this form of work relationship and has no interest in changing to either (full-time) dependent employment or increase their independence and engage on the outside market.

Table 6.7 Overview on the personal characteristics and findings of the interviews conducted

No.	Sex	Age	Education level	Private status	Business service sector	Satisfaction	Office at contractor's place	Control	Working hours per week	Higher income
1	M	30	University (FH)	Family	Financial	No	Yes	No	30	No
2	M	25	Technical college	Single	Computer	Yes	Yes	Yes	25	Yes
3	M	25	University (FH)	Single	Consulting	Yes	Yes	No	70	Yes
4	F	35	TTC	Single	Consulting	Yes	Yes	No	50	Yes
5	M	45	Technical college	Family	Consulting	Yes	Yes	No	70	Yes
6	M	25	Technical college	Single	Computer	Yes	Yes	Yes	30	Yes
7	F	25	University	Single	Research	No	Yes	Yes	25	No
8	F	30	TTC	Single	Financial	No	Yes	No	30	No
9	M	45	University	Family	Consulting	Yes	No	No	70	No
10	F	30	Business college	Family	Book keeping	Yes	Yes	Yes	20	No
11	M	30	University (FH)	Single	Financial	No	Yes	Yes	40	No
12	M	20	High school	Single	Financial	Yes	Yes	No	70	Yes
13	F	60	Studies not finished	Family	Research	No	No	Yes	30	No
14	M	30	Technical college	Single	Computer	Yes	Yes	No	60	Yes

Note: FH = Fachhochschule (Applied College); TTC = teachers training college.

Some interview partners, especially those who have other responsibilities, such as university studies to finish or a child to take care of, are satisfied with their current situation, as it gives them the needed time flexibility and a 'stable' income from one major contractor. However, they can envisage increasing the size of their business and working for more companies when their other responsibilities become less important.

> I'm very satisfied with my job, I have fun, my colleagues are cool and it's easier to manage job, university studies and leisure time. At the moment it's the perfect form of employment for me. In the long run, I can also image to extend the business, probably together with a friend of mine. The market for IT-specialists is still good. (I 2)

> I'm satisfied with my job as a self-employed person. With my child, I don't have time at the moment to look for more companies. However, I can image increasing my business, if possible. The pros are flexible time management, more challenge and more fun. The negative side of being in self-employment is the permanent pressure to find new companies and new jobs and the worse social security protection, missing holiday and sick pay, and so on. (I 10)

Not surprisingly, those who had no alternative but to take the job under the conditions offered are not satisfied and want to change to dependent employment as soon as possible (see Table 6.7). Furthermore, not only the voluntary or involuntary decision is the pivotal factor for the level of satisfaction but also working conditions (i.e. flexibility of time, freedom to decide, interesting job, relationship to colleagues/team) and the financial situation have a strong influence.

> Actually the job itself is ok. However, for the next year, it is still not clear, if there will be a budget for me. If not, I'm trying to get fixed employment instead. I'd prefer to have a constant income instead of muddling through as a small subcontractor always on the risk of loosing the client. (I 6)

It seems that the former employment status of the worker also has an influence on their satisfaction and future preferences, as those who were dependent employees and still prefer an employment relationship want to become employees again. Those who actively decided for (dependent) self-employment, coming from dependent employment, do not want to go back into employment, but even intend to increase their independency by spreading business activities.

6.4 Dependent self-employment in the Austrian freight industry

6.4.1 Recent developments in the Austrian freight industry

During the last years the economic and legal backgrounds for forwarders have changed substantially. Due to the expansion of cross-boarder transactions (especially with the countries of eastern Europe) the total volume of transports has grown considerably. Competition has become keener due to the liberalisation of road transport, increasing the number of foreign forwarders entering the Austrian market. These forwarders take advantage of lower labour costs and a less restrictive legal framework in their home country, allowing them to offer their services at a lower price than their Austrian competitors. This implies that Austrian forwarders are forced to reduce their costs as well to be able to compete with these new rivals.

Reacting to the harsher competition, Austrian forwarders pursue different strategies. First, they have been restructuring their businesses to reduce costs, in particular fixed overheads. Second, mergers and acquisitions enabled them to benefit from economies of scale, making them more competitive. Third, we observe a concentration on core business and niche strategies. Specialisation can help a company to place itself on the market in a unique way and none of its rivals can enter this niche.

Outsourcing the fleet of trucks has to be seen in this context. First of all a company-owned car pool is a significant cost factor, which consists mainly of fixed overheads. Thus, outsourcing physical transport reduces these fixed costs substantially. Secondly, for many forwarders physical transport is not part of their core business and is therefore outsourced for strategic reasons. The organisation of transport is an integrated part of the core business of forwarders. This implies that the main emphasis lies on the planning, organising and managing of shipping activities but not on the actual physical transport. Therefore many forwarding agents cooperate with trucking firms for carrying out road transport. In fact, there are only few forwarding agencies which would perform all the physical transport themselves without cooperating with trucking firms (Sladky 1994: 2).

156 Dependent Self-Employment

The interviews carried out for this case study have confirmed that forwarders increasingly reduce the number of company-owned vehicles. None of the companies interviewed acts exclusively with company-owned vehicles. Those companies who have their own car pool have decided to either reduce the number of trucks or not to increase the number of vehicles despite an increasing volume of orders. Four of the ten companies interviewed have no company-owned vehicles at all. They either have completely outsourced their fleet of trucks or started business without ever owning vehicles.

The interviews highlight that the companies have chosen various strategies for externalising their fleet of trucks. First, some companies pursue a dual strategy by sourcing out only part of the car pool. These forwarders employ drivers who transport goods with company-owned trucks, but also cooperate with external trucking firms. Usually, the companies own as many trucks as they can fully deploy over the year. Thus, if the number of orders surpasses the internal transport capacities, additional orders will be executed in cooperation with subcontractors (capacity outsourcing). The interviews have revealed different ways to organise the cooperation with trucking firms. To guarantee a stable service level and appropriate quality standards, the forwarders are generally interested in establishing long-term business relationships with their subcontractors.

Second, four of the ten companies interviewed decided to outsource the entire fleet of trucks. In these cases outsourcing primarily resulted from a strategic decision. These companies intended to concentrate on the core business. They do not consider physical transport as part of their core business and, thus, contracted it out either to one trucking company or to individual small subcontractors (specialisation outsourcing). Selling the entire fleet to only one trucking company, however, can cause severe problems since the forwarder will then be extremely dependent on this trucking firm (creating a hold-up problem). If the forwarder decides to source out the trucks to various small subcontractors this dependency can be reduced. The interviews have shown that three of the companies that sourced out the entire car pool have pursued a combined strategy. They have outsourced part of their vehicles to a big trucking firm and part of the trucks to self-employed carriers, some of them former employees.

Third, two of the companies participating in the survey have run their business without ever possessing a company-owned car pool. In these two cases it was argued already at the time of the foundation of the company, which dates back several decades, that it would be more advantageous for a forwarder to cooperate with carriers in organising transport than to perform physical transport internally. Both companies stress the importance to cooperate with many different carriers, implying that their subcontractors are mainly small carriers. They are located in different regions and countries and therefore subject to different economic and legal conditions. This variety permits the forwarder to diversify its own risk and reduce its dependency on the individual carriers.

6.4.2 The contractual organisation of dependent self-employment in the Austrian freight industry

To avoid that dependent outsourcing jeopardises continuity in the production process it is crucial to define the rights and duties of both parties in a written contract. All of the interviewed companies, which cooperate with self-employed carriers, have drawn up written contracts with their subcontractors. In these contracts only the main issues of the cooperation are laid down. As in the insurance industry we find that written contracts regulate only the basic framework of the business relationship, while the actual organisation is based on unwritten agreements and codes of conduct. The written framework contracts are usually subject to a period of notice of 3–6 months and state binding prices for freight room. Furthermore, they frequently include the following typical provisions.

First, exclusive partnership. Eight out of ten forwarders interviewed work with self-employed carriers. Six of them insisted on an exclusive partnership with the subcontractors, which means that the subcontractors are not allowed to work with further forwarders. However, taking in orders from different companies would allow the self-employed to diversify the economic risk and to become economically independent. One logistic reason for an exclusive partnership is to guarantee that the self-employed carriers have enough loading space available. The interviews have shown two different forms of exclusive partnerships. The forwarders either demand that all trucks of the self-employed are used exclusively for carrying out their orders or that only specific trucks are designated to the forwarder. With the latter alternative the self-employed is free to buy other trucks and offer their shipping room to other customers as well.

Second, most of the companies, which have an exclusive partnership with their subcontractors guarantee them a minimum turnover. This helps to reduce the economic risk for the self-employed carriers. Due to the fact that under an exclusive partnership the self-employed are not allowed to take in orders from other customers, managers stressed that it was the responsibility of the forwarders to guarantee them at least a yearly minimum turnover.

Third, most forwarders insist on a uniform design of the trucks to promote the company. A standardised appearance of the fleet usually has the aim that the trucks are identified as vehicles of the forwarder on the road even if they do not belong to the forwarder but to a subcontractor. Since the trucks will be identified as vehicles of the forwarder, it is of importance that the forwarder takes care that all vehicles, no matter if they are company-owned or vehicles of subcontractors, meet the required safety standards because in the case of an accident it will also be the forwarder having to deal with the negative publicity. For the self-employed this uniform appearance of the trucks implies that it will be even harder to get orders from other customers and therefore they become even more dependent on the forwarder.

6.4.3 Motives for outsourcing the fleet of trucks

The main motive for sourcing out the fleet of trucks is to reduce costs, but also to change the cost structure. Cost-cutting has gained importance due to the fact that harsher competition has forced forwarders to restructure their businesses and to become more competitive. Managers stressed costs for personnel as one of the most important cost-factor of a company-owned fleet also due to the fact that forwarders need additional drivers to replace employees being ill or on paid vacation. Moreover, outsourcing the fleet of trucks also implies that not only labour costs but also costs for searching and training employees is sourced out.

A substantial part of the costs caused by a company-owned fleet of trucks are fixed overheads (i.e. personnel, insurance, depreciation and so on). However, since the order intake of forwarders fluctuates considerably, high fixed overheads cannot be covered in times of low order intake, implying that a company-owned fleet of trucks can only be profitable if the trucks will be used in (rather) full capacity throughout the whole year. Contracting out physical transport produces mainly variable costs which are only caused in the case of an order placed with an outside carrier. This means that if the volume of orders rises, more orders will be contracted out and thus, costs and profit will increase. If, however, the volume of orders declines, profit will decrease and costs will be reduced as well. Furthermore, even in times of high order intake additional orders can be taken in, since contracting out helps avoiding capacity bottlenecks.

Most of the ten companies analysed for this case study cooperate with self-employed carriers. Only two companies stated not to work with self-employed carriers. The cost advantages of self-employed carriers mainly result from the flat organisational structure and from the possibility of organising the production process more flexibly. Managers highlight that self-employed carriers have lower administrative costs than bigger trucking firms. This cost advantage becomes even more important if the forwarder offers certain services (e.g. using the firm-owned garage and so on) to the self-employed and if both present themselves on the market jointly, which enables the self-employed to profit from economies of scale (e.g. procurement of gasoline, trucks, insurances and so on). Both strategies can be seen frequently with exclusive contracts where a subcontractor only works for one forwarder.

Since self-employed carriers often work alone (or with only few employees) they can offer the forwarder non-standard working times and working overtime at low costs. These flexible working arrangements are considered by the majority of the interviewed managers as the most important cost advantage of small self-employed carriers. However, many also pointed out that this flexible organisation of the working time often results in self-exploitation of the dependent self-employed worker. Since they are beyond employment law, they are not paid extra for working overtime, implying that the working conditions of self-employed carriers deteriorate compared to those of employed drivers. Thus, interviews have clearly shown that small self-employed carriers are usually able to offer their services at a more favourable price than big trucking firms.

In this context managers frequently pointed out the importance to pay the self-employed a 'fair price'. For forwarders it is crucial to ensure a stable quality of services and are, thus, interested in long-term business relations with their subcontractors to keep their pool of subcontractors as stable as possible. Serious price-cutting, however, may result in subcontractors going bankrupt or switching to other contractors, resulting in losing experienced partners, which could jeopardise the reliability and quality of its service. However, the interviews have generally shown that the economic situation for small carriers is difficult and many of them go bankrupt already during their first years.

By contracting out, physical transport forwarders also pass part of their economic risk onto their subcontractors because costs resulting from internal over- and under-capacity of shipping space need not be born by the forwarder. Managers emphasised that this enables forwarders to calculate prices more tightly, increasing their competitiveness.

Additionally, outsourcing physical transport permits forwarders to avoid specific risks of carriage by road. In the case of an accident, for example, the company has to bear not only the costs of damage to the vehicles and the goods but can also be made responsible for casualties and negative impacts on the health of people and on the environment. Thus, most of the risk induced by road transport will be passed from the forwarder to the carrier. However, interviews have shown that most of the companies do not take the risk themselves but are covered by private insurance contracts. Therefore outsourcing of physical transport basically implies a reduction of insurance and administrative costs for the forwarders. However, outsourcing physical transport does not imply that the forwarder does not have to take any risk of road transport. In many cases the trucks on the road will be identified as vehicles of the forwarder and not necessarily as those of the carrier. Thus if a truck is involved in a media-covered accident, it is the forwarder who has to deal with negative publicity, no matter whether the truck was company-owned or belonged to one of the subcontractors.

Interestingly, the survey has shown that the reduction of capital commitment was not considered to be an important motive for the externalisation of the car pool. Although selling the trucks can help to raise new capital, the trucks had been usually used already for several years and thus, they had almost been written off completely. Therefore the only capital savings that could be achieved resulted from a reduction of replacement investments. Interviewed managers stressed that it is generally easier to achieve considerable savings by reducing the personnel working in physical transport than by reducing the number of trucks.

Forwarders can become more flexible by sourcing out to a great pool of small subcontractors to increase the number of cooperations. Due to this diversified pool of partners the forwarder can better fulfil the various needs of different customers. Particularly in the international business a great diversity of partners can be an advantage. Primarily, different geographic locations of the partners help the forwarder to execute customers' orders worldwide more rapidly and less costly. Furthermore, specific knowledge of the subcontractors (languages, experiences with different customs procedures, expertise with special transports and so on) enables the forwarder to work for different groups of customers. This greater diversity finally strengthens the economic position of a company since it will become more independent from the development of a specific industry or region.

Those forwarders who opted for sourcing out the entire fleet of trucks highlighted that the concentration on the core business by sourcing out physical transport produced positive effects on the core business. These forwarders contracted out not only physical transport but also all administrative processes in connection with physical transport, implying additional management capacities for the core business.

Moreover, managers emphasised various gains due to specialisation. Since road transport involves high risks there are a range of legal restrictions governing carriage by trucks. The legal framework regulates driving hours, transport of dangerous goods, customs duty and so on. For the forwarders this tight legal framework often results in substantial administrative costs. In addition, in many cases costly expertise is necessary to organise transports according to the legal restrictions. Some managers argue that outsourcing permits them to benefit from external expertise. For certain transports (e.g. transports of dangerous goods) it is advantageous to hire a specialised carrier. Since these specialised carriers receive orders from a number of different customers, resulting in a greater volume of specialised orders, they generate specific knowledge which would be too costly to be developed by a forwarder. As a result, specialisation guarantees that transports can be carried out more quickly and less costly. However, such expertise in the freight business is rather found with big trucking firms than with small self-employed carriers, implying that dependent outsourcing of physical transport is rather capacity outsourcing than specialisation outsourcing.

6.4.4 Effects, risks and consequences of outsourcing

The case study has shown that by cooperating with an external carrier a forwarder looses part of the control over the production process since the physical transport can no longer be influenced directly. In contrast to carrying out physical transport internally, a cooperation with a carrier involves that the forwarder is dependent on the performance of the carrier and therefore has to rely on the carrier to execute the order to the customer's full expectations.

Since forwarders and carriers often have diverging company goals, a cooperation can cause inconsistencies in carrying out an order, however. Meeting the customers' expectations means that the goods have to be delivered according to the contract, undamaged and on time. It also implies that the drivers are friendly and the trucks are clean and equipped according to the usual safety standards. On the other hand, the main goals for a carrier usually are full usage of shipping capacity, efficient route planning and profitability objectives. Thus, for a successful cooperation it is important that the different goals of both companies are coordinated properly. A successful cooperation needs to bring together these diverging goals in order to prevent a low quality of the service and not to loose customers. Interviews have shown that the companies which still have own trucks prefer to carry out those orders internally which they consider as important and sensible in terms of quality. The argument put forward is that the forwarder can supervise and control the quality of the service more closely in the case of employed drivers. In addition, almost all of the managers interviewed indicate that they have higher confidence in their own employees than in external drivers. Consequently, the loss of control over the production process also creates dependency on the subcontractor. The majority of the interviewed companies try to keep its own dependency as low as possible by selling their trucks to different partners so that they can cooperate with several different trucking firms. Splitting the fleet of trucks between several companies, however, means to risk a loss of economies of scale and specialisation gains.

In addition, managers emphasised that they want to avoid that their subcontractors are too dependent on them. Cooperating with only one forwarder, the advantage of a synergy-potential which could be used by taking in orders from other companies as well is reduced, resulting in higher prices. Furthermore, a strong dependency of the subcontractors can also have a negative impact on the forwarders' flexibility. Most of the managers interviewed argued that it is problematic to reduce the orders of one subcontractor if such a step could cause bankruptcy for the subcontractor.

In other words, we observe mutual dependency in those tied business relationships. As a result, choosing the appropriate partner is pivotal for the success of outsourcing since both partners will become dependent on each other in their production process. Setting up a written contract would help both partners to agree on certain standards and define measures and sanctions should one of them fail to meet the targets. However, written contracts cannot clarify all possible contingencies. As discussed above, the written contracts we found in the freight industry rather regulate only the basic framework of the business relationship. A certain degree of trust between the two partners is therefore necessary for a prosperous cooperation. Interviewed managers and dependent self-employed workers agreed that they were trying to establish long-term relationships for transport services. Even if there is no written arrangement suggesting a long-term relationship, the subcontractors can rely on follow-up orders if their services meet the standards of the forwarder. Managers stress that they have a great interest in working together with well-known subcontractors where they know that orders will be carried out properly. They argue that the customer usually identifies the forwarder with the delivery and not the subcontractor. Any shortfalls in the delivery will be attributed to the forwarder. The forwarding agency then risks losing customers and ruining its reputation. Most managers emphasise that their companies were willing to pay higher prices to their subcontractors for physical transport if they had already had positive experience with them.

The interviews have shown that many forwarders consider it an important advantage of dependent outsourcing that the potential partners frequently are already known to the forwarder. In many cases the new subcontractors are either former employees of the forwarder or of already existing subcontractors of the company. This basically implies that the working fields of the former drivers remain the same and therefore they have already acquired experience, know the customers, addresses, driving routes and so on, so that they need no specific training. Furthermore, the forwarder already knows the motivation, working style and reliability of these workers, facilitating the establishment of trust. Thus, the interviews have drawn the following picture: in most cases forwarders try to carry out orders of particular importance internally or together with carriers whom they have known already for a longer time and hence with whom they have established mutual trust. Orders surpassing this capacity and being considered as less sensible are subcontracted to other trucking firms on the spot market which are frequently not known very well by the forwarder.

Some managers even stressed that outsourcing physical transport often results in an increase in quality. One argument for this gain in quality was that outsourcing enables the company to use external expertise as already stressed above. Another argument put forward in this context is that the driving personnel of a specialised trucking firm is often better qualified and motivated because these employees work in the core business of the trucking firm. An additional claim is that it is sometimes easier to ensure a high quality standard with outside carriers because in the case of under-performance it is easier to end the business relation with a subcontractor than with an employed driver.

Also dependent outsourcing may lead to higher quality. In most of the cases the interviewed managers have confirmed that the quality of the service in fact has increased due to the cooperation with self-employed carriers because self-employed carriers are better motivated. Some managers indicated that the self-employed acted more like entrepreneurs and therefore, they were more dedicated to offering a good service. This can also be explained by the fact that self-employed carriers are eager to meet the customers' expectations since otherwise they might risk losing orders.

The externalisation of the fleet of trucks usually involves a knowledge transfer from the forwarder to the trucking firm. This is mainly due to the fact that the trucking firm which agrees to buy the trucks from the forwarder usually also takes over the drivers and, thus, also their knowledge. On the one hand this is an advantage for the forwarder because the trucking firm incorporates the necessary expertise and experience to meet the customers' expectations, not jeopardising the quality of the service. The drivers who have switched from the forwarder to the trucking firm are already familiar with the specific needs of customers, they know the addresses of the customers, the best routes and the time necessary for going there. On the other hand, one could argue that this transfer of knowledge bears the risk that the trucking firm takes advantage of the acquired expertise and starts entering into the market of the forwarder. However, interviewed managers did not consider this danger as very important.

In general, the employees mostly affected by the outsourcing decision are those who were formerly working for the outsourcing firm. These employees are mainly afraid of losing their jobs or losing privileges already achieved by switching to another employer. Basically the externalisation of the fleet of trucks implies for the employees either to become self-employed or to switch to another employer. Even if in the majority of the cases the outsourcing decision did not result in the dismissal of employees, they usually disapprove the outsourcing plans of the management.

The interviewed managers confirmed that higher motivated small self-employed carriers sometimes set new benchmarks, putting pressure on the employed drivers. This seems reasonable as for self-employed carriers their income is directly related to the numbers of orders carried out. In other words, the more orders self-employed can execute to the customers' full expectations the more they can earn. By contrast, the salary will not change for employed drivers, no matter how many deliveries they carry out during their working time.

Furthermore, some of the interviewees have stated that in many cases of dependent outsourcing it has been the higher motivated and qualified employees who have decided to buy a truck and to become self-employed. These employees are frequently young drivers who expect higher job satisfaction and better career opportunities by starting their own business and thus, they are usually willing to work harder and are willing to work longer hours.

6.5 The creation of dependency

The case studies above and Bertolini and Muehlberger (2006) have shown that dependency is shaped not only by the formal contract and the exclusiveness of the business relationship but also by relational contracts. Basically, a self-employed worker's dependence on an outsourcing company is created by two main facts. First, companies offer their self-employed subcontractors a wide range of support in order to solve the principal-agent problem. These supporting measures are also designed to bind the worker more tightly to the company, imposing high costs for changing contract partner. Second, most outsourcing companies have developed sophisticated schemes of controlling tied agents. The result of these managerial control instruments, however, is that the outsourcing company introduces elements of hierarchy into the business relationship which makes the actual work organisation of the self-employed workers similar to that of employees.

6.5.1 Dependency as a result of support

Outsourcing companies support the business activities of their self-employed workers in various ways. Essentially, this support can be classified under two categories. Firstly, different kinds of financial support (in all three industries) and secondly, the provision of business know-how and management skills (especially in the insurance and business service industry). Although we found some differences across the industries which is due to a different work process and skill level, we did not find substantial differences in support measures between the countries.

When tied agents in the insurance industry start their own business, an important source of support from the insurance company they contract with is financial. Most insurance companies offer their new tied agents a loan to open their business and in addition to this pay them a higher rate of commission during the first year (or first 2 years) than in the subsequent. In addition to various financial packages for business start-up, insurance companies financially support the purchase of office and IT equipment or marketing material. In the business service industry we also found that workers receive financial support through low-interest loans, payments in advance or the provision of office room and equipment. In the freight industry we mainly observed that outsourcing companies sell the trucks to the outsourced workers at a favourable price or that the workers can buy a truck via the firm for better conditions. Outsourcing companies also financially support the redesign of the trucks so that they bear the sign and logo of the company.

Additionally, they have the possibility to buy gasoline and insurance products at low prices and to use the firm-owned garage. The reason for this financial support is not only to tie the self-employed worker closer to the company but also to make sure that the worker represents the company accordingly. Managers in both the service and the insurance industry stressed, for instance, that self-employed workers get financial support for office equipment only if they fulfil the company's criteria.

The second important source of support is provided in terms of know-how and business skills. Due to the difference in skill levels in the industries investigated, we found this kind of support important only in the insurance (stronger) and business service industries (weaker). In the insurance industry, support in this area starts with the development of the business plan. Some insurance companies develop a business plan for the tied agent, while other companies simply offer the tied agent their entrepreneurial knowledge for the preparation of a business plan. Besides assistance for business start-ups, insurance companies provide entrepreneurial know-how for accounting, IT, tax consultancy and business management. Although we found similar support methods in the business service industry, this is less an issue since most self-employed workers are highly educated and possess high management skills. Nevertheless, in most cases dependent self-employed workers get back-office support for which they have to pay partly.

Another key issue is training. According to legal regulations in the British and Austrian insurance industry, tied agents are obliged to have professional experience, which means that insurance companies do not have to provide basic training. Nevertheless, special product training and further sales training are crucial for briefing the tied agent, first, to sell those products the insurance company wants to sell and, second, to sell the products in the way intended by the insurance company. Basically, insurance companies use two different methods to finance these various support measures. Either insurers pay their tied agents a lower rate of commission to finance their services or they pay their tied agents a higher rate of commission (i.e. roughly equal to that paid of brokers), but the tied agents must (partially) pay for the services they use. Interviews with tied agents, however, have shown that the first method is sometimes misinterpreted, because some argue that the services are free of charge. Some managers argue that the first method has the advantage of obliging the tied agent to take part in training. In both the business service and the freight industry we also find that many dependent self-employed workers are provided with training courses either at a reduced price or without directly charging them.

In sum, the various kinds of support help the insurance company to gain closer managerial control over the business activities of their self-employed workers and to tie them to the company. Consequently, dependency is created not only by the fact that dependent self-employed workers are only allowed to contract with one company (exclusiveness) but also by the actual organisation of the work relationship. On the one hand, support and service help the workers to manage their business, but some measures also increase their degree of dependence. The consequence of support and the resulting dependency, however, is that the borderline between employment and self-employment becomes blurred.

6.5.2 Dependency as a result of managerial control

The issue of managerial control over self-employed workers is central for an outsourcing company in deciding whether to work with them or not. Companies that work with dependent self-employed workers have developed sophisticated mechanisms for controlling their work. However, compared to employees, controlling dependent self-employed workers demands different instruments since direct disciplinary measures are largely inapplicable. Nevertheless, by working with self-employed workers who are closely tied to only one company, the latter wish to have, on the one hand, managerial control over their workers similar to that over employees and, on the other hand, to profit from the advantages of outsourcing.

Managers of insurance companies that do not deploy tied agents claim that the lack of managerial control over tied agents is one of the main reasons for not working with them. The example of a British general insurer that has only recently started to hire agents on the basis of an employment contract rather than on a self-employed basis illustrates well the importance of managerial control. The main goal of this organisational change was to intensify control over the sales force. One of the key problems in the old organisation was that the company suspected their tied agents of selling products from other companies, although they were only allowed to sell the products of the outsourcing company. As a result, the company tried to put a stop to these practices by employing people.

In the insurance industry managerial control over tied agents is exercised in various ways. British tied agents, for example, report that the insurance companies check whether the products sold are appropriate for the customers. Furthermore, a compliance team is responsible for controlling the tied agents' work according to regulatory rules. Regular meetings with company managers and supervisors ensure that the insurance company is permanently informed about business development and other issues. Moreover, insurance companies try to ensure that the tied agents comply with the company's corporate culture. This refers not only to issues such as marketing, advertising and corporate design but also to how they appear on the market and how they interact with customers. One British manager, to give an explicit example, reports that even advertisements by tied agents in local communities have to be cleared by the head office. An Austrian manager, to give another example, states that the company occasionally mandates a trustee to audit some of their tied agents.

An additional method of controlling tied agents is undertaking customer surveys to check the quality of the interaction with customers. As already mentioned above, insurance companies permanently exercise control through their local and regional managers who are in direct and regular contact with the tied agents. Another way of governing tied agents is through training. While introducing products to their tied agents and training them in new sales methods, insurance companies influence the sales practices of their tied agents. Finally, a further important source of managerial control is IT as it facilitates control and reduces control costs substantially.

Another, more subtle, way of controlling tied agents is by offering specific incentives. The interviews have shown that insurance companies use different incentive structures to influence managerial control and corporate governance. Incentives are pivotal in understanding how tied agents behave in organisations. Moreover, incentive structures are important instruments for companies to solve the classical principal-agent problem, since disciplinary measures are largely inapplicable in tied agency. One classical instrument is, of course, money. Insurance companies may thus influence not only overall performance but also customer structure or the products that are sold through a specific mix of commission and bonification. For example, when insurance companies aim at boosting the long-term insurance business, they (temporarily) change the commission and bonification for these products. This, in turn, means that payment for specific performances varies and is subject to change without renegotiation. In other words, the tied agents' income also depends on a flexible incentive structure, which is determined by the insurance company on a unilateral basis. Furthermore, insurance companies control the performance of their tied agents by demanding a minimum performance level be fulfilled in order to keep their contract. Besides pecuniary incentives, insurance companies use non-cash incentives to motivate and control tied agents. Insurance companies use a variety of different non-cash incentives such as internal firm newspapers where the best selling agents are presented, conference trips, contests between agents or firm-internal clubs for high-performers.

Also in the business service industry managerial control is exercised through various mechanisms. Many dependent self-employed workers in the Italian and Austrian business service industry work at the employer's premises, being tightly integrated into the firm and those daily firm-internal routines. If they do not have an office at the company's premises, they are, of course, in constant contact via e-mail and telephone and have regular meetings with supervisors. Furthermore, many jobs in the business service industry are fulfilled within a team, which often is constituted of both self-employed workers and employees, additionally blurring the boundaries between the two labour market states. Some dependent self-employed workers report to have to hand over working time plans and to be subject to control over the work process. In the Austrian freight industry direct control is mainly executed by the amount of orders the self-employed worker has to handle and by inquiring whether the delivery has been carried out to the customer's satisfaction. Furthermore, most workers report that they pass by the office of the company on a daily basis to take over the paper work and to agree on the daily route.

6.5.3 Relational risk and mutual dependency

The last two sections have demonstrated the ways the self-employed workers' dependency on the outsourcing firm is created. However, dependency may also be mutual, creating relational risk. In the insurance industry we observed that issues such as the loss of direct access to customers, the difficulty of controlling tied agents, increased risk exposure, problems of loyalty, the importance of the brand and the uncertain long-term costs of tied agency are pivotal reasons for insurance companies to not work with tied agents. Of course, some of these issues are, in turn, the problems tied-agent-deploying companies struggle with, creating mutual dependence. The main issues of mutual dependency that managers address are access to customers and treatment of the brand. Direct access to customers is essential not only for customer-specific marketing, but also for influencing the customer's decision as to whether they renew a contract or place another contract. Consequently, insurance companies that deploy tied agents are keen to improve direct contact with customers in order to gain access to their information and influence their decisions. However, tied agents, in turn, have an interest in reducing the communication between the company and their customers. The client bank (i.e. the files of the customers' details) legally belongs to the insurance company in all countries investigated. However, both sides realise that this is only theoretical, because in the end it is the clients who decide with whom they wish to do business. Thus, insurance companies are highly aware of the fact that customers develop a relationship with their advisers and not with the company. Hence, according to the business contract tied agents are not allowed to take their customers with them in the case that they change company. Some insurance companies try to solve this problem by 'buying' the client bank from the tied agent when the business contract is terminated.

Another source of mutual dependence in all industries is the treatment of the brand. The entrepreneurial success of self-employed workers is pivotal for the company since they represent the brand to customers. Additionally, if a self-employed worker goes bankrupt, the outsourcing company is likely to lose the money they have invested in the form of support measures.

In the business service industry mutual dependency is created through various mechanisms. As in the insurance industry, the loss of direct contact with clients was particularly stressed. Since dependent self-employed workers in the business service industry are mainly high skilled and often rather specialised, the sourcing out of knowledge and the dependence on specialised skills are further issues that create problems for the company. As above, the appearance and success of dependent self-employed workers is seen as crucial for the brand and the reputation of the company.

In the freight industry we find that outsourcing companies are highly aware of the relational risk. Those companies who work with both employees and self-employed workers carry out sensible orders internally as they can control their employees more closely. In order to reduce the dependency upon one subcontractor and prevent a hold-up problem, most companies prefer to source out their business to several, small subcontractors.

6.6 Dependency, relational contracts and the creation of hybrid forms of organisational governance

In the introductory chapter of this book, we distinguished between economic and personal dependence. While economic dependence refers to the entrepreneurial risk that is transferred from the principal (i.e. the outsourcing company) to the agent (i.e. self-employed worker), personal dependence refers to dependence in terms of time, place and content of work and work processes. The last section has empirically documented how economic and personal dependence is created in dependent business relationships, highlighting that dependency is created both by formal and informal means.

The support methods illustrated above mainly create *economic* dependence since they tie the agent closely to the principal and reduce the value of outsider options due to high switching costs. Financial support helps the self-employed workers, on the one hand, to build up their business, but on the other hand considerably reduces the possibility to change contract partner, since the favourable conditions of financial support are linked to an existing contract. If the agents withdrew from the contract, they would be confronted with new, less favourable terms of repayment. Additionally, outsourcing companies financially support their agents to solve the principal-agent problem, that is to make sure that they work according to the companies' criteria. Thus, self-employed workers invest both money (e.g. office design, software, marketing material, equipment) and human resources (e.g. training) to fulfil these criteria, which in turn increases switching costs. Consequently, financial support enhances dependency by increasing the costs of alternative options. In sum, support measures that provoke long-term commitment strengthen dependency.

Assistance for accounting, IT, tax consultancy or business management, furthermore, binds the agent to the company since it has greater control over the agent. Managerial control over agents as described above generates *personal* dependence because it determines the way tied agents carry out their work. We have argued that company managers control the work of the self-employed workers, checking not only marketing material or customer files, but also whether the agents work according to regulatory or company rules. In addition, companies reported to check the accounting of their agents and may undertake customer surveys. These layers of managerial control, together with control via specific pecuniary or non-pecuniary incentives, allow the companies to strongly determine the work organisation of agents.

In Chapter 5 we argued that dependent business relationships use both an authority and a price control mechanism to reduce opportunism. On the one hand, control is executed using authority structures similar to those found in employment relationships, as described above. On the other hand, the price mechanism is fortified by the competition of other governance structures, further enhancing control. We have shown that most companies that work with closely tied self-employed workers also have employees (hierarchy) and deploy subcontractors from the spot market. The case studies have demonstrated is that competition from other channels enhances the control of the price mechanism by reducing the bargaining power of dependent self-employed workers.

However, these two control mechanisms are also strengthened by a third mechanism. In Chapter 5 we argued that dependency is not only created by formal but also by informal contracts. Indeed, interviews have shown that in all industries only some specific rights and duties of both parties are formally codified in the contract between the outsourcing company and the self-employed workers. Of course, we have seen that the contents of formal contracts vary not only between the industries but also between companies and even between the self-employed workers of the same company, depending on the negotiations between the two contract partners. However, most written contracts only regulate the basic framework of the business relationships. Basically, self-employed workers with more qualifications and experience in the business are able to negotiate a contract that allows them more autonomy. Yet outsourcing companies are well aware of the fact that they have to be very careful not to include any authority or routine mechanisms in the written contract. For instance – referring to the specific support measures discussed above – written contracts usually do *not* regulate issues such as training responsibilities, provision of business know-how and management skills, assistance in (or control of) accounting, IT, tax consultancy, details of regular business meetings with company managers or non-pecuniary incentive schemes. Furthermore, contracts do not normally define in detail how much of the administration surrounding the sale of products or services is expected to be carried out by the self-employed worker or by the outsourcing company (e.g. handling claims, exhorting customers in case of a delay in payment). The most important topics regulated by the private contract between a self-employed workers and a company is, first, the exclusiveness of the business relationship, second, the payment and, third, the external appearance. Some managers report that the contract also determines details of financial support, minimum turnover or whether and how self-employed workers are paid for their customer stock when one party terminates the contract.

We thus see that contracts mainly regulate clearly definable issues. Whether self-employed workers have broken the clause of exclusiveness or whether they have fulfilled a minimum turnover is both observable and contractible. Consequently, it is possible to include these topics in a formal contract. However, more complex matters such as how much management support or training are more difficult to clarify in a written contract. Additionally, it is not in the companies' interest to regulate any authority or control issues, in order to avoid conflict with legal regulations and exposure to opportunism. Thus, companies use informal, relational contracts to circumvent difficulties in formal contracting. In Chapter 5 we defined relational contracts as based on informal agreements, unwritten codes and understandings that powerfully affect the behaviour of the parties involved. The empirical evidence we have collected in the three industries shows that most of the issues that define the actual organisation of dependent outsourcing are based on informal agreements, unwritten codes and understandings. Furthermore, we found that many companies mainly recruit former employees. Hence, these companies build up business relations with their agents on the basis of existing social relations and common understandings, facilitating the establishment of relational contracts.

The differentiation between written and relational contracts also determines the observed mechanisms of conflict resolution. Those issues that are clearly written in contracts are, of course, enforceable by courts. However, conflicts concerning matters that are not contractible and, thus, are based on relational contracts are solved by the self-enforcing nature of relational contracts. Additionally, outsourcing companies use administrative fiat to solve conflicts. As analysed above, company managers control the daily work of the self-employed workers, checking files, accounting, marketing material and so on. Consequently, companies use administrative fiat if problems concerning these issues arise.

This partial hierarchical subordination not only creates dependency but also the imprecise position of self-employed workers in the organisational structure of the outsourcing company. Interviews with both managers and self-employed workers have depicted the hybrid position of the latter in the organisational structure of the companies. On the one hand, they work on the basis of a private business contract. On the other hand, they have a close relationship with the company which includes hierarchical elements, resulting in a hybrid status.

6.7 Power and trust in dependent business relations

In the last section we argued that dependency is created by both formal and relational contracts. It was also shown that relational contracts are self-enforcing since the short-term gains of cheating are smaller than the long-term gains of the business relation. Thus, relational contracts are powerful because they create commitment and trust.

Trust is one of the most frequently analysed characteristics of inter-organisational relations or networks (Gambetta 1988; Lane and Bachmann 1998; Bachmann 2001; Nooteboom 2002). Basically, this literature argues that only hybrid forms of coordination are based on trust as a central mode of control. Trust, it is argued, helps to overcome problems of opportunistic behaviour and incomplete contracting and, hence, produces an economic value. However, the vast literature on the issue of trust also demonstrates that the concept of trust is defined in numerous ways. While one string of research views trust as based on calculation and rationality (e.g. Coleman 1990; Hardin 1996; Gibbons 2000b), the other accentuates that trust is value- and norm-based (e.g. Granovetter 1985; Gambetta 1988; Lorenz 1999). We do not intend to directly take part in or to review this discussion,[13] but to concentrate instead on its relevance for the subject matter of this book. Consequently, this section asks which role trust plays in dependent business relations and which mode of trust is produced.

Grimshaw and Rubery (2005) argue that existing theories of inter-organisational contracting assume that organisations are treated as if they have the same status within networks. This assumption, so they claim, hides those differences in power that shape the kind of trusting relations that are established. It follows that 'in an economy with heterogeneous organizations, where the option of breaking from the agreement is more costlessly available to one partner than the other(s), power exists as an alternative mechanism to trust to control the structure and dynamics of inter-organisational contracting' (Grimshaw and Rubery 2005: 1042). Thus, they suggest that power drives out trust between unequal partners or, in other words, that trust and power are mutually exclusive in unequal business relationships (a similar argument can also be found in Nooteboom 2002: 88f and 199).

The empirical case studies above have without doubt shown that outsourcing companies are extremely powerful in relation to their dependent self-employed workers. Does this mean – in the logical context of Grimshaw and Rubery (2005) – that if companies are too powerful to be trusted, they have no incentive *not* to renege on their commitments? Are companies capable of making credible commitments to their self-employed workers and thus, of building up trust?

Research on the control mechanisms in business relationships shows that it is important to consider forms of trust between unequal parties since the majority of inter-organisational relations are based on *both* power *and* trust (Farrell 2004). We argue that trust is also generated in business relationships with strong asymmetries of trust, as observed in dependent business relationships.

According to Knight (1992) exercising power means affecting the alternatives available to the other party. We have seen that outsourcing companies exercise power over their self-employed workers by strongly affecting the alternatives available to them by using both formal (i.e. the contractual clause of exclusiveness) and informal (i.e. support measures that increase the costs of alternative options and control) means. This, in turn, affects the trustworthiness of the workers because they are interested in a long-term relationship. The discussion of the various support measures, such as financial support, has shown that the short-run value of reneging is lower than the long-run value of the relationship. Thus, we observe that these relational contracts are self-enforcing.

Since dependent self-employed workers are (forced to be) interested in a long-term relationship, they must eventually take the interests of the outsourcing companies into account. In other words, they have a strong incentive to behave in a trustworthy (or reliable) manner. Consequently, it is rational for the worker to behave trustworthily because of the long-term economic benefits (or, the other way around, the costs of the breakdown of the business relationship in the short run). The outsourcing company, in turn, trusts the worker because it knows that it is in the worker's interest to attend to the interests of the outsourcing company.

Hence, we observe trust despite unequal power. However, asymmetries of power may lead to asymmetries in trust relationships, and therefore affect the form of cooperation as argued by Grimshaw and Rubery (2005) and Farrell (2004). Our empirical evidence shows that outsourcing companies use these asymmetries of power to introduce hierarchical elements in order to increase their managerial control over workers. Thus, companies use their power to determine the structural framework of the business relationship. However, they must design a framework in which the workers have an incentive to trust and to behave trustworthily – otherwise it is not possible to reach a cooperative equilibrium from which both parties benefit. We suggest that this argument also holds when assuming a push effect (i.e. self-employed workers have been pushed into this labour market status by the external pressures of industrial restructuring and/or unemployment). The important point is that the structural frameworks of these dependent business relations are set up in such a way that both parties have an incentive to behave trustworthily. In sum, we observe trust in such business relationships because both parties are interested in continuing the relationship and have, therefore, to take the other's interest into account or, in other words, to behave in a trustworthy manner. As a result, trust can co-exist even when strong asymmetries of power are present, as observed in dependent business relations.

However, behaving in a trustworthy way depends on the value of alternative options or on how the parties value the relationship. If one party values the relationship less, it has less incentive to behave trustworthily. Consequently, trust also depends on the value of the relationship the partners offer as compared to alternative options (Nooteboom 2002; Farrell 2004). The limits of trust and commitment are therefore determined by the value the business relations produces for both parties. Workers with low productivity who thus win low profits for the outsourcing company will run into troubles. However, companies that offer contracts, which bring no additional benefits compared to alternative options, will find it hard to recruit self-employed workers. The interviews with managers and self-employed workers have shown that this is additionally strengthened by a reputational mechanism. If one insurance company treats their self-employed workers badly, they will find it difficult to recruit new, successful self-employed workers who are already working in the industry.

The trust we find in dependent business relations involves considered expectations about the interests of others to behave in a trustworthy manner. Trust will be observed as long as one party believes that the other party has an interest in fulfilling that trust. Trust here clearly deviates from trust in hybrid business relations. Dore (1983) and Lorenz (1999) have found in referring to goodwill trust or moral contracts. Furthermore, we cannot confirm Granovetter's (1985) argument that social content rather than institutional arrangements leads to trust and abstention from opportunism. Instead, we found that it is the institutional set-up of the dependent business relation that generates trust. Consequently, trust in dependent business relations is limited to very particular matters that are based on a quid pro quo logic.

6.8 Conclusions

This chapter brought together empirical research on dependent forms of self-employment in the British, Italian and Austrian insurance industry, the Italian and Austrian business service industry and the Austrian freight industry. It discussed the organizational governance of dependent forms of self-employment along the dimensions of dependency, relational contracts and trust. We analysed by which means dependency is created, what role relational contracts play and whether we observe trust in this asymmetrical power relationships.

In all the industries in the three countries, we have observed that dependent self-employment is increasingly used. The motives for sourcing out to self-employed workers and simultaneously integrating them rather strongly into the company are around issues of reducing costs for personnel by transforming fixed into variable costs and thus increasing financial flexibility as well as circumventing labour protection and thus profiting from more flexible working hours and reducing costs of labour protection.

Furthermore, we have analysed the creation of dependency in these work relationships. We have demonstrated that dependency is created not only by formal but also by informal means. The interviews have highlighted that companies offer their self-employed workers a wide range of support to solve the principal-agent problem. These support measures can be grouped into financial and know-how support. However, these support measures also tie the worker closer to the company, increasing the costs of alternative options and, thus, economic dependence. However, informal and formal control of tied agents determines how they carry out their work and, consequently, creates personal dependence. On the other hand, we have also argued that dependency is often a mutual one because outsourcing also means for companies to reduce managerial control, to increase risk exposure (e.g. the risk of damaging the brand) or to battle with lower loyalty.

Moreover, outsourcing companies use both authority and price control mechanisms to control self-employed workers and reduce opportunism, creating hybrid forms of organisational governance. Most control and support measures rely on informal, relational contracts that are self-enforcing because the short-term gain of reneging is smaller than the long-term benefit of the business relationship. Outsourcing companies increase the costs of alternative options, generating incentives for the worker to cooperate on a long-term basis. We have argued that this institutional structure generates calculative trust despite asymmetrical power relations.

7
Conclusions

7.1 Explaining dependent self-employment: an evaluation of the research questions

7.1.1 The key features of dependent business relationships

In Chapter 5 we have developed research questions that aim to explain the logic of dependent business relationships along the dimensions of the normative basis, the control mechanism, the methods of conflict resolution, the tone or climate, the amount of commitment and the degree of flexibility. The following sections evaluate these research questions according to the empirical findings of Chapter 6.

7.1.1.1 The normative basis of dependent self-employment

In Chapter 5 we have argued that dependent business relationships are based on both formal and relational contracts. Looking at dependent business relationships in the insurance, business service and freight industry in three countries, we have seen that formal contracts only regulate the basic framework of the relationship, while the details are managed by informal agreements, unwritten codes and understandings (or relational contracts). For instance, formal contracts determine the exclusiveness of the business relationship, the payment and, in some reported cases, also the details of the financial support, a minimum turnover or the treatment of the files of the customers after the termination of the contract. On the other side, formal contracts do not regulate issues such as the organisation of administration, training, provision of business know-how and management skills, assistance in (or control of) accounting, IT, tax matters, organisation of business meetings with company managers or non-pecuniary incentive schemes.

The rationales behind the simultaneous use of formal and relational contracts are the following. First, in order to avoid conflicts with legal regulations, outsourcing companies have to ensure not to include any authority or routine mechanisms in legal contracts that raise suspicion of an employment relation. Thus, they have an intrinsic interest in using a formal contract for the basic set-up of the business relationship and a relational contract that allows them to have a certain amount of control over their self-employed workers. Second, writing a complete contract would require to foresee and describe all the relevant contingencies. Moreover, the parties must be able to determine the actions to be taken for each possible contingency. Since it is not possible to write such contracts (and if possible, they would be too costly) due to bounded rationality problems, the parties have to restrict the formal contract to clearly definable issues as described above. Most issues of the actual organisation of the business relationship are therefore governed by relational contracts.

In Chapter 6 it has been argued that the normative basis of the business relationships described in this study is the agent's dependency upon the principal, expressed by formal and informal means. On the basis of the definition of dependency in the introductory chapter, we have empirically observed both forms of dependency, that is economic and personal dependency. Economic dependence is mainly created by the exclusiveness of the business relationship and financial support measures that tie the agent closely to the principal by increasing the costs of outsider options. Personal dependence is created by support measures that increase the control over the agent, such as assistance for accounting, IT, tax issues or business know-how. These different layers of control in combination with specific pecuniary and non-pecuniary incentive schemes strongly determine the organisation of work of tied agents.

7.1.1.2 The control mechanism

The empirical analysis in the insurance industry has demonstrated that outsourcing companies not only use elements of markets and hierarchies but also relational contracts to control their self-employed workers. First, control through the price mechanism is mainly exercised by asset ownership and distribution channel competition. The most important asset in the business relationships described in this study is the client bank (i.e. the files of the customers and, thus, the knowledge about customers) and the project-specific knowledge. In the insurance industry, the client bank is theoretically owned by the insurance companies. However, it is the insurance agent who has direct access to customers and thus an influence on the decisions of customers. Consequently, the tied agents de facto own the produced asset 'client bank'. This creates an implicit price for which the downstream party would have to buy the client bank after the termination of the business relationship. This price mechanism helps to provide the upstream party with the information they need to make coherent decisions and to motivate them to undertake activities that increase the value of their de facto asset, ideally enhancing efficiency and mitigating the principal-agent problem. Furthermore, competition by other governance structures – that is hierarchy (employees) and spot markets (occasional business partners) – strengthens the price mechanism by reducing the bargaining power of self-employed workers.

Second, as already argued above, the downstream party deploys authority (hierarchy) mainly by relational contracts in order not to get in conflict with legal regulations. Chapter 6 has revealed that outsourcing companies have developed sophisticated mechanisms of controlling the work of self-employed workers. The main source of control is regular meetings with company managers as well as bureaucratic checks by the supervisors. Moreover, interviewees have reported that control is executed through trustees (such as chartered accountants), customer surveys, training obligations or internal regulations of market appearance. Subtler layers of control are specific pecuniary (e.g. commission structure) and non-pecuniary (e.g. contests) incentive schemes. The authority mechanism is, additionally, facilitated by the fact that most insurance companies deploy individuals of their former direct sales force and can thus apply firm-specific routines.

Third, dependent business relationships are controlled by relational contracts. In Chapter 5, we have argued that relational contracts have two major aims in dependent business relationships. On the one hand, they help to circumvent difficulties in formal contracting and to be compliant with legal rules as already discussed above. On the other hand, they provide incentives for both parties not to behave opportunistically. The non-specificity of relational contracts implies that they are not enforceable by courts. Consequently, they must be self-enforcing, which means that the short-run value of reneging must be less than the long-run value of the relationship, thus reducing opportunistic behaviour. Interviews have proven that the business relationship between outsourcing companies and their self-employed workers is organised in a way so that both parties profit in the longer term. For instance, the self-employed workers get better conditions, higher payment and have less hierarchical control the longer (and better) the business relationship goes. However, we found that this mechanism is stronger in the insurance and the freight industry and weaker in the business service industry, which is strongly based on project work. Further, the conditions of the financial support improve over time, reducing the dependency due to credits. Of course, also the outsourcing companies profit from a long-term perspective of the business relationship since the discounted (or present) value of training and recruiting costs as well as costs of supporting self-employed agents decrease over time. In sum, one of the specific characteristics of dependent business relationships is the interplay of different layers of control. The long-term incentive structure of relational contracts is fortified by hierarchies and the market mechanisms.

7.1.1.3 Methods of conflict resolution

Despite the control exercised by relational contracts, hierarchical and market structures and the resulting mitigation of the principal-agent problem, conflicts between the upstream and the downstream parties regularly occur. Examples of conflicts are a low quality of customer service, the sale of unsuitable products, an inappropriate external appearance on the market, the breach of the clause of exclusiveness or a slow information flow. This raises the question how conflicts are solved in dependent business relationships.

Basically, the resolution of conflicts is determined by the separation of formal and implicit relational contracts. Conflicts that relate to issues that are clearly defined in a formal contract are enforceable by third parties such as courts. However, as we have discussed above, formal contracts only regulate the basic framework of the business relationship. Consequently, third party enforceability refers only to some basic issues such as the exclusiveness of the contract or the amount of the commission for products sold.

Conflicts concerning issues that are governed by implicit relational contracts (e.g. the quality of customer service and the appearance on the market) are solved by administrative fiat and/or the self-enforcing nature of relational contracts. Interviews have proven that these conflicts are solved in a similar way as conflicts with employees. If the outsourcing company finds that self-employed workers do not work according to the implicit relational contract, the company manager in charge (or the 'supervisor') will discuss the matter with the worker and if no subsequent changes are observable after some time, the company cancels the contract.

7.1.1.4 Tone or climate

The climate of dependent business relationships is both bureaucratic and characterised by mutual benefits produced by self-enforcing relational contracts. As argued above, bureaucracy and administrative fiat plays a crucial role in dependent business relationship. We have seen that outsourcing companies have developed a large range of bureaucratic control over their self-employed workers similar to employment relationships. This is additionally strengthened by the fact that many companies supervise their workers through the same managers that control employees. Moreover, most tied agents were previously employed by the same company, also reinforcing the bureaucratic climate.

Nevertheless, this study has also shown that the nature of self-enforcing relational contracts creates mutual benefits in the long run and thus trust. We have argued that, on the one side, self-employed workers have an incentive to behave trustworthily because they are interested in a long-term relationship due to the high costs of alternative options in the short run. The outsourcing company, on the other side, trusts the worker because it takes the rationales of the worker into account. Thus, we found that the institutional framework of the dependent business relationships we have described in this study produces incentives for both parties to behave trustworthily despite the asymmetries of power. The resulting trust is defined as calculative, rational trust, where parties behave 'as if' they trusted the other party due to the institutional framework of the business relationship.

7.1.1.5 Commitment

The amount of commitment the business parties generate is strongly determined by the underlying self-enforcing relational contracts and the resulting creation of trust. The downstream party is interested in getting a high-value work from the upstream party. Since it is difficult to write a contract, which determines high-value work (despite the fact that it may be observable), the parties agree upon relational contracts that provide – as discussed above – the necessary incentives to carry out work with an observable but non-contractible high value due to the long-term value of the relationship. Hence, the nature of long-term relational contracts provides incentives to show a high level of commitment in order to profit from future payoffs. Additionally, the hierarchical control mechanism in dependent business relationships forces the upstream party to show a substantial amount of commitment in order to retain the business contract.

7.1.1.6 Degree of flexibility

We have seen that deploying dependent agents can be seen as the start of an investment in a long-term relationship. On the one hand, the downstream party financially and organisationally supports the upstream party in order to have control over the upstream party and to create ties and thus dependency. However, this implies that the downstream party loses a certain amount of flexibility due to high hiring and firing costs of dependent agents. On the other hand, the downstream party (partly) transfers risk to the upstream party and transforms fixed into variable costs, gaining financial flexibility. We have seen that this is a major incentive for firms to create dependent forms of outsourcing.

7.1.2 The factors determining the creation of dependent business relationships

In Chapter 5 we have also theoretically analysed the factors determining the creation of dependent business relationships. On the basis of relevant sociological approaches to business organisations, we have identified issues of resource dependency, environmental and institutional changes, imitative behaviour, routines and norms as well as the influence of the state as pivotal for the creation of dependent business relationships. The following sections evaluate these research questions on the basis of the empirical findings of the previous chapter.

7.1.2.1 Managing resource dependency

In Chapter 5 we discussed the resource dependence approach which argues that firms reduce their external resource dependence by introducing elements of authority into the market. This strategy allows the firm to gain stronger control over critical resources, reducing uncertainty. Chapter 6 has proven that outsourcing companies use dependent outsourcing to benefit from the advantages of outsourcing while (partly) avoiding its disadvantages by introducing elements of authority. On the one hand, outsourcing means to (partly) transfer the entrepreneurial risk to the worker, to transform fixed into variable costs thus gaining financial flexibility, to circumvent labour and social security law, to weaken the bargaining power of internal labour, to circumvent institutionalised hierarchical structures and to increase incentive pay structures. On the other hand, sourcing out workers through dependent forms of outsourcing mitigates some disadvantages of outsourcing such as the loss of control and loyalty and vulnerability to opportunism. Chapter 6 illustrated that companies introduce hierarchical elements into the outsourcing relationship by controlling their self-employed workers' agent using administrative fiat, but also self-enforcing relational contracts which establish 'trust' and loyalty. Companies use various control mechanisms to determine the work process such as the control of accounting or marketing material. Consequently, they reduce the uncertainty that is usually connected with outsourcing by establishing long-term relational contracts and hierarchical structures.

7.1.2.2 The influence of environmental changes

Chapter 6 has made evident that the decision to deploy dependent self-employed workers was also heavily influenced by changing environmental conditions. All three industries investigated have been confronted with fundamental changes in the industrial environment. For instance, Austrian insurance companies saw a dramatic increase in competition through deregulation aimed at opening the market following accession to the European Union. This development has led to pressure to reduce costs and increase flexibility. Consequently, companies searched for new modes of governance which allowed them to adapt to the new environment and introduced tied agency. In the British insurance industry, re-regulation of the sales process following the consequences of deregulation in the 1980s has demanded tighter control over sales agents. This development basically had three effects on the distribution of insurance products. First, some insurance companies that previously worked with tied agents ceased to deploy (or reduced) them. Second, deploying tied agents is a shrinking option for insurance companies. Third, insurance companies have progressively increased their use of IFAs and insurance brokers in order to source out not only labour but also legal liability.

7.1.2.3 The influence of institutional changes

We have seen that labour law and industrial regulation partly explain the different outcomes in the three countries. The differences between labour and social security law are a major reason why we observe different outcomes across countries. In Italy and Austria, the highly regulated labour law in combination with high social security contributions and labour taxes provides strong incentives to source out labour. In the UK, in contrast, these incentives are comparatively few. Especially in the insurance industry we have seen that the industrial regulation of tied agency – and, thus, the legal feasibility of establishing dependent business relations – considerably differs between the countries under investigation. Italian and Austrian insurance law recognises composite insurers, which allows insurance agents to sell insurance products from both the general and the life insurance business. However, although Austrian insurance law permits tied agents, it does not regulate tied agency, thus increasing the incentives for insurers to benefit from this legal void. British insurance law, on the contrary, distinguishes between general and life insurers. While tied agents in the life business are only allowed to sell the products of one life insurer, tied agents in the general business are able to offer products of up to six general insurers. Thus, dependent self-employment is mainly restricted to the life insurance business in the UK.

Nevertheless, companies do not necessarily adapt in similar ways to laws and regulations. So far, we have argued that the regulatory environment provides more incentives for dependent outsourcing in Italy and Austria than in the UK. The empirical investigation in Chapter 6 has indeed shown that Austrian insurance companies use dependent forms of outsourcing more intensively than their British counterparts. However, we have also observed organisational diversity in the three countries. Thus, national laws and regulations do not necessarily lead to similar organisational adaptations. This empirical observation is caused by factors such as diverse cultural-historical development of the firms and their institutionalisation but also by the influence of internationalisation (e.g. when foreign mother companies introduce new governance structures). In the Austrian insurance industry, for instance, it was the companies with a tied agent system in the country of origin that pioneered tied agency in Austria as a result of pressures to do so from the mother company. This leads to organisational homogenisation across countries but also to organisational diversity within national borders to some extent.

7.1.2.4 The role of imitative behaviour

Especially in the insurance industry, we have seen that imitative behaviour played a crucial role. Chapter 6 has highlighted that the radical change in governance structures of Austrian insurance companies towards dependent outsourcing was also strongly influenced by imitation. In Chapter 5 we discussed new institutional theory which argues that mimetic behaviour is often a result of uncertainty. We have shown that the adaptation of dependent outsourcing in the Austrian insurance industry was heavily based on imitative behaviour. The insurer that was the first to introduce the tied agent system in Austria entered the market at a time when the insurance business had been strongly restructured following deregulation as already mentioned above. The innovative behaviour of the new market entrant during this period of uncertainty due to regulative and competitive transformations induced most major insurance companies to introduce tied agency.

7.1.2.5 The role of organisational routines and norms

The establishment of dependent self-employment was also facilitated by the fact that the most outsourcing companies initially mainly recruited from their employees. Thus, they were able to build up business relations with their self-employed workers on the basis of existing social relations and common understandings, facilitating the establishment of trust. Expressed differently, companies used organisational routines and norms known to both parties. For instance, in order to use well-established routines and norms, most companies deploy the same hierarchical structure for employees and dependent self-employed workers so that the same company managers are responsible for both.

7.1.2.6 The influence of the state

Comparing different countries allows us, furthermore, to move beyond the analysis of the firm and the industry towards a focus on the influence of the state. As discussed above, the observed organisational changes within the three industries were heavily determined by the state that changed the market rules. In Austria, we saw a strong increase in competition in a formerly strongly protected market due to deregulatory measures (especially in the insurance and the freight industries). In the UK, in contrast, a tighter regulation of the sales process of insurance products due to previous market failures reduced incentives to source out labour without simultaneously sourcing out legal liability. In Italy, companies massively started to reduce insider protection by transferring workers outside of the highly protected area. Thus, we argue that the transformations in the observed markets were a result of exogenous forces induced by the state. Furthermore, we have argued that the costs of Italian and Austrian labour and social law additionally increase the incentives for outsourcing, while British companies have less motivation to do so with respect to labour costs.

The division of employment and self-employment in a legal system indirectly involves an assessment of how certain social and economic risks are to be shared between employers, workers and the state. While employees have access to specific social security benefits and the protection of certain expectations of continuing security of income and employment, self-employed persons have only restricted or no access to these social benefits. However, employees do not have the same opportunities as the self-employed to set off their work-related expenditures against income tax (Burchell et al. 1999).

7.2 The borders of dependent self-employment and legal regulation

Outsourcing and subcontracting is not a new phenomenon in the organisation of labour. Rather, the subcontracting system was the dominant market form in the late 18th and during the 19th century. In the 20th century, employment became the dominant form of labour organisation. Although the market has still been seen as an efficient and flexible solution for transactions, the employment relationships emerged.

Marsden (1999: 23–27) sees five major reasons for this development. First, employing workers on the basis of an open-ended employment contract guarantees employers availability of labour when it is needed. Especially in times of high labour demand, the subcontracting system was riddled with a high 'labour turnover, absenteeism and general instability'. Second, the subcontracting system lacked the incentives of firm-specific skill acquisition. The subcontractors had no interest in investing in skills to the particular needs of a specific employer since a productivity improvement would have only created a hold-up situation due to post-contractual opportunism. Third, mistreatment of capital equipment in order to maximise short-term output increasingly became a problem with rising capital investments. Fourth, the lack of attachment in the subcontracting system increased transactions costs such as negotiating new contracts or finding new contractors. Finally, a common phenomenon of the subcontracting system was the social disorder due to the uncertainty of contracts, high earning differentials among workers, competitive bargaining and short-term employment.

Marsden (1999) argues that these problems attached to the subcontracting system became increasingly important with the industrial changes of the 20th century. Fordist mass production of standardised goods, high capital investments as well as increasing and stable demand led to the emergence of standard full-time, open-ended employment relationships (especially for male workers), embedded in vertically structured, bureaucratic organisations. Eventually, the institutions of the welfare state, which have been growing in importance since the 1950s, were built on the basis of the predominance of employment and labour, and social security law helped to institutionalise the employment relationship (e.g. Crouch 1999; Audretsch and Thurik 2001; Supiot 2001).

Despite the recent changes of product and labour markets (see Chapter 1), the vast majority of work relationships are still based on employment contracts. Marsden (1999: 27) suggests that this is due to 'the great flexibility of the employment relationship, and the considerable benefits it provides to both parties'. An employment relationship sets the limits of managerial authority to direct work so that firms gain sufficient flexibility while providing workers with sufficient protection. However, the re-emergence of outsourcing and subcontracting activities suggests that recent changes in product and labour markets have a significant effect on the organisation of labour. Firms do not longer 'hoard' labour but have introduced more flexible forms of work such as agency work, part-time work, fixed-term work and dependent forms of subcontracting. High and persistent levels of unemployment and the downsizing of the welfare state have, furthermore, weakened workers' threat point for gaining protection.

Reviewing the five reasons for the emergence of the employment relationship as discussed in Marsden (1999) with respect to the results of this study, we find that dependent forms of outsourcing are able to, first, guarantee employers the availability of labour by long-term, relational contracts, second, create incentives of firm-specific skill acquisition by both training opportunities and obligations, third, solve the problem of capital mistreatment by transferring ownership and, fourth, reducing transaction costs by long-term, relational contracts. However, the fifth reason – that is the social disorder due to high uncertainty – is only partly solved by dependent forms of outsourcing due to the weak legal protection of dependent self-employed workers in most European countries. Still, only a small group of workers is affected so far. Nevertheless, we have identified dependency, power asymmetries and the weak legal protection as a major problem for dependent self-employed workers. Even so, this study has demonstrated that dependent forms of outsourcing are also capable of setting limits to managerial authority, giving the outsourcing firm sufficient flexibility while providing workers with sufficient protection through long-term relational contracts. Thus we argue that market relationships that are laced with elements of hierarchy can show very similar characteristics to employment relationships. Marsden (1999) draws a too narrow picture of markets, seeing them as transaction forms based on an ex ante definition of obligations. Consequently, there must be other forces at work that explain why the employment relationship is still the predominant form of work organisation.

In other words, the limits of dependent form of outsourcing are set by various constraints as discussed in Chapter 5. On the one side, the border to spot market relationships is determined by the discounted value of the relationship. If the transaction is either fairly standardised in terms of the product and the process or has a low frequency, the value of the business relationship itself will be low because there are no incentives to invest in the relationship. Thus, spot markets are usually a logical (or efficient) form to handle standardised transactions or transactions with a low frequency. On the other side, the border to employment is shaped by both the value of the incentives from asset ownership and the discounted value of risk-sharing. In Chapter 6 we have argued that the asset – know-how about customers and project-specific know-how – is de facto owned by the dependent self-employed workers, which increases their motivation to raise the value of the asset. As a result, if the value of the incentives from asset ownership and the value of risk-sharing are higher than the value of an employment relationship, the firm will decide to source labour out on a dependent basis. The value of an employment relationship is determined, firstly, by the closer control of employees and, secondly, by the institutions in which employment relationships are embedded. For instance, due to factors such as the regulations of labour law, the limits of managerial authority, the societal rules of employment and organisational routines, both workers and firms know what to expect from an employment relationship, reducing uncertainty (Marsden 1999).

However, these borders between different forms of work are, of course, strongly determined by legal constraints. As argued in Chapters 1 and 3, the re-emergence of outsourcing and the creation of dependent forms of self-employment has resulted in an active legal and political debate on possible reforms on a national, EU-wide and international level. So far, labour law in most European countries is founded on a distinction between workers' subordination (employment) and independent work on a self-employed basis. However, as discussed above, fundamental changes in the organisation of production call for legal reforms. The binary distinction between subordinate employment and self-employment no longer reflects the work organisation of the 'Post-fordist' firm. Not only has the technical and operational independence of employees risen ('work empowerment'), but also self-employed persons working closely with a main principal are observed to show characteristics of dependence (Supiot 2001; Perulli 2003; Sciarra 2004).

However, Sciarra (2004) and Perulli (2003) point out that it is most difficult to assess dependent forms of self-employment due to its complexity and ambiguity. On the one hand, we observe different levels of dependency and autonomy, and on the other, very heterogeneous circumstances of industries and professions. The motivation of this study was to show how dependency is created in some specific industries and professions in three different countries in order to draw some broader conclusions on the re-emergence of dependent forms of self-employment.

According to the legal tests that European courts apply to prove the labour market status of an individual (see Chapter 3), we find that the circumstances of dependent self-employed workers in all industries investigated are substantially close to that of employees. First, dependent self-employed workers are strongly controlled by the downstream party (control test). Second, they are de facto considerably integrated into the business of the downstream party (integration test). Third, they bear a large part of the risk due to the economic dependency (dependency test). Finally, they are more or less obliged to accept any work that is offered (mutuality of obligation test). However, due to the unequal power of the business partners and financial constraints of the upstream party, only few cases, where conflicts arise, are brought to court. Furthermore, most issues of the business relationship are governed by implicit relational contracts, complicating the use of legal tests.

Most labour lawyers agree that dependent self-employed workers lack labour protection. For instance, the Supiot Report (2001: 220) stresses that 'those workers who cannot be regarded as employed persons, but are in a situation of economic dependence vis-à-vis a principal, should be able to benefit from the social rights to which this dependence entitles them'. However, there are different approaches proposed in the legal literature on how to expand labour protection to dependent self-employed workers. First, creating a new third category of employment, second, full extension of labour law to also cover dependent self-employed workers and, third, creating a circle of basic social rights applicable to all work relationships and additional circles for protection of different kinds of work (Engblom 2003: Chapter 4; Perulli 2003: 112–116).

There is strong evidence that the European Union will follow the third approach – as proposed by Supiot (2001), Perulli (2003) and Sciarra (2004) in their reports to the European Commission. Supiot (2001: 54f) defines social rights according to three major concentric circles.[1] The first circle covers basic universal social rights guaranteed to all individuals irrespective of work (e.g. health insurance, family benefits, equal treatment for men and women). A second circle defines additional rights for persons in occupational activities (e.g. health and safety regulations, anti-discrimination law). Finally, a third circle of protection for workers in subordination, providing a scale of rights related to the degree of the subordination (Supiot 2001: 55). However, it is important to note that Supiot (2001: 22) defines 'para-subordination' only in terms of economic dependence which means that protection is graded according to the degree of economic dependence in this approach.

With respect to the findings of our study, this approach has two major disadvantages. While it appears to be unproblematic to define the outer circle, legal theorists will find it difficult to determine the border between the inner and the second circle and to draw the line between different degrees of dependency. This study has shown that dependency does not only refer to economic but also to personal dependence. Thus, similar to employees, dependent self-employed workers may be economically dependent *and* subject to subordination, which complicates drawing the line. Furthermore, we have seen that both forms of dependency are created by formal and informal means, making it even more problematic to define dependency. Another problem with this approach is that creating a legal definition for dependent self-employed workers and assigning rights to this group creates costs. These costs, in turn, generate incentives to circumvent the law by placing workers far out in the circles.

Consequently, an important element in counterbalancing dependency is the entitlement of basic rights to all persons in employment. Of course, it would be politically unrealistic to presume that the EU or European nation states would go further than granting basic rights to this group. Another point is that defining dependency only on the basis of economic dependency would not capture the dependent element of the business relationships described in this study. Thus, it is important to apply a multi-level test. Finally, the complexity and ambiguity of dependent forms of self-employment due to very heterogeneous circumstances of industries and professions enhances the importance of collective agreements at both the national and the EU level.

7.3 Within-system diversity and mixed governance structures

In the introductory chapter we have argued that the 'varieties of capitalism' literature is too rigid in the dualistic view of organising capitalism.

In contrast, we have found that specific combinations of institutional forces produce the particular result of a higher degree of outsourcing in the Italian and Austrian than in the British insurance industry, which would not have been predicted by the 'varieties of capitalism' literature. For instance, high labour protection measures in combination with a legal grey zone of dependent self-employment and the weak regulation of the sales process in Italy and Austria increase the incentives for firms to source out labour on a dependent basis. Thus, it is a mix of high employment protection and low industrial regulation that produces this result (i.e. within-system diversity). In the UK, on the contrary, a mix of low labour protection for employees and a high regulation of the sales process creates an incentive to either employ agents to have strong control over the sales process or to source out labour on an independent basis (i.e. independent financial advisers) in order to source out the risk that is related to the sales process, too. Finally, we have demonstrated that the mixing of organisational governance structures (again within-system diversity) creates new forms of organisational governance that cannot be explained by the dualistic view of the 'varieties of capitalism' literature.

In Chapter 5 we have argued that dependent forms of outsourcing can neither be explained by the traditional market-versus-hierarchy approach nor by theoretical research on hybrids. Instead, we have put forward the argument that dependent outsourcing introduces elements of hierarchies into the market by using relational contracts. The market-versus-hierarchy approach sees these two different modes of governance as two alternative mechanisms for performing tasks, arguing that firms choose the mode associated with the lowest transaction costs. The trend of vertical disintegration and the emergence of business networks since the 1980s, however, has stimulated research on hybrid forms, that is inter organisational relationships mainly based on relational contracts.

Williamson (1985) describes the dimensions of asset specificity, uncertainty and frequency as being critical for the establishment of a specific governance system. The argument is that these three dimensions together determine the governance structure. The higher the degree of these three dimensions, the higher the probability of vertical integration (hierarchy). However, this study has proven that firms find other ways than vertical integration to mitigate problems of hold-up and opportunism. The key argument is that firms have established governance structures based on markets, hierarchies *and* relational contracts so that they are able to keep a substantial amount of control despite of sourcing out transactions. In other words, by creating close (dependent) ties, the downstream party improves the trade-off between incentives (typically linked to market transactions) and control (typically linked to hierarchy). Relational contracts are not only used to deal with non-contractible issues as suggested by the organisational economics literature but also to increase the power of the downstream party through control and dependency.

The organisational economics literature argues that every transaction can be linked to a most efficient organisational arrangement. This study, however, has found that it is misleading to investigate single transactions, as some are embedded in others. The case studies presented in Chapter 6 have shown that firms simultaneously make, buy *and* cooperate rather than follow the classical make-or-buy dichotomy. We have seen that transactions that are controlled by one mechanism have an impact on transactions controlled by another mechanism. For instance, insurance companies simultaneously use different distribution channels in order to foster competition between the different channels, which mitigates the bargaining power of the upstream parties. Information gained in one channel through similar control mechanisms is used to reduce uncertainty and opportunistic bargaining in other channels.

Economic models of the boundaries of the firm mainly analyse the efficiency of transactions and do neither refer to the issues of 'control' and 'risk' nor to environmental influences on organisational structures. In this study, however, we have found that the main logic of dependent forms of outsourcing is to introduce elements of hierarchy into the outsourcing relationship. This organisational structure allows firms to source out part of the risk while keeping control over their agents. Of course it is the legal system that determines to what extent risk can be transferred. We have argued that dependent self-employment is still widely unregulated in most countries. Surely, this is partly explained by the administrative lag caused by the time that is usually needed to legally meet new societal developments, but also due to the complexity of the issue as argued above. Another part of this story, however, is that governments purposely choose not to regulate the grey zone between independent self-employment and dependent employment in order to foster business start-ups.

Closely connected with the issue of legally regulating dependent forms of self-employment is the regulation of employment and social security law. We have argued that employment and social security law powerfully drive the incentives for outsourcing in an economy. While a strongly regulated Italian and Austrian labour market induces firms to circumvent regulations by sourcing out labour on a close-tie basis, the British labour market regulation seems to provide less incentives to do so. Another important source of environmental influence is industrial regulation. This case study has proven that the specific industrial regulation in the three countries analysed strongly explains the different outcomes between them. While British insurers need to tighten the control over their agents due to industrial regulation (leading to hierarchy), their Austrian counterparts are mainly concerned with gaining financial flexibility and improving incentive structures, leading to dependent outsourcing.

In addition to influences from the macro- and the meso-levels, we also found evidence for micro-level factors that are important in understanding the reasons for dependent forms of outsourcing. We have claimed that factors such as the cultural-historical development of firms and the influence of international mother companies have also an effect on the organisation of the governance system. Finally, we have identified herd behaviour and imitation in an uncertain environment as an important factor in explaining the massive trend in outsourcing in Austria. Consequently, the interaction of the institutional factors on all three levels determine the organisational structures of firms.

This study has shown that the dimensions of risk and control are crucial in analysing both the boundaries of the firm and the boundaries of the employment relationship. Firms are blurring their established boundaries not only by forms of collaboration with independent firms as stressed by recent work of organisational theorists but also by sourcing out labour and establishing close ties with the outsourced self-employed workers.

Notes

1 The blurring boundaries between employment and self-employment

1. *Outsourcing* (*Dependent*) and *subcontracting* (*dependent*) are used synonymously in this book to describe the process of contracting out part of the production to other firms. The notion *dependent self-employment* refers to the employment status of the dependent subcontractor.
2. We use the terms *subcontractors, agents, self-employed* (*dependent*) *workers* synonymously in this book.
3. The expressions *principal* and *company* (*outsourcing*) are used interchangeably throughout the text.
4. These analytical definitions, however, do not necessarily fit with legal definitions. For legal definitions and problems in the three countries investigated in this study see Chapter 3.
5. Even if we assume that the dependent self-employed person also does occasional extra jobs, he or she nevertheless generates the vast majority of his or her income from the business relationship with the main contractor.
6. Consequently, we use the terms *business relationship* and *work relationship* interchangeably throughout the text.
7. See Chapter 6 for an empirical investigation of dependent self-employment in the freight industry.
8. Of course, dependent self-employed workers have the possibility to buy private insurance protection against the risk of an interruption in business arising through no fault of the worker.
9. See Chapter 6 of this book for a detailed analysis of dependent self-employment in the insurance industry.
10. This depends on the tax system, however. Nevertheless, in most European countries self-employed persons are able to set off a larger amount of their work-related expenditures against income tax compared to employees.
11. Typically associated with closely connected firms (dense networks of cross-shareholding, membership in influential employers' associations), strong trade unions, powerful works councils, high levels of employment protection, less fluid labour markets, longer job tenures, coordinated wage-setting, collaborative training schemes and standard-setting by industry associations (Hall and Gingerich 2004).
12. Typically associated with transparent equity markets and dispersed shareholding, weak industrial regulation, weak trade unions, low employment protection, fluid labour markets, individual wage-setting, lack of collaborative training programmes and competitive markets (Hall and Gingerich 2004).

2 Work on the border between employment and self-employment

1. Note, however, that according to international guidelines, most statistics on self-employment exclude unpaid family workers. They are not treated as entrepreneurs, but rather as assistants of entrepreneurs, probably leading to an understatement of the true level of women's entrepreneurship.
2. We regard franchising as a special case of dependent self-employment because the relationship between the franchisor and the franchisee are mostly based on written explicit contracts that are often standardised as shown in Felstead (1993). Dependent self-employed workers, however, do not necessarily have strong explicit contracts with their employing entity as demonstrated in the empirical study in Chapter 6.
3. Examples of contractual terms are that the franchisor reserves the right to take over franchisees if performance is not sufficiently high or that the franchisor may locate new franchisees close to existing ones.
4. A total of 40 per cent of the self-employed individuals in this survey entered self-employment due to redundancy. Nevertheless, a clear majority subsequently came to prefer self-employment.
5. Canada (Charest 2003) and the USA (Philips 2003) are found to be strongly dependent on the various state regulations and the unionisation of the area where the construction firm is located.

3 The institutional factor: Labor law and regulations across Europe

1. Council Directive 97/81/EC of 15 December 1997 concerning the Framework Agreement on part-time work concluded by UNICE, CEEP and the ETUC.
2. Council Directive 99/70/EC of 28 June 1999 concerning the Framework Agreement on fixed-term work concluded by UNICE, CEEP and the ETUC. The UK implemented this directive in 2002 by the Fixed-term Employees (Prevention of Less Favourable Treatment) Regulations (SI 2002/2034), which transform fixed-term contract into contracts of indefinite duration under specific conditions (Freedland 2003: 317).
3. The historical legal dichotomy of the categories 'employees' and 'self-employed persons' – and the social protection or non-protection that goes along with these categories – is based on the Fordist production regime and the paternalistic welfare state as observed between the late 1940s and the late 1970s. Both changing employment systems and welfare state regimes demand a conceptual change in national labour laws (Crouch 1999; Collins 1990).
4. Please note that, in a *legal* perspective, false self-employment differs from dependent self-employment since the latter refers to – per definition – unlawful work relationships.
5. Council Directive 2000/78/EC of 27 November 2000 establishing a general framework for equal treatment in employment and occupation.
6. Freedland (2003) and Burchell et al. (1999) provide a comprehensive overview of the factors British courts take into account when deciding the issue of employment statuses.

7. See Freedland (2003: Chapter 1) for a thorough discussion of the historical development of the expansion of the boundaries of employment protection.
8. The Working Time Regulations 1998, SI 1998/1833, Reg 2(1).
9. National Minimum Wage Act 1998, Section 54(3).
10. Disability Discrimination Act 1996, Section 68.
11. The Part-time Workers (Prevention of Less Favourable Treatment) Regulations SI 2000/1551, Art 2.
12. Employment Rights Act 1996, Section 13.
13. British legislation introduced the category of 'workers' to cover a wider range of subordinate employees, but also contracts for the personal execution of any work or labour whereby the party receiving the service or work 'is not by virtue of the contract that of a client or customer of any profession or business undertaking carried on by the individual' (The main statutory definition of 'worker' set out in Section 230(3) of the Employment Rights Act 1996, quoted in Freedland 2003: 24). Thus, this definition excludes those who sell products or services that do not result from their own work (Engblom 2003: 163).
14. As, for instance, in Italy or Germany.
15. The classical legal distinction between employees and self-employed persons in the UK is that the former works under a 'contract of employment', while the latter has a 'contract for services' (Freedland 2003: Chapter 1).
16. Recognising that there are various types of work relationships which cut across the distinction of 'contract of employment' and the semi-dependent 'worker' contract, Freedland (2003: 26–35) proposes to establish the category of the 'personal employment contract'. Freedland (2003: 28) defines this category as 'comprising contracts for employment or work to be carried out normally in person and not in the conduct of an independent business or professional practice'. Although this definition is close to that of the definitions of 'workers' and 'employed persons', it relaxes the personal character of the work to be carried out and it includes those with a contract of employment, establishing a new approach to subsume both employees (i.e. contract of employment) and semi-dependent workers into one legal category (with subcategories for both types of work).
17. In the UK, the scope of labour law for employees is much more restricted than in Italy and Austria. Employment protection in the UK depends on the numbers of hours worked per week and the length of continuous service.
18. That is, whether the 'worker' has to carry out the work personally or not.
19. For instance, collective agreements, firm agreements, working time act, protection in case of insolvency of the firm, holiday act and equal treatment act.
20. They are excluded, for example, from collective agreements and do not get any money in case of illness or when they are prevented from carrying out their work. The working time act, the health protection measures, the maternity leave act and so on are not applicable for WerkvertragsnehmerInnen.
21. Disputes in court mainly refer to cases where formally self-employed individuals try to get recognition of an employee status in order to benefit from employment protection that only cover employees (e.g. unfair dismissal) (Eiro 2002).

22. The right to receive a pension is obtained at the age of 57 years after a minimum of 5 years of contribution to the fund. The minimum amount of the pension is given by the non-contributory pension ('pensione sociale') plus 20 per cent (INPS 2001). The annual contribution of collaborators is around half of the contribution paid by employees with the same wage. Thus, the future pensions of collaborators will be substantially lower than that of employees.
23. Mainly in the public sector, in sport activities, for business agents and for firms' auditors.
24. The initial contribution to the INPS fund was set at 10 per cent of gross income (1/3 paid by the worker and 2/3 paid by the employer) which was subsequently increased to 13 per cent (in 1997) and will reach 19 per cent by 2018, compared with 33 per cent of employees.
25. The new Italian left-wing government who came into power in 2006 plans to enlarge the employment and social security rights of co.co.co. workers.
26. Two exemptions refer to an anti-discrimination and a freedom of speech law (Engblom 2003: 102).

4 The supply side: Identifying workers on the border between employment and self-employment

1. For a discussion of the research design see Chapter 6.
2. While the number of *Neue Selbständige* in the 4th quarter of 1998 was 7722, this rose to 24 120 in the 1st quarter of 2002. Similarly, the number of *freie DienstnehmerInnen* rose from 9611 in January 1998 to 25 168 in May 2002. Of course, changes in legislation may also have had an influence on rising numbers.
3. The BLFS relies on the self-reporting of the employment status, which does not necessarily correspond to the legal classification. Burchell et al.'s (1999) survey of a representative sample of 4000 workers found that 30 per cent have an ambiguous employment status, and that 8 per cent of them were legally classified as 'self-employed'. Another classification problem could arise from the fact that some individuals may be classified as employees in tax issues, but as self-employed in employment issues (or vice versa) and it is not clear which labour market status these individuals report for the BLFS. In addition, we might classify some 'genuine' self-employed as dependent self-employed because of temporary fluctuations in the number employed or the number of customers, or both.
4. In the INPS data it is necessary to distinguish between actual and registered contributors. Since it is not required to withdraw from the fund at the end of a contract, the number of contributors is lower than the number of registered workers.
5. Rilevazione Continua delle Forze Lavoro (RCFL).
6. 'Co.pro.' are included into the 'co.co.co.' category in the ILFS.
7. By using the information on different rates of contribution to the fund it is possible to identify 'pure' collaborators also in the INPS dataset (Berton et al. 2005).

8. In 2002, the INPS data show that 46.2 per cent of contributors are women, while they represent only 37.7 per cent of the total labour force.
9. In Italy, two part-time workers are more expensive for the firm than one full-time worker.

5 The organisational governance of dependent forms of self-employment

1. In Coase's words: 'But in view of the fact that it is usually argued that co-ordination will be done by the price mechanism, why is such organisation necessary? Why are there these "islands of conscious power"?' (Coase 1937: 388).
2. In this context, relational contracts refer to informal agreements, unwritten codes and unwritten understandings that powerfully affect the behaviour of individuals within firms.
3. Examples of limitations on a firm's size are the costs of bureaucracy, the weakening of individual incentives and the hazards of internal politicking.
4. For instance, when the employee does not receive a bonus for a specific performance despite an ex ante informal agreement.
5. Some of the following sociological approaches originally focused on organisations in a broader sense and not only on business organisations. In this section, however, the focus will be on business organisations, and therefore mainly draws on those parts of the theories which refer to these.
6. While *organisational structure* refers to formalisation, vertical and horizontal differentiation, bureaucratisation, centralisation, complexity and integration, *organisational context* is operationalised in terms of organisational size, technology and specific environmental characteristics (e.g. uncertainty, competition) (Nohria and Gulati 1994: 539).
7. Inter-organisational power depends on the extent to which organisations control resources needed by others and to what extent they can reduce their resource dependency on others.
8. Resource dependence theory assumes that although organisations are constrained by their environment, they also undertake actions that alter those environments (Pfeffer 1982: 198).
9. Since institutional approaches to organisations have a very long tradition and are, moreover, strongly rooted across different disciplines and directions, the following focuses on the current institutional theory of 'New Institutionalism' in organisational analysis. Scott (1995) gives a comprehensive overview of old and new institutional thinking in sociology, economics and political science. Scott and Meyer (1994) and Powell and DiMaggio (1991) highlight the new institutionalism in organisational analysis.
10. The term 'property rights' refers to rules that determine the conditions of ownership and control of means of production. 'Governance structures' relates to rules that define relations of competition and cooperation, and the organisational structure of firms. 'Conception of control' means market-specific agreements between firms, which allow actors to interpret their world and act to control situations. 'Rules of exchange' define the

conditions of business deals (e.g. transport, insurance, payment, enforcement of contracts).
11. A 'stable market' is defined as follows: '[A] market in which the identities and status hierarchy of firms (the incumbents and the challengers) are well known and a conception of control that guides actors who lead firms is shared' (Fligstein 1996: 663).
12. The state's role is however variable and depends on the nature of the markets. It is not seen as pivotal in every economic process.
13. Examples of these laws are competition laws or anti-trust laws.

6 The creation of dependent self-employment in comparative perspective

1. One interview in Austria was conducted in March 2004.
2. These platforms are: work@professional, work@flex, work@social, work@IT, work@education, work@external, work@migration. These platforms cover atypical employees in different sectors and from different backgrounds.
3. The difference between the data of the microcensus, the British Annual Employment Survey and the Labour Force Survey is due to differences in the statistical sample procedure.
4. For an overview, see, for instance, Edwards (2003).
5. However, the Financial Services Authority (FSA) stresses that these figures have to be interpreted carefully since insurance companies registered many employees as dealing with customer advice in the early years.
6. In the late 1980s, the Conservative Government changed the pension system, giving individuals the option of not taking part in company pension schemes. Additionally, individuals were actively encouraged to set up their own private pension schemes. The weak regulation of the insurance industry in the late 1980s and early 1990s, however, created a pension mis-selling scandal where those who had taken private pension schemes rather than that provided by their employer, ended up far worse off. In 1993, the Securities and Investment Board (SIB), the predecessor of the Financial Services Authority (FSA), conducted an investigation into the sales practices of insurers. On the basis of this investigation the SIB concluded that many of the practices of the insurance sales force were unethical. It was found that the sales force of insurance companies and independent financial advisers (IFAs) sold policies that were not in the best interest of the policyholders (Hunte 1998: 107f). More precisely, the SIB review showed that personal pensions were sold between 1988 and 1994 to people who should have stayed in, or joined, an occupational pension scheme. As a result of these findings, SIB urged product providers and IFAs to conduct proactive reviews of all personal pension transactions between 1988 and 1994. They had to identify customers who were inappropriately advised to invest in personal pensions and, where appropriate, to provide redress. Estimations show that around 2 600 000 pension schemes were potentially affected (ABI 1998).
7. The British Treasury has drawn up guidelines on Charges, Access and Terms known as CAT Standards. ISA Stands for Individual Savings Accounts which

the Government introduced in 1999. ISAs offer tax-free benefits on a wide range of investments.
8. For instance, mortgages are typically backed with life insurance contracts.
9. Since we are interested in dependent forms of self-employment, the empirical analysis mainly focuses on the British long-term insurance industry where tied agents are only allowed to be tied to one long-term insurance company.
10. Eventually, the company was recently sold to an Austrian insurance company.
11. The following analysis refers to the situation at the time of the interviews (between November 2000 and May 2001). Changes that have occurred since then are not considered.
12. This finding is in line with Lafontaine and Shaw (2005) who argue that brand value (measured in terms of advertising fees and media expenditure) is an important determinant in the ownership decision of franchisors. They show that firms with a strong and high value brandname are more likely to own their outlets because they need greater direct managerial control over the quality of the brandname.
13. For an overview of this discussion on the issue of trust, see, for instance, Lane (1998). Referring to proponents of the value- and norm-based trust view such as Gambetta (1988) or Zucker (1986), Lane (1998: 6) states that 'trust begins where rational prediction ends'. Some authors in this debate argue that trust based on calculation is not really trust at all. We agree that calculative trust is indeed a different kind of trust – or, in other words, the cognitive basis of trusting is different from value-based trust. We nevertheless use the same word ('trust') because we argue that the outcome – i.e. trust – is the same although the reason or cognitive basis differs. Expressed differently, in calculative trust, parties behave 'as if' they trusted the other party – thus, the outcome in the business relationship is the same, when compared to value- or norm-based trust.

7 Conclusions

1. A fourth circle, which is omitted here, refers to unpaid work (e.g. voluntary work).

References

ABI (Association of British Insurers) (1998): *Parliamentary Briefing on Pensions Mis-selling*, Information Sheet, June 1998, http://www.abi.org.uk/ (08/03/01).

ABI (Association of British Insurers) (1999): *Insurance. Facts, Figures and Trends*, London.

ABI (Association of British Insurers) (2000): *Insurance. Statistics Yearbook, 1989–1999*, London.

ABI (Association of British Insurers) (2001): *Insurance. Statistics Yearbook, 1990–2000*, London.

ABI (Association of British Insurers) (2002): *Insurance Trends. Quarterly Statistics and Research Review*, October, Issue 34, London.

ABI (Association of British Insurers) (2003a): *Insurance Trends. Quarterly Statistics and Research Review*, January, Issue 35, London.

ABI (Association of British Insurers) (2003b): *Insurance Trends. Quarterly Statistics and Research Review*, January, Issue 36, London.

Abraham, K. G. and Taylor, S. K. (1996): Firms' use of outside contractors: theory and evidence, *Journal of Labor Economics*, 14 (3), 394–424.

Acs, Z. J., Audretsch, D. B. and Evans, D. S. (1994): *Why Does the Self-employment Rate Vary Across Countries and Over Time?* Centre for Economic Policy Research, Discussion Paper No. 871, London.

Allen, M. (2004): The varieties of capitalism paradigm: not enough variety? *Socio-Economic Review*, 2, 87–106.

Altieri, G. and Oteri, C. (2004): *Il lavoro interinale come sistema. Bilancio di un quinquennio.* Roma: Ediesse.

Amable, B. (2003): *The Diversity of Modern Capitalism*, Oxford: Oxford University Press.

Arruñada, B., González-Díaz, M. and Fernández, A. (2004): Determinants of organizational form. Transactions costs and institutions in the European trucking industry. *Industrial and Corporate Change*, 13 (6), 867–82.

Arum, R. and Müller, W. (2004): *The Reemergence of Self-Employment: Comparative Findings and Empirical Propositions.* New Haven: Princeton University Press.

Atkinson, J. (2000): *Employment Options and Labour Market Participation*, Report for the European Foundation for the Improvement of Living and Working Conditions, Dublin.

Audretsch, D. B. and Thurik, A. R. (2001): What's new about the new economy? Sources of growth in the managed and entrepreneurial economies, *Industrial and Corporate Change*, 10 (1), 267–315.

Audretsch, D. B., Carree, M. A., Van Stel, A. J. and Thurik, A. R. (2005): *Does Self-Employment Reduce Unemployment?* Discussion Paper Industrial Organization, Centre for Economic Policy Research.

Bachmann, R. (2001): Trust, power and control in trans-organizational relations, *Organization Studies*, 22 (2), 337–65.

Baker, G. P. and Hubbard, T. N. (2003): Make versus buy in trucking: asset ownership, job design and information, NBER Working Paper 8727, Cambridge (MA), *American Economic Review*, 93 (3), 551–72.
Baker, G. P. and Hubbard, T. N. (2004): Contractibility and asset ownership: on-board computers and governance in U.S. trucking, *Quarterly Journal of Economics*, 119 (4), 1443–79.
Baker, G., Gibbons, R. and Murphy, K. J. (1999): Relational contracts and the theory of the firm, mimeo, MIT Sloan School, *Quarterly Journal of Economics*, 117 (1), 39–84.
Baumann, A. (2002): Path-dependency or Governance? The Emergence of Labour Market Institutions in the Media Production Industries in the UK and Germany, PhD Thesis, European University Institute, Department of Political and Social Sciences, Florence.
Bertolini, S. and Muehlberger, U. (2006): *The Organizational Governance of Work Relationships Between Employment and Self-employment*. Paper presented at the SASE Annual Congress 2006, Trier.
Berton, F., Pacelli, L. and Segre, G. (2005): Il Lavoro Parasubordinato in Italia. Tra Autonomia Del Lavoratore e Precarietà del Lavoro. *Rivista Italiana degli Economisti*, 10, 57–99.
Bewley, T. F. (1999): *Why Wages don't Fall during a Recession*, Cambridge, MA and London: Harvard University Press.
Blanchflower, D. G. (2000): *Self-employment in OECD Countries*, NBER Working Paper 7486, Cambridge (MA).
Blanchflower, D. G. and Oswald, A. J. (1998): What makes an entrepreneur? *Journal of Labor Economics*, 16 (1), 26–60.
Blaschke, S. (2001): Austria: Corporatist regulation of service labour markets, in: Dølvik, J. E. (ed.), *At Your Service? Comparative Perspectives on Employment and Labour Relations in the European Private Sector Services*, Brussels: Peter Lang.
Blau, D. (1987): A time series analysis of self-employment in the United States, *Journal of Political Economy*, 95 (3), 445–67.
Blau, P. and Scott, R. (1962): *Formal Organizations: A Comparative Approach*, San Francisco: Chandler Publishing.
Bögenhold, D. and Staber, U. (1991): The decline and rise of self-employment, *Work, Employment and Society*, 5, 223–39.
Bosch, G. and Philips, P. (2003): Introduction, in: Bosch, G. and Philips, P. (eds), *Building Chaos. An International Comparison of Deregulation in the Construction Industry*, London and New York: Routledge, 1–23.
Bosch, G. and Zühlke-Robinet, K. (2003): Germany. The labor market in the German construction industry, in: Bosch, G. and Philips, P. (eds), *Building Chaos. An International Comparison of Deregulation in the Construction Industry*, London and New York: Routledge, 48–72.
Bredach, J. L. and Eccles, R. G. (1989): Price, authority, and trust: from ideal types to plural forms, *Annual Review of Sociology*, 15, 97–118.
Burchell, B., Deakin, S. and Honey, S. (1999): *The Employment Status of Individuals in Non-standard Employment*, Report for the British Department of Trade and Industry.
Byrne, J. and van der Meer, M. (2003): Spain. Spain down the low track, in: Bosch, G. and Philips, P. (eds.), *Building Chaos. An International Comparison*

of *Deregulation in the Construction Industry*, London and New York: Routledge, 138–160.
Campbell, J. and Lindberg, L. (1990): Property rights and the organization of economic activity by the state, *American Sociological Review*, 55, 3–14.
Castells, M. (1996): *The Information Age. Economy, Society and Culture*, Volume 1, The Rise of the Network Society, Oxford: Blackwell.
Charest, J. (2003): Canada. Labor market regulation and labor relations in the construction industry: the special case of Quebec within the Canadian context, in: Bosch, G. and Philips, P. (eds), *Building Chaos. An International Comparison of Deregulation in the Construction Industry*, London and New York: Routledge, 95–113.
Child, J. (1987): Information technology, organization, and the response to strategic challenges. *California Management Review*, 30, 33–50.
Clarke, K. and Drinkwater, S. (2000): Pushed out or pulled in? Self-employment among ethic minorities in England and Wales, *Labour Economics*, 7 (5), 603–28.
CNEL (2004): Rapporto sul mercato del lavoro 2003, Roma.
Coase, R. H. (1937): The nature of the firm, *Economica*, New Series, IV, November, 386–405.
Coleman, J. S. (1990): *The Foundations of Social Theory*, Cambridge (MA): Harvard University Press.
Collins, H. (1990): Independent contractors and the challenge of vertical integration to employment protection laws, *Oxford Journal of Legal Studies*, 10 (3), 353–80.
Cowling, M. and Taylor, M. (2001): Entrepreneurial women and men: two different species. *Small Business Economics*, 16, 167–75.
Crouch, C. (1999): *Social Change in Western Europe*, Oxford: Oxford University Press.
Crouch, C. (2003): Institutions within which real actors innovate, in: Mayntz, R. and Streeck, W. (Hg.), *Die Reformierbarkeit der Demokratie. Innovationen und Blockaden*, Frankfurt/Main: Campus.
Crouch, C. (2005): *Capitalist Diversity and Change. Recombinant Governance and Institutional Entrepreneurs*. Oxford: Oxford University Press.
Crouch, C. and Streeck, W. (eds) (1997): *Political Economy of Modern Capitalism. Mapping Convergence and Diversity*, London: Sage.
Datamonitor (1999): *Managing Multi-channel Distribution*, London.
Davies, P. and Freedland, M. (2000): Employees, workers and the autonomy of labour law, in: Simon, D. and Weiss, M. (Hg.), *Zur Autonomie des Individuums, Liber Amoricum Spiros Simitis*, Baden-Baden: Nomos.
Davis-Blake, A. and Uzzi, B. (1993): Determinants of employment externalisation: a study of temporary workers and independent contractors, *Administrative Science Quarterly*, 38 (2), 195–223.
De La Rica, S. and Iza, A. (2005): Career planning in Spain: do fixed-term contracts delay marriage and parenthood? *Review of Economics of the Household*, 3 (1), 49–73.
Deakin, S. and Morris, G. S. (1998): *Labour Law*, 2nd edition, London: Buttersworth.
Dex, S., Willis, J., Paterson, R. and Sheppard, E. (2000): Freelance workers and contract uncertainty: the effects of contractual changes in the television industry, *Work, Employment and Society*, 14 (2), 283–305.

References 205

Dietrich, H. (1996): *Empirische Befunde zur 'Scheinselbständigkeit'*. Ergebnisse des IAB-Projekts 4-448V 'Freie Mitarbeiter und selbständige Einzelunternehmer mit persönlicher und wirtschaftlicher Abhängigkeit', edited by the German Federal Ministry of Labour and Social Order, Bonn.

DiMaggio, P. J. (ed.) (2001): *The Twenty-First-Century Firm. Changing Economic Organization in International Perspective*, Princeton: Princeton University Press.

DiMaggio, P. J. and Powell, W. W. (1983): The iron cage revisited. Institutional isomorphism and collective rationality in organizational fields, *American Sociological Review*, 48, 147–60.

Dolvik, J. E. (ed.) (2001): *At Your Service? Comparative Perspectives on Employment and Labour Relations in the European Private Sector Services*. Brussels: Peter Lang.

Dore, R. (1983): Goodwill and the spirit of market Capitalism, *The British Journal of Sociology*, 34 (4), 459–82.

Dunlop Commission (1994): Final Report. Commission on the Future of Work-Management Relations.

Ebbinghaus, B. and Manow, P. (2001): Introduction: studying varieties of welfare capitalism, in: Ebbinghaus, B. and Manow, P. (eds.), *Comparing Welfare Capitalism. Social Policy and Political Economy in Europe*, Japan and the USA, London: Routledge.

Ebbinghaus, B. and Visser, J. (2000): *Trade Unions in Western Europe since 1945*, Basingstoke: Macmillan.

Eccles, R. G. (1981): The quasifirm in the construction industry, *Journal of Economic Behavior and Organization*, 2, 335–57.

Edwards, P. (ed.) (2003): *Industrial Relations*, 2nd edition, Oxford: Blackwell Publishing.

Eiro (European Industrial Relations Observatory on-line) (2002): *Economically Dependent Workers, Employment Law and Industrial Relations*, EU countries, http://www.eiro.eurofound.eu.int/2002/05/study/tn0205101s.html (28/09/04).

EIRR (European Industrial Relations Review) (1995): *Nonstandard Forms of Employment in Europe: Part-time Work, Fixed Term Contracts and Temporary Work Contracts*, Issue 252, London: Eclipse.

Eisenhardt, K. M. (1989): Building theories from case study research, *Academy of Management Review*, 14, 532–50.

Engblom, S. (2001): Equal treatment of employees and self-employed workers, *The International Journal of Comparative Labour Law and Industrial Relations*, 17 (2), 211–31.

Engblom, S. (2003): *Self-employment and the Personal Scope of Labour Law. Comparative Lessons from France, Italy, Sweden, the United Kingdom and the United States*, PhD Thesis, European University Institute, Department of Law, Florence.

Esping-Andersen, G. (1990): *The Three Worlds of Welfare Capitalism*, London: Polity Press.

Evans, D. S. and Jovanovic, B. (1989): An estimated model of entrepreneurial choice under liquidity constraints, *Journal of Political Economy*, 97 (4), 808–27.

Evans, D. S. and Leighton, L. S. (1989): Some empirical aspects of entrepreneurship, *American Economic Review*, 79 (3), 519–35.

Evans, J. A., Kunda, G. and Barley, S. R. (2004): Beach time, bridge time, and billable hours: the temporal structure of technical contracting, *Administrative Science Quarterly*, 49, 1–38.
Fairlie, R. W. and Meyer, B. D. (1996): Ethnic and racial self-employment differences and possible explanations, *Journal of Human Resources*, 31 (4), 757–93.
Farrell, H. (2004): Trust, distrust, and power, in: Hardin, R. (ed.), *Distrust*, New York: Russell Sage Foundation.
Felstead, A. (1993): *The Corporate Paradox. Power and Control in the Business Franchise*. London and New York: Routledge.
Fernández, A., Arruñada, B. and González, M. (1998): *Contractual and Regulatory Explanations of Quasi-integration in the Trucking Industry*, Universitat Pompeu Fabra WP Series, Ref. 292, Barcelona.
Fernández, A., Arruñada, B. and González, M. (2000): Quasi-integration in less-than-truckload trucking, in: Ménard, C. (ed.), *Institutions, Contracts and Organization. Perspectives from New Institutional Economics*, Cheltenham: Edward Elgar.
Ferrera, M. (1997): *Le Trappole del Welfare*, Bologna: Il Mulino.
Fink, M., Riesenfelder, A. and Tálos, E. (2001): *Atypische Beschäftigungsverhältnisse. Geringfügige Beschäftigung und frei DienstnehmerInnen*, Wien.
Fligstein, N. (1990): *The Transformation of Corporate Control*, Cambridge (MA): Harvard University Press.
Fligstein, N. (1996): Markets as politics: a political-cultural approach to market institutions, *American Sociological Review*, 61, 656–73.
Fligstein, N. (2001): *The Architecture of Markets. An Economic Sociology of Twenty-first-century Capitalist Societies*, Princeton and Oxford: Princeton University Press.
Fligstein, N. and Freeland, R. (1995): Theoretical and comparative perspectives on corporate organization, *Annual Review of Sociology*, 21, 21–43.
Freedland, M. (2003): *The Personal Employment Contract*, Oxford: Oxford University Press.
FSA (Financial Services Authority) (2002): *Reforming Polarisation. Making the Market Work for Consumers*, Consultation Paper 121, London.
Gambetta, D. (1988): Can we trust trust?, in: Gambetta, D. (ed.), *Trust. Making and Breaking of Cooperative Relations*, Oxford: Blackwell.
Gibbons, R. (2000a): *Why Organizations Are Such a Mess (and What an Economist Might Do About It)*, Draft, MIT, mimeo.
Gibbons, R. (2000b): Trust in social structures. Hobbes and Coase meet repeated games, MIT, mimeo, in: Cook, K. (ed.), *Trust in Society*, New York: Russell Sage Foundation.
Glancy, S. (1998): *Managing Multi-channel Distribution. Evolution and Revolution*, Financial Times Finance Management Reports, London.
González-Díaz, M., Arruñada, B. and Fernández, A. (1998): Regulation as cause of firm fragmentation: the case of the Spanish construction industry. *International Review of Law and Economics*, 18 (4), 433–50.
González-Díaz, M., Arruñada, B. and Fernández, A. (2000): Causes of subcontracting. Evidence from panel data on construction firms, *Journal of Economic Behavior and Organization*, 42, 167–87.

References 207

Granovetter, M. (1985): Economic action and social structure: the problem of embeddedness, *American Journal of Sociology*, 91, 481–510.

Granovetter, M. (1995): Coase revisited. Business groups in the modern economy, *Industrial and Corporate Change*, 4 (1), 93–130.

Grimshaw, D. and Rubery, J. (2005): Inter-capital relations and the network organization: redefining the work and employment nexus, *Cambridge Journal of Economics*, 29, 1027–51.

Grossman, S. J. and Hart, O. D. (1986): The costs and benefits of ownership: a theory of vertical and lateral integration, *Journal of Political Economy*, 96 (4), 691–719.

Gstöttner-Hofer, G. (ed.) (1997): Was ist morgen noch normal? Gewerkschaften und atypische Arbeitsverhältnisse. Wien: ÖGB Verlag.

Gulati, R. (2004): Alliances and networks, in: Reuer, J. J. (ed.), *Strategic Alliances*, Oxford: Oxford University Press.

Hall, P. and Gingerich, D. (2004): *Varieties of Capitalism and Institutional Complementarities in the Macroeconomy: An Empirical Analysis*, MPIfG Discussion Paper 04/5.

Hall, P. and Soskice, D. (eds) (2001): *Varieties of Capitalism. The Institutional Foundations of Comparative Advantage*, Cambridge: Cambridge University Press.

Hannan, J. and Freeman, J. (1977): The population ecology of organizations, *American Journal of Sociology*, 49, 149–64.

Hannan, J. and Freeman, J. (1989): *Organizational Ecology*, Cambridge (MA): Harvard University Press.

Hardin, R. (1996): Trustworthiness, *Ethics*, 107, 26–42.

Harrison, B. and Kelley, M. R. (1993): Outsourcing and the search for 'Flexibility', *Work, Employment and Society*, 7 (2), 213–35.

Hart, O. (1995): *Firms, Contracts, and Financial Structure*, Clarendon Lectures in Economics, Oxford: Clarendon Press.

Harvey, M. (2003): The United Kingdom. Privatization, fragmentation, and inflexible flexibilization in the UK construction industry, in: Bosch, G. and Philips, P. (eds), *Building Chaos. An International Comparison of Deregulation in the Construction Industry*, London and New York: Routledge, 188–209.

Helper, S., MacDuffie, J. P. and Sabel, C. (2000): Pragmatic collaborations: advancing knowledge while controlling opportunism, *Industrial and Corporate Change*, 9 (3), 443–88.

Houseman, S. N. and Polivka, A. E. (2000): The implications of flexible staffing arrangements for job stability, in: Neumark, D. (ed.), *On the Job. Is Longterm Employment a Thing of the Past?* New York: Russell Sage Foundation, 427–62.

Hunte, C. (1998): *The European Life Insurance Market*, Financial Times Finance Report, London.

Hyytinen, A. and Rouvinen, P. (2006): *The Labour Market Consequences of Self-Employment Spells: European Evidence*. EUI Working Paper, RSCAS No. 2006/08.

ILO (2003): *The Scope of the Employment Relationship*, Report V, International Labour Conference, 91st Session, Geneva, http://www.ilo.org/public/english/standards/relm/ilc/ilc91/pdf/rep-v.pdf (22/10/04).

INPS (2001): 1^0 Rapporto sul lavoro subordinato, in: Alzoni, A., Bombelli, S., Legini, A. and Santoro, G. (eds), Roma.

IRES (2005): Nuovo contratto. Stessi Problemi. Gli effetti della legge 30/2003 nel passaggio dalle collaborazioni coordinate e continuative al lavoro a progetto, Roma.
Kalleberg, A. L., Reskin, B. F. and Hudson, K. (2000): Bad jobs in America: standard and nonstandard employment relations and job quality in the United States, *American Sociological Review*, 65 (2), 256–78.
Kitschelt, H., Lange, P., Marks, G. and Stephens, J. D. (eds) (1999): *Continuity and Change in Contemporary Capitalism*, Cambridge: Cambridge University Press.
Klein, R., Crawford, R. G. and Alchian, A. A. (1978): Vertical integration, appropriable rents, and the competitive contracting process, *Journal of Law and Economics*, 21 (2), 297–326.
Knight, J. (1992): *Institutions and Social Conflict*, Cambridge: Cambridge University Press.
Kogut, B. (2004): Joint ventures: theoretical and empirical perspectives, in: Reuer, J. J. (ed.), *Strategic Alliances*, Oxford: Oxford University Press.
Kunda, G., Barley, S. R. and Evans, J. (2002): Why do contractors contract? The experience of highly skilled technical professionals in a contingent labor market, *Industrial and Labor Relations Review*, 55 (2), 234–61.
Lafontaine, F. and Shaw, K. L. (2005): Targeting managerial control: evidence from franchising, *RAND Journal of Economics*, 36 (1), 131–50.
Lane, C. (1998): Introduction. Theories and issues in the study of trust, in: Lane, C. and Bachmann, R. (eds), *Trust Within and Between Organizations. Conceptional Issues and Empirical Applications*, Oxford: Oxford University Press.
Lane, C. and Bachmann, R. (eds) (1998): *Trust Within and Between Organizations. Conceptional Issues and Empirical Applications*, Oxford: Oxford University Press.
Lautsch, B. A. (2002): Uncovering and explaining variance in the features and outcomes of contingent work, *Industrial and Labor Relations Review*, 56 (1), 23–43.
Lawrence, P. and Lorsch, J. (1967): *Organization and Environment*, Boston: Harvard Business School.
Lewin-Solomons, S. B. (1998): *The Plural Form in Franchising: A Synergism of Market and Hierarchy*, University of Cambridge, mimeo.
Linder, M. (1999): Dependent and independent contractors in recent U.S. labor law: an ambiguous dichotomy rooted in simulated statutory purposelessness, *Comparative Labor Law and Policy Journal*, 21 (1), 187–230.
Lorenz, E. (1999): Trust, contract and economic cooperation, *Cambridge Journal of Economics*, 23, 301–15.
Lubanski, N. (2003): Denmark. Searching for innovation, in: Bosch, G. and Philips, P. (eds), *Building Chaos. An International Comparison of Deregulation in the Construction Industry*, London and New York: Routledge, 73–94.
Lyon-Caen, G. (1990): *Le Droit du Travail Non-salarié*, Report for the Commissariat général du Plan, Paris.
Macaulay, S. (1963): Non-contractual relations in business: a preliminary study, *American Sociological Review*, 28, 55–67.
Macneil, I. (1978): Contracts. Adjustments of long-term economic relations under classical, neoclassical, and relational contract law, *Northwestern University Law Review*, 72, 854–906.
MAPS (Market Assessment Publications Ltd) (1998): *Issues and Challenges in the UK Life Assurance Market 1998*, London.

Marchington, M., Grimshaw, D., Rubery, J. and Willmott, H. (eds) (2004): *Fragmenting Work. Crossing Boundaries and Disordering Hierarchies*, Oxford: Oxford University Press.

Marsden, D. (1999): *A Theory of Employment Systems. Micro-foundations of Societal Diversity*, Oxford: Oxford University Press.

Mayerhuber, C. and Url, T. (1999): Kurze Beschäftigungsdauer dominiert den österreichischen Arbeitsmarkt, *WIFO Monatsberichte*, 72, 693–703.

Meager, N. (1992): Does unemployment lead to self-employment? *Small Business Economics*, 4, 87–103.

Meager, N. (1998): United Kingdom, *SYSDEM Trends*, No. 31, Winter, 74–9.

Mesch, M. (Hg.) (1998): *Neue Arbeitsplätze in Österreich. Die Beschäftigungsentwicklung im österreichischen Dienstleistungssektor*, Wien: Manz.

Mühlberger, U. (2000): *Neue Formen der Beschäftigung. Arbeitsflexibilisierung durch atypische Beschäftigung in Österreich*, Wien: Braumüller.

Mühlberger, U. (2002): *Outsourcing, Dependency and Quasi-integration*, Dissertation at the Vienna University of Economics and B. A.

Muehlberger, U. and Pernicka, S. (2007): *Transferring the labour-capital conflict into the domain of corporate associations: The case of dependent forms of self-employment*, Paper presented at the SASE Annual Meeting, Copenhagen.

Nagel, B. (2002): Scheinselbständigkeit in Österreich und Großbritannien. Vergleich der gesetzlichen Rahmenbedingungen und empirische Analyse, MA Thesis at the Vienna University of Economics & B. A.

Naldini, M. (2003): *The Family in the Mediterranean Welfare States*, London and New York: Routledge.

Nelson, R. and Winter, S. (1982): *An Evolutionary Theory of Economic Change*, Cambridge (MA): Harvard University Press.

Nisbet, P. (1997): Dualism, flexibility and self-employment in the UK construction industry, *Work, Employment and Society*, 11 (3), 459–79.

Nohria, N. (1992): Is a network perspective a useful way of studying organizations? In: Nohria, N. and Eccles, R. G. (eds), *Networks in Organizations: Structure, Form, and Action*, Boston: Harvard Business School Press, 1–22.

Nohria, N. and Gulati, R. (1994): Firms and their environments, in: Smelser, N. J. and Swedberg, R. (eds), *The Handbook of Economic Sociology*, Princeton and New York: Princeton University Press and Russell Sage Foundation, 529–55.

Nooteboom, B. (2002): *Trust. Forms, Foundations, Functions, Failures and Figures*, Cheltenham: Edward Elgar.

O'Reilly, J. and Fagan, C. (eds) (1998): *Part-time Prospects: An International Comparison of Part-time Work in Europe, North America and the Pacific Rim*, London: Routledge.

O'Reilly, J., Cebrián, I. and Lallement, M. (eds) (2000): *Working-time Changes. Social Integration Through Transitional Labour Markets*, Cheltenham: Edward Elgar.

OECD (2000): *Employment Outlook 2000*, Working party on employment, draft Chapter 5, Recent developments in self-employment, mimeo, Paris.

ONS (Office for National Statistics) (1997): Results of the 1996 Annual employment survey, *Labour Market Trends*, November 1997, London: The Stationery Office, 461–7.

ONS (Office for National Statistics) (1998): Trade union membership and recognition 1996–97: an analysis of data from the certification officer and the LFS, *Labour Market Trends*, July 1998, London: The Stationery Office, 353–64.

ONS (Office for National Statistics) (2001a): *Labour Market Trends*, London: The Stationery Office.

ONS (Office for National Statistics) (2001b): *Annual Abstract of Statistics*, London: The Stationery Office.

ÖSTAT (Österreichisches Statistisches Zentralamt) (2000): *Statistisches Jahrbuch 1999:2000*, Wien.

Parry, D. (2000): *The Future of European Insurance*, Datamonitor for Reuters Business Insight, London.

Perulli, A. (2003): *Economically Dependent/Quasi-subordinate (Parasubordinate) Employment: Legal, Social and Economic Aspects*, Study for the European Commission, http://europa.eu.int/comm/employment_social/labour_law/docs/parasubordination_report_en.pdf (06/10/04).

Pfeffer, J. (1982): *Organizations and Organization Theory*, Boston: Pitman.

Pfeffer, J. and Nowak, P. (1976): Joint-ventures and interorganizational interdependence, *Administrative Science Quarterly*, 21, 398–418.

Pfeffer, J. and Salancik, G. (1978): *The External Control of Organizations*, New York: Harper & Row.

Philips, P. (2003): The United States. Dual worlds: the two growth paths in US construction, in: Bosch, G. and Philips, P. (eds), *Building Chaos. An International Comparison of Deregulation in the Construction Industry*, London and New York: Routledge, 161–87.

Piore, M. J. and Sabel, C. F. (1984): *The Second Industrial Divide: Possibilities for Prosperity*, New York: Basic Books.

Podolny, J. M. and Page, K. L. (1998): Network forms of organization, *Annual Review of Sociology*, 24, 57–76.

Powell, W. W. (1990): Neither markets nor hierarchies: network forms of organization, in: Frances, J., Levacic, R. and Mitchell, J. (eds), *Markets, Hierarchies and Networks*, London: Sage, 265–76, an adapted version from: Research in Organizational Behavior, 12, 295–336.

Powell, W. W. (2001): The capitalist form in the twenty-first century. Emerging patterns in western enterprises, in: DiMaggio, P. (ed.), *The Twenty-first Century Firm. Changing Economic Organization in International Perspective*, Princeton: Princeton University Press, 33–68.

Powell, W. W. and DiMaggio, P. J. (eds) (1991): *The New Institutionalism in Organizational Analysis*, Chicago and London: The University of Chicago Press.

Purcell, K., McKnight, A. and Simm, C. (1999): *The Lower Earning Limit in Practice. Part-time Employment in Hotels and Catering*, EOC Research Discussion Series, Manchester.

Regalia, I. (2003): *Lavoro autonomi economicamente dipendente / lavoro parasubordinato – Una ricognizione so tutele e rappresentanza in Europa*. Mimeo

Reithofer, H. (1997): Der Österreichische Versicherungsmarkt, in: *Versicherungs-Handbuch*, Bildungswerk der Österreichischen Versicherungswirtschaft, Vienna.

Robson, M. T. (1998): The Rise in Self-employment Amongst UK Males, *Small Business Economics*, 10, 199–212.

Rubery, J. (1999): *The Shaping of Work and Working Time in the Service Sector*. Manchester School of Management: Mimeo.

References

Rubery, J., Earnshaw, J. and Burchell, B. (1993): *New Forms and Patterns of Employment: The Role of Self-employment in Britain*, Baden-Baden: Nomos Verlagsgesellschaft.

Rubery, J., Earnshaw, J., Marchington, M., Cooke, F. L. and Vincent, S. (2002): Changing organizational forms and the employment relationship, *Journal of Management Studies*, 39 (5), 645–72.

Schindler, R. (2000): Arbeitnehmerbegriff – Abgrenzung und Schutzzweck, in: Resch, R. (Hg.) *(Schein-)Selbständigkeit. Arbeits- und sozialrechtliche Fragen*, Wien: Linde.

Schuetze, H. J. (2000): Taxes, economic conditions and recent trends in male self-employment: a Canada–US comparison, *Labour Economics*, 7 (5), 507–44.

Schwarz, W. and Löschnigg, G. (1997): *Arbeitsrecht. Gesetze und Kommentare*, Wien: Verlag des ÖGB.

Sciarra, S. (1991): Franchising and contract of employment. Notes on a still impossible assimilation, in: Joerges, C. (ed.), *Franchising and the Law. Theoretical and Comparative Approaches in Europe and the United States*, Baden-Baden: Nomos Verlagsgesellschaft.

Sciarra, S. (2004): *The Evolution of Labour Law (1992–2004)*, General Report, Project for the European Commission, http://www.europa.eu.int/comm/employment_social/labour_law/docs/generalreport_en.pdf (08/10/04).

Scott, W. R. (1995): *Institutions and Organizations*, Thousand Oaks: Sage.

Scott, W. R. and Meyer, J. W. (1994): *Institutional Environments and Organizations. Structural Complexity and Individualism*, Thousand Oaks: Sage.

Semlinger, K. (1991): New developments in subcontracting: mixing market and hierarchy, in: Ash, A. and Dietrich, M. (eds), *Towards a New Europe? Structural Change in the European Economy*, Aldershot: Edward Elgar.

Semlinger, K. (1993): Small firms and outsourcing as flexibility reservoirs of large firms, in: Grabher, G. (ed.), *The Embedded Firm: On the Socioeconomics of Industrial Networks*, London and New York: Routledge.

Simon, H. (1951): A formal theory of the employment relationship, *Econometrica*, 19, 293–305.

Sladky, S. (1994): *Die österreichische Speditionsbranche und ihre Erfolgsfaktoren*, MA Thesis, Vienna University of Economics and B.A.

Smeaton, D. (2003): *Self-employed Workers: Calling the Shots or Hesitant Independents? A Consideration of the Trends*. London: Policy Studies Institute.

Soskice, D. (1999): Divergent production regimes. Coordinated and uncoordinated market economies in the 1980s and 1990s, in: Kitschelt, H., Lange, P., Marks, G. and Stephens, J. D. (eds), *Continuity and Change in Contemporary Capitalism*, Cambridge: Cambridge University Press.

Statistik Austria (2002): *Statistische Nachrichten*, 5/2002, Wien.

Statistik Austria (2003): *Statistisches Jahrbuch*, Wien.

Storey, J., Salaman, G. and Platman, K. (2005): Living with enterprise in an enterprise economy: freelance and contract workers in the media, *Human Relations*, 58 (8), 1033–54.

Supiot, A. (2001): *Beyond Employment. Changes in Work and the Future of Labour Law in Europe*, Oxford: Oxford University Press.

Taylor, M. P. (1996): Earnings, independence or unemployment: why become self-employed? *Oxford Bulletin of Economics and Statistics*, 58 (2), 253–65.

Thompson, G. F. (2003): *Between Hierarchies and Markets. The Logic and Limits of Network Forms of Organization.* Oxford: Oxford University Press.
Thompson, J. D. (1967): *Organizations in Actions*, New York: McGraw-Hill.
Tolbert, P. S. and Zucker, L. G. (1996): The institutionalization of institutional theory, in: Clegg St. R., Hardy, C. and Nord, W. R. (eds), *Handbook of Organization Studies*, London: Sage, 175–90.
Tufft, R. (1998): *The Future of UK Insurance to 2005*, Datamonitor for Reuters Business Insight, London.
Underhill, E. (2003): Australia. The Australian construction industry: union control in a disorganized industry, in: Bosch, G. and Philips, P. (eds), *Building Chaos. An International Comparison of Deregulation in the Construction Industry*, London and New York: Routledge, 114–37.
Ursell, G. (2000): Television production: issues of exploitation, commodification and subjectivity in UK television labour markets, *Media, Culture and Society*, 22, 805–25.
Uzzi, B. (1996): The sources and consequences of embeddedness for the economic performance of organizations: the network effect, *American Sociological Review*, 61, 674–98.
Van der Meer, M. (2003): The Netherlands. Rules in revision: high-quality production in the Dutch construction industry, in: Bosch, G. and Philips, P. (eds), *Building Chaos. An International Comparison of Deregulation in the Construction Industry*, London and New York: Routledge, 24–47.
Van Husen (2000): Zum Begriff (Neue) Selbständigkeit gemäß § 1 Abs 3 GewO, *Österreichische Zeitschrift für Wirtschaftsrecht*.
VVO (Verein der Versicherungsunternehmen Österreichs) (2000): *Statistik über die Verteilung der Vertriebswege*, Wien.
Weber, M. [1922] (2002): *Wirtschaft und Gesellschaft, Grundriß der verstehenden Soziologie*, Tübingen: Mohr.
Williamson, O. E. (1975): *Markets and Hierarchies: Analysis and Antitrust Implications, A Study in the Economics of Internal Organization*, New York: The Free Press.
Williamson, O. E. (1979): Transaction cost economics: the governance of contractual relations, *Journal of Law and Economics*, 22, 233–61.
Williamson, O. E. (1985): *The Economic Institutions of Capitalism: Firms, Markets, Relational Contracting*, New York: The Free Press.
Yin, R. K. (1993): *Applications of Case Study Research*, Applied Social Research Methods Series, 34, Newbury Park: Sage Publications.
Yoon, J. H. and Kang, B.-G. (2003): Republic of Korea. The drivers for change in the Korean construction industry: regulation and deregulation, in: Bosch, G. and Philips, P. (eds), *Building Chaos. An International Comparison of Deregulation in the Construction Industry*, London and New York: Routledge, 73–94.
Zagler, M. (2003): *Sectoral Shifts and Dependent Self-employment*, Free University of Bozen-Bolzano, School of Economics and Management Working Paper No. 38, Bozen-Bolzano.
Zucker, L. G. (1986): Production of trust. Institutional sources of economic structure, 1840–1920, *Research in Organizational Behavior*, 8, 53–111.
Zucker, L. G. (1987): Institutional theories of organization, *Annual Review of Sociology*, 13, 443–64.

Index

ABI, 114, 120, 126, 200, 202
adviser, independent financial, 51, 94,
    108, 120, 192, 200
agency, 67, 71, 73, 124
agent system, tied, 125, 140, 185–6
agents, 3, 4, 11, 21, 25, 112, 115, 121,
    129, 136–8, 140–1, 167, 169–71,
    173, 179, 183–4, 192–5
    employed, 51, 132, 137, 141
    forwarding, 110, 155
    independent, 6, 7, 11–12, 124
    multi-tied, 108, 121, 124, 127
    self-employed, 121, 181
agreements, collective, 11, 30, 43,
    112, 115, 133, 191, 197
alternative-use value, 90–1
asset
    ownership, 26–7, 92, 96, 179, 189,
      203
    specificity, 27, 83–5, 192
Austria, ix, 8–12, 14–15, 20–2, 36,
    42–3, 54–5, 57–8, 108–9, 114–15,
    120, 123–6, 128–34, 140, 142,
    185–6
Austrian
    freight industry, vii, 50, 53, 108,
      110, 155, 157, 169, 176
    insurance industry, vi, 108, 110–12,
      120, 128, 166, 176, 185
    labour law, 39, 40
    service industry, vi, 143, 145
Austrian Trade Union Federation,
    112–13
Austrian Trade Union of Salaried
    Private Sector Employees, 109
authority, 5, 39, 92, 95–6, 98–9,
    171–3, 177, 179, 183, 203
    managerial, 188–9
    mechanisms, 92, 94, 99, 180

Blurring Boundaries, v, 1, 3, 5, 7, 9,
    11, 13, 15, 17, 195

boundaries, 1, 9, 13, 26–7, 82, 85–6,
    106–7, 169, 193–4, 197
British insurance companies, 116,
    118, 128, 131–2, 134–5, 137, 139
business
    networks, 83, 86–7, 99, 192
    organisations, 1–3, 13, 86–7, 97,
      102, 183, 199
    relations, dependent, vii, 173–6
    relationships, 1, 3–5, 7, 12–13, 27,
      41–2, 80, 87–90, 96, 105, 162,
      165, 172, 174–5, 177–82,
      189–91
    service industry, 13–14, 144, 165–6,
      169–70, 181

capital, human, 7, 49, 50, 77, 79
collaboration, coordinated, 42, 67, 69
company culture, vi, 132, 139–40
composite insurer, 131, 185
conflict resolution, vii, 95–6, 173,
    178, 181
conflicts, 32, 94, 96, 173, 179–81, 190
construction industry, 12, 28–30,
    203–5, 207–8, 210, 212
contingent work, 25, 208
contract
    for services, 38, 197
    workers, 211
contracting, 4, 84, 158–9, 195
    classical, 84
    inter-organisational, 174
    neoclassical, 84
contractors, 21–3, 25–6, 28, 31, 33,
    40–1, 44, 50, 85, 93, 109, 144–5,
    147, 149, 154, 159
contracts, 1, 5, 7, 8, 12, 21–5, 34–40,
    42–4, 52, 67, 78, 146, 167–9,
    171–3, 181–2, 196–8, 206–8
    complete, 89, 179
    incomplete, 83
    informal, 99, 172

contracts – *continued*
  written, 9, 145, 157, 162, 172–3
Control, 4, 7, 8, 16, 28–9, 38–9, 43–4, 95–6, 98–9, 103–4, 108–9, 135–8, 167–72, 174–5, 177–81, 183–4, 192–4
  company managers, 171, 173
  costs, 132, 168
  direct, 11, 169
  layers of, 179, 181
  mechanisms, vii, 16, 27, 94–6, 172, 174, 178–9, 193; hierarchical, 105–6, 182
cooperation, 88–9, 109, 145, 156–7, 160–1, 163, 175, 199
coordination, 4, 8–10, 12, 28, 42, 54, 174
costs, 23, 69, 81–3, 86, 128, 132–4, 139–40, 155, 158–60, 171, 175, 177, 179, 181, 184, 191
  variable, 132–3, 158, 177, 183
culture, 101–2, 105, 129–30, 204, 212

dependence, 6, 8, 22–3, 35–6, 170–1, 189–90
  mutual, 169–70
dependency, vii, 5, 16, 95, 99, 105, 107–8, 147, 156–7, 162, 165, 167, 169–73, 177, 179, 190–1
  economic, 40, 190–1
  mutual, vii, 93, 162, 169
  personal, 39, 40, 179
dependent
  business relationships, vi, vii, 2, 94, 96–7, 171, 175, 178, 180–3
  forms: of outsourcing, v, 20, 97; of self-employment, 1, 15, 21, 36, 42, 54, 98, 176, 189–91, 201, 209
  outsourcing, vi, 4, 9, 16, 26–7, 33, 81, 83, 92, 94–5, 99, 100, 102–3, 105–7, 109–10, 163–4, 185; key features of, 16, 81; logic of, 9, 13, 107
  self-employed workers, 5–8, 13–14, 16, 28–9, 36–7, 43–5, 50–2, 54–8, 61–2, 77–9, 107–10, 113, 144–5, 147–50, 166–7, 188–91

self-employment, v–vii, 4–8, 10–2, 14–6, 20–2, 28–30, 35–8, 40–2, 50, 52–4, 57–8, 76–8, 106–52, 154–78, 184–6, 192–6
  dependent forms of self-employment, 81, 83, 85, 87, 89, 91, 93, 95, 97, 99, 101, 103, 105
deregulation, 30–1, 44, 111, 142, 144, 184, 186, 203–4, 207–8, 210, 212
distrust, 206
diversity, within-system, viii, 11, 17, 191–2

economics, transaction cost, 85–6, 212
elements of authority, 5, 16, 96, 98–9, 105, 183
employees
  atypical, 34, 200
  fixed-term, 34, 196
  status, 6, 7, 12, 38, 41, 124, 197
  traditional, 37–8
employment
  contract of, 5, 21, 37–8, 197, 211
  contracts, 1, 3, 11, 35, 38, 167, 188; personal, 197, 206
  law, 21, 36–7, 45, 159
  protection, 7, 15, 17, 30, 34–5, 39, 41–2, 45, 53, 195, 197
  relationships, 1, 28, 37, 41, 82, 94–5, 112, 154, 171, 182, 187–9, 194, 207, 211
entrepreneurial risk, 3–7, 40, 170, 183

family, 10, 47, 67, 110, 130, 152–3, 209
firms, 3, 10, 12–13, 16, 23–5, 27–8, 69, 80–3, 85–8, 90–3, 96–105, 183, 188–9, 192–5, 198–202, 211–12
  existence of, 81
  hierarchical, 82
  independent, 85, 121, 194
flexibility, vii, 6, 8, 23, 26, 49, 54, 77–8, 94–5, 97, 99, 128, 145, 149–52, 183–4, 188
formal contracts, 80, 83, 92, 94–7, 99, 105, 165, 172, 178–9, 181
forms, network, 46, 87, 210
forwarders, 14, 26, 41, 155–64

Index 215

franchising, v, 15, 22, 87, 196, 208, 211
freelancers, 18, 31–2, 40–1, 113, 144–5, 149
freelance workers, 32, 113, 205

governance, 2, 27, 84, 87, 92, 101–2, 107, 184, 203, 212
structures, ix, 13, 16, 28, 81, 84–6, 94–7, 99, 102–4, 108, 171, 180, 185, 192, 199

hierarchical
structures, 1, 2, 184, 186
subordination, 4, 14
hierarchies, vi, 1, 2, 16, 52, 81–3, 85, 91–2, 94, 97, 172, 179–81, 192–4, 208, 210–12
hold-up problems, 1, 27–8, 156, 170

imitative behaviour, vii, 102, 183, 185–6
incentives, 3, 17, 28, 30, 34, 49, 53, 79, 82, 90–1, 93, 132, 168, 174–6, 182–9, 191–4
independent contractors, v, 5, 23, 25, 44, 90, 92, 204, 208
industrial
regulation, vi, 17, 134, 184–5, 194
relations, 9, 21, 24, 111–12, 114, 144, 205
industries
freight, 45, 108, 162, 165–6, 170, 178, 181, 186, 195
media, 12, 15, 26, 32–3
trucking, 12, 26–7, 33, 206
informal agreements, 80, 86, 94–5, 105, 145, 173, 178, 199
institutional theory, new, 100–1, 106
institutions, 10–11, 32, 101, 105–6, 187, 189, 202, 204, 206, 211
insurance, 8, 12, 16, 45, 115, 120, 123, 144, 158–60, 165–6, 178, 181, 186, 200, 202
industry, vi, 11–14, 50, 52, 93, 108, 111–13, 115, 121, 132, 140, 157, 166–7, 169–70, 179, 185
integration, 38, 85, 90–1, 199

vertical, 27–9, 33, 83–6, 91, 192, 204, 208
interactions, 4, 64, 70, 101, 103, 113, 145, 168, 194
Italian insurance companies, 51
Italian Labour Force Surveys, ix, 8, 15, 66, 68

job tenure, 59, 61, 65, 69, 70, 74–6, 195

labour
contract, 40, 116, 125
law: personal scope of, 34, 37, 44; protection, 15, 38, 44
market: outsider, 11, 16, 79; regulation, 19, 49; status, 19, 54, 61, 67, 75–6, 78, 175, 190, 198; structures, 50, 77
protection, 177, 190
secondary, 29
Labour Law and Regulations, v, 34–5, 37, 39, 41, 43, 45
loyalty, 132, 136, 169, 184

management of resource dependencies, 87, 92
managerial control, vi, vii, 134–5, 137–8, 167–9, 171, 175, 177, 208
model, repeated game, 89
multi-channel distribution, x, 109, 116, 127–8, 131

non-cash incentives, 169
non-integration, 90–1
non-standard employment, 144, 203
norms, vii, 87, 101, 103, 183, 186

opportunism, 82–3, 85, 87, 89, 95–6, 171, 173, 176–7, 184, 192, 207
organisational
boundaries, 3, 4
field, 104
forms, ix, 31, 90, 100–1, 111
governance, 9, 13, 80–1, 92, 97, 105, 109, 177, 192, 199
routines, vii, 103, 186, 189
sociology, 80

organisational – *continued*
  structures, 31, 92, 97–8, 100–3, 105–6, 109, 112, 148–9, 173, 193–4, 199; formal, 80
organisations, 4, 9, 14, 27–9, 34, 80, 83, 87–8, 93–4, 98–103, 105–6, 120, 167–8, 173–4, 178–9, 199
  modes of, 82
  network forms of, 87
outsourcing, v–vii, 1–4, 8, 9, 11–13, 15–16, 20–4, 26–8, 80–1, 91–2, 108–11, 132–4, 139–42, 160–4, 183–4, 186–9, 192–5
  dependent forms of, v, vi, 2–4, 8, 9, 11–13, 16, 26–8, 33, 80–1, 91–2, 95, 99, 105, 183, 185, 188, 192–4
  relationship, 184, 193
  spot, 90–1

part-time, 34–5, 60, 64, 68, 70, 73, 144
  employment, 111, 113, 143
  jobs, 69, 78, 113
  workers, 34, 65, 197, 199
  working, 66–7, 69, 70, 75, 78
partnership, exclusive, 157
personal dependence, 5, 6, 40, 42, 170–1, 177, 179, 191
population ecology, 99, 100, 207
power, vii, 50, 93, 96, 98, 107, 173–6, 193, 198, 202, 206
preferences, individual, 49, 77
price mechanism, 81, 92, 96, 171–2, 179–80, 199
principal-agent problem, 165, 171, 177, 180–1
productivity, vi, 109, 132, 140–1, 143

reciprocity, vi, 80, 86–8, 92–3, 95
relational
  contract theory, 92
  contracts, vi, vii, 1, 13, 16, 28, 80–9, 91–2, 94–7, 105, 108, 165, 170, 173–5, 177–82, 188, 192–3; implicit, 181, 190; long-term, 93, 105, 182, 188; non-specificity of, 89, 180; self-enforcing, 16, 90, 95, 182, 184

resource dependence theory, 98–9, 101, 199
risk, vii, 11, 29, 31–2, 40, 62–3, 70–1, 74, 76, 78, 92, 122, 128, 152, 160–4, 192–5
  economic, 6, 7, 133, 157, 159, 186
  exposure, vi, 132, 134–6, 177
  relational, vii, 169–70
routines, 82, 94–5, 101, 103, 180, 183, 186

sales forces, direct, 120, 126–7, 137
scandal, mis-selling, 116, 120, 135–6, 200
self-employed
  persons, 4, 7, 15, 35, 37, 40, 53, 57, 61, 67, 69, 75, 110, 154, 187, 195–7; dependent, 4, 5, 109, 195; independent, 4, 5, 37
  workers, 1, 12–13, 29, 35, 38, 47, 58, 97, 144, 151, 165–7, 169–77, 179–82, 184, 186, 205
self-employment, v, ix, 1, 2, 3, 4, 5, 7, 8, 9, 11, 13–15, 17, 18–22, 23, 25, 26, 27, 28–33, 35–6, 40–2, 44–50, 52–4, 189–91, 195–6, 201–5, 209–11
service sector, 3, 57, 69, 109, 111–12, 114, 142–4, 210
short-term contracts, 31–2
social
  relations, 13, 80, 88, 173, 186
  security, 35, 39, 42, 44–5, 53, 55, 151–2; law, 1, 3, 15, 34, 37, 42, 183–4, 188, 193; system, 15, 34, 36, 40–1
  structures, 88, 92, 94, 103, 206–7
subcontracting, 4, 21, 23–4, 29, 30, 32, 52, 187–8, 195, 206, 211
subcontractors, 4–6, 27–9, 53, 80, 110, 145–9, 154, 156–60, 162–3, 170, 187, 195
subordination, 6, 8, 14, 35–6, 39, 42, 57, 189, 191
support, vii, 24–5, 29, 51, 83, 109, 117, 121–2, 134, 141, 147–8, 152, 165–7, 171, 177

tied
  agency, 13, 51, 53, 109, 115, 117, 122, 124–6, 130–4, 137, 140–1, 168–9, 184–6
  agents, 6, 7, 12–13, 51, 94, 108–9, 112–13, 115–17, 120–41, 165–71, 177, 179, 182, 184–5, 201
transaction costs, 82, 120, 122
trucking firms, 155–6, 159, 161–3
trust, vii, 1, 13, 16, 80, 83, 88–9, 93, 96, 105, 129–30, 173–7, 182, 201–3, 206, 208–9
  calculative, 16, 177, 201
  norm-based, 201

uncertainty, 29, 31–2, 82–4, 93, 99, 101–3, 106, 184–6, 192–3, 199
unemployment, 3, 46–7, 52, 77, 175, 188, 209, 211

ventures, joint, 83, 86–7, 92, 99, 208

work
  organisation, 34, 54, 165, 171, 189
  relationships, 1, 4, 16, 21, 36, 41–4, 66, 147, 152, 167, 177, 188, 190, 195, 197
workers
  contingent, 25, 44
  outsourced, 113, 165;
  self-employed, 194